(GOD) AFTER AUSCHWITZ

(GOD) AFTER AUSCHWITZ

TRADITION AND CHANGE IN
POST-HOLOCAUST JEWISH THOUGHT

Zachary Braiterman

PRINCETON UNIVERSITY PRESS

PRINCETON, NEW JERSEY

PUBLISHED BY PRINCETON UNIVERSITY PRESS, 41 WILLIAM STREET,

PRINCETON, NEW JERSEY 08540

IN THE UNITED KINGDOM: PRINCETON UNIVERSITY PRESS, CHICHESTER, WEST SUSSEX

LIBRARY OF CONGRESS CATALOGING-IN-PUBLICATION DATA

BRAITERMAN, ZACHARY, 1963–

(GOD) AFTER AUSCHWITZ : TRADITION AND CHANGE IN POST-HOLOCAUST

JEWISH THOUGHT / BY ZACHARY BRAITERMAN.

P. CM.

INCLUDES BIBLIOGRAPHICAL REFERENCES AND INDEX.

ISBN 0-691-05941-1 (CLOTH : ALK. PAPER)

1. HOLOCAUST (JEWISH THEOLOGY). 2. THEODICY.

3. JUDAISM—20TH CENTURY. I. TITLE.

BM645.H6B69 1998 296.3'1174—DC21 98-16318

THIS BOOK HAS BEEN COMPOSED IN GALLIARD

THE PAPER USED IN THIS PUBLICATION

MEETS THE MINIMUM REQUIREMENTS

OF ANSI/NISO Z39.48-1992 (R 1997)

(*PERMANENCE OF PAPER*).

HTTP://PUP.PRINCETON.EDU

PRINTED IN THE UNITED STATES OF AMERICA

3 5 7 9 10 8 6 4 2

CONTENTS

ACKNOWLEDGMENTS

ARTS OF THIS BOOK were published under separate cover. The following journals have kindly allowed me to reprint those materials here. Portions of Chapter 4 appeared as "'Hitler's Accomplice'?! The Tragic Theology of Richard Rubenstein," in *Modern Judaism* 17 (1997); portions of Chapter 5 appeared as "Anti/theodic Faith in the Thought of Eliezer Berkovits," in *Journal of Jewish Thought and Philosophy* 7, no.1 (fall 1997); and portions of Chapter 6 appeared as "Fideism Redux: Emil Fackenheim and the State of Israel," in *Jewish Social Studies* 4, no. 1 (fall 1997).

I would also like to thank the faculty and staff at the University of Judaism where I spent the academic year 1995–1996 as a Finkelstein postdoctoral fellow. This generous support allowed me the opportunity to expand intellectual and social horizons.

Most of all, I am happy to acknowledge enormous intellectual debts this project has accrued. In particular I want to thank Van Harvey, David Biale, Edith and Michael Wyschogrod, Steven Zipperstein, Hester Gelber, Einat Ramon, James Hyman, Ken Koltun-Fromm, Aryeh Cohen, Elliot Dorff, David Ellenson, David Myers, Naomi Seidman, and the anonymous reviewers at the aforementioned journals. I owe special gratitude to Arnold Eisen for closely reading countless drafts as supervisor of what was then my doctoral dissertation. His line-for-line eye shaped and sharpened this project (both in terms of content and form) from the very start. Great thanks also go to Steven Kepnes and the anonymous reader for their acute attention to this manuscript for Princeton University Press. These people all forced me to grapple with questions that by myself I overlooked or underplayed. Their comments combined rigor and concern for this project's coherence. The book's faults are my own responsibility. Last, I owe immeasurable gratitude to my brother Jared Braiterman and to Margaret Karalis for their sense of style, boundless humor, and critical insight.

(GOD) AFTER AUSCHWITZ

INTRODUCTION

MODERNITY SURPASSED

JEWISH RELIGIOUS THOUGHT AFTER AUSCHWITZ

> Once upon a time we were dreaming of sweet and imaginary
> fires and of crumbling wedding canopies, but he, Sutzkever,
> beheld man in his utter ugliness, in his physical and
> spiritual degradation.
> (Marc Chagall)

ZYGMUNT BAUMAN was certainly not the first to note that "the Holocaust was born and executed in our modern rational society, at the high stage of our civilization and at the peak of cultural achievement, and for this reason it is a problem of that society, civilization and culture."[1] Indeed, catastrophic suffering belongs to the entire twentieth century—a century in which mass murder and mass death marked the convergence of modern organization, modern technology, and human propensities for violence and apathy. The Holocaust, two world wars, the Armenian genocide, the Stalinist gulag, Hiroshima and Nagasaki, Maoist purges, killing fields in Cambodia, Bosnia, and Rawanda, along with the specters of nuclear apocalypse, global environmental, disaster and the spread of AIDS all combine to haunt the Western imagination. To be sure, this all-too-familiar litany has already become rote, piously intoned, then easily ignored. But these names still work to different effect on those who take the time to linger over them. The litany retains its power to undermine the value of the human person, the meaning of history and modernity, and the significance of human cultural practice and social organization (along with belief in God). The endemic suffering that has riddled the entire twentith century confronts theologians, philosophers, artists, novelists, and poets with the dilemma of orienting human life and thought around the experience and memory of profound negativity and broken cultural traditions.[2]

Jewish religious thought provides a focal node with which to analyze postmodern (post-Holocaust) attempts at refiguring cultural and intellectual praxis. In the following pages, I examine how catastrophic suffering and its memory absorb the work of three pivotal contemporary Jewish thinkers: Richard Rubenstein, Eliezer Berkovits, and Emil Fackenheim. Their writings have framed post-Holocaust religious discourse, defining its left wing, its right wing, and its center. Assuming that religious reflection intersects with reading, my focus is twofold: theological and literary. In the late 1960s and throughout the 1970s, Rubenstein, Berkovits, and Fackenheim began to rework received notions about God and covenant by rereading traditional Jewish texts. In the process (and despite fierce disagreements among themselves), they have articulated a uniquely post-Holocaust theological sensibility dominated by what we are about to call *antitheodicy*.

Theodicy is a familiar technical term, coined by the German philosopher Gottfried Wilhelm Leibniz to mean "the justification of God." We expand this to include any attempt to justify, explain, or find acceptable meaning to the relationship that subsists between God (or some other form of ultimate reality), evil, and suffering. In contrast, *antitheodicy* means refusing to justify, explain, or accept that relationship. Although it often borders on blasphemy, antitheodicy does not constitute atheism; it might even express stubborn love that human persons have for God. After all, the author of a genuine antitheodic statement must believe that an actual relationship subsists between God and evil in order to reject it; and they must love God in order to be offended by that relationship. *Antitheodicy* is my own neologism.[3] I use it in order to account for a particular religious sensibility, based (in part) on fragments selectively culled from classical Jewish texts, that dominates post-Holocaust Jewish thought.

It will become apparent in the chapters that follow that my use of *theodicy* is intentionally broad. Critical readers might even object that I have applied it too broadly, that I have found theodicy where none in fact exists. This will appear especially to be the case when I turn to Jewish thinkers like Joseph Soloveitchik and Mordecai Kaplan—thinkers who ostensibly reject the very project of theodicy, along with other "God's eye" explanatory frameworks. I would only point out that theodicy constitutes a large family of different (and often contradictory) types of religious utterance. These include theories of just deserts, spiritual or ethical catharsis, the free-will argument, privation theories of evil that deny its ultimate existence, and epistemological doubts about the human capacity to know the ways of God or theologically interpret moral experience. Some theodicies ascribe blame to victims, others merit. The author of one type of theodic statement interprets suffering as a punishing sign of divine displeasure. Another might understand it as a sign of God's passionate love for the persons suffering. Another might profess the human inability to read such signs. My purpose in casting so wide a net is to show how these contradictory types of religious utterance are made to function to the same effect: to justify God and providence in the face of evil and suffering. In my view, *any* utterance that attributes positive spiritual or moral "meaning" to genuine evil, any attempt to "redeem" suffering, risks entering into this family resemblance. Readers will find this author largely unsympathetic to this task, but not entirely. Indeed, I suggest at the end of Chapter 3 that religious thinkers must sometimes take this risk in ultimately desperate attempts to draw good out of evil.

My own suspicions regarding theodicy and my sympathies towards antitheodicy do not overlook the point that neither represent stable entities. Theodicy and antitheodicy are but second order, heuristic categories with which to evaluate the meaning of a given religious utterance. As such, both remain subject to intense interpretive play. A statement that is theodic in one context (e.g., "God is good because God rewards the righteous in the world-to-come") can become antitheodic in another semantic context (e.g., "God misgoverns this-world and so defers reward until the world-to-come"). The same slippage holds true of antitheodic statements. The notion that we can never explain the ways of God by means of speculation can turn theodic when followed by statements that justify God and affirm the ultimate moral value of suffering. Indeed, such statements may sometimes even follow claims that a religious thinker rejects theodicy! I make these points at the end of Chapter 2 and in my discussion of Soloveitchik and Kaplan in Chapter 3. In the meantime, I want to suggest the following about the authorial intent of religious thinkers: whether or not a particular thinker consciously understands herself to have explicitly employed theodicy does not mean that she has not made implicit use of it.

It is not coincidental that post-Holocaust Jewish thinkers make little to no such use of theodicy—explicit or implicit. The collapse of theodicy in their work speaks to vexing questions surrounding the Holocaust's historical and theological uniqueness. Rubenstein and Fackenheim have argued that the Holocaust represented a unique and radical evil in human history that has ruptured traditional theological categories like theodicy. Against Rubenstein and Fackenheim, other scholars maintain that the Holocaust was only one of many catastrophes in Jewish history; as such, it neither requires nor has generated any unique theological response. It will become clear that I disagree with both positions. On the one hand, the Holocaust and post-Holocaust thought occur within broader historical and theological contexts. One cannot properly understand the Holocaust outside of the larger context of modern mass death. Nor can one understand contemporary Jewish response to catastrophe without reflecting upon the shape of classical and modern Jewish thought. At the same time, Auschwitz represents a theological point of no return. A uniquely modern catastrophe with uniquely modern implications befell the Jewish people in the twentieth century. In turn, this catastrophe and its memory have profoundly reshaped the given theodic and antitheodic contours of its religious culture.

We return to the question concerning the uniqueness of the Holocaust at the end of this introduction. Narrowing our focus for now, we see that the Holocaust has radically complicated the project of twentieth-century Jewish modernism. By "Jewish modernism," I mean a series of disjointed efforts to renew traditional ideational, social, and textual patterns broken by the uneven encounter with Western culture. Modern Jewish thinkers sought to "make it new" by turning against nineteenth-century views of progress and other canons of Enlightenment reason and historicism. Examples include the neo-Hasidism of Martin Buber and Abraham Joshua Heschel, Gershom Scholem's rehabilitation of Kabbalah's intellectual respectability, Franz Rosenzweig's return to revelation and ritual, Soloveitchik's phenomenological analysis of Halakha, and general reappraisals of the Hebrew Bible and rabbinic aggadah. These projects paralleled the use of traditional motifs in the poetry, novels, and paintings of Hayim Nahman Bialik, Shai Agnon, Marc Chagall, and so many others. In turn, these Jewish thinkers and artists reflected the Orientalist turn to archaic, Eastern, and "primitivist" tropes in the varied works of Wassily Kandinsky, Paul Klee, Thomas Mann, Hermann Hesse, Ezra Pound, James Joyce, and other avant-garde modernists. In our view the Holocaust has posed unique theological problems to those Jewish thinkers who fall under this rubric. Not surprisingly, little to no "post-Holocaust" thought appears among ultra-Orthodox Jews, who have wanted nothing from either modernity or modernism.[4]

The Holocaust intensified an already-strained relation between Judaism and modern cultural currents. It did not take the Holocaust for Kant, Hegel, Marx, Nietzsche, and Freud, and the proponents of historicism and positivism to cast doubt upon the cogency of a traditional narrative pattern based on [1] a transcendent deity who [2] created the world, [3] chose one particular people, [4] and revealed to that people one particular set of commandments encoded in a particular textual corpus that would [5] lead them toward privileged messianic and otherworldly futures. Jewish thinkers like Buber, Baeck, Rosenzweig, Heschel, Soloveitchik, and Kaplan responded to the challenge posed by modernity by recasting traditional Jewish texts, tropes, and narrative structures. Judaism was made to accord with modern intellectual and cultural trends while calling the hegemony of Enlightenment reason into question. The Holocaust, however, has exacerbated extant questions about God, Torah, Israel, mitzvah, and covenant by placing them before the historical presence of monumental horror. By the end of the twentieth century, European history has undermined modern Jewish life and thought more thoroughly than did nineteenth century German *Geistesgeschichte*.

Modern Jewish religious thinkers like Buber, Heschel, Soloveitchik, and Kaplan made only haphazard and oblique reference to the Holocaust immediately after the war. Some scholars and critics have suggested that they suffered from a state of psychological shock—like mourners and terminally ill patients who undergo a transitional period of denial and disbelief. In this view a prolonged psychic distress rendered modern Jewish theologians mute.[5] However, we will see in Chapter 3 that despair, anxiety, and disillusionment had already begun to mark the theological literature of the 1950s and early 1960s. In the face of tragedy, Buber, Heschel, Soloveitchik, and Kaplan sought to affirm *guardedly* optimistic appraisals of God, the ultimate direction of providence, the human person, society, Jewish destiny, and the abiding relevance of traditional texts. They ignored neither tragedy nor the Holocaust. Instead, Auschwitz represented a silent but as yet unnamed presence in their postwar writings.

Discursive factors explain this relative silence better than psychologism. Buber, Heschel, Soloveitchik, and Kaplan lacked a widespread discourse with which to discuss the Holocaust. A flurry of memoirs, literature, film, and scholarship would begin to chronicle the Holocaust in graphic detail. Such texts disseminated a vocabulary, a body of knowledge without which one could only have referred to the Holocaust in passing and general terms. Indeed, the very word *Holocaust* appeared relatively late. Some time elapsed before the name Auschwitz or phrases like "Arbeit macht frei" assumed their current iconographic status. Without a sufficiently developed discourse, there was simply no language with which to talk about the Holocaust, no pastiche of image, figure, phrase, slogan, narrative, and reflection with which to rivet the religious imagination.

Religious thought cannot operate in a discursive vacuum. In our case, post-Holocaust theology owes its origin to a larger discourse taking shape throughout the 1960s and 1970s. The 1963 Eichmann trial, the testimony it generated, and Hannah Arendt's formulation of the "banality of evil" constituted central moments in its formation. The work of Elie Wiesel played a pivotal role, providing Jewish theologians images of hunted, hanging, and burning children, death marches, concentration camp life, the figure of the survivor, a language of witness, and an antiaesthetic of bitter despair and resistance. Primo Levi left Jewish theologians with the figure of the "Musselmann"—the camp denizen broken by what Jean Amery called the Nazi "logic of destruction." Alexander Donat used the term "Holocaust Kingdom" to designate a specific place in the history of human suffering. The critic Terrence De Pres in his study of Holocaust memoirs suggested the image of "excremental assault." In addition to memoirs and literary representations, the 1960s and 1970s saw the historical studies of Lucy Dawidowicz and Raul Hilberg, and the psychological reflections of Elie Cohen, Viktor Frankl, and Bruno Bettelheim. The documentary film *Night and Fog* visualized the Holocaust, providing macabre images of warehoused human hair and typhus-ravaged bodies bulldozed into mass graves. This extensive Holocaust discourse did more than dominate post-Holocaust religious thought. It constituted the very condition of possibility for any sustained theological encounter with the Holocaust.

Rubenstein was one of the first Jewish theologians to respond to this literature, practically inventing post-Holocaust theology *de novo* in 1966 with the publication of *After Auschwitz*. At the time Rubenstein was a campus rabbi at the University of Pittsburgh. The enfant terrible of Jewish theology, Rubenstein would soon suffer what Michael Berenbaum called bureaucratic excommunication for advancing radical conclusions in the wake of catastrophic suffering. With the publication of *After Auschwitz*, Rubenstein found himself pilloried by the organized Jewish community and unable to find academic work. He eventually took a teaching post at Florida State University in Tallahassee. At present he is president of the University of Bridgeport—an academic institution associated with Rev. Moon's Unification Church. Rubenstein had dared to argue that the Holocaust radically sundered Jews from biblical and rabbinic ideas about God, covenant and election, suffering and redemption found. According to Rubenstein, the "Judeo-Christian" tradition posits belief in an omnipotent and just God, the ultimate author of history. Rubenstein argued that if such a God exists, the Holocaust had to represent divine will. Rejecting that theology, Rubenstein declared "the death of God." He argued that contemporary Jews who honestly confront the Holocaust can no longer orient their lives around cherished beliefs and texts. Instead, he advanced what he called an insightful paganism. In an absurd universe, the suffering person does not represent a figure of guilt and redemption, but a victim of tragic happenstance.

In stark contrast, Berkovits denied that the Holocaust posed any unique theological challenge to traditional belief and Jewish texts. Ordained at the modern Orthodox Hildesheimer Rabbinical Seminary in Germany, Berkovits taught Jewish philosophy at the Hebrew Theological College in Skokie, Illinois, before immigrating to Israel. In *Faith after the Holocaust* (1973) and *With God in Hell* (1979), Berkovits argued that traditional Judaism retains its integrity after Auschwitz. He criticized Rubenstein for using Christian terms like "the death of God" and for addressing the Holocaust out of historical context. Berkovits was a self-styled champion of tradition, who sought to define and defend the nature of "authentic" Jewish faith. According to Berkovits, Jewish tradition had confronted the problem of evil throughout a long history of exile. At the surface, Berkovits argued that the notions of human freedom and messianic trust remain philosophically and theologically cogent after the Holocaust and Israel's military victory in 1967. In fact, the Berkovits I describe in Chapter 5 was more complex than this quick sketch suggests.

The traditionalism informing Berkovits's thought belied an edge no less radical than Richard Rubenstein's.

With his own rhetoric of rupture and repair, Fackenheim assumed a position roughly between Rubenstein and Berkovits. Like Berkovits, Fackenheim was born in Germany, where he was ordained (at the liberal *Hochshule fur die Wissenschaft des Judentums*). Fackenheim escaped the war and settled in Toronto where he taught philosophy for many years. He now lives in Jerusalem. Fackenheim became best known for claiming that a 614th mitzvah commands the Jewish people after the Holocaust. In *God's Presence in History* (1970), he argued that "The Commanding Voice of Auschwitz" commands Jews to remember the Holocaust and survive as Jews without despairing of God, world, or "man."[6] Fackenheim paradoxically asserted that post-Holocaust Jews must mend a radical rupture in Jewish life, belief, and tradition. Culling insights from Bible, midrash, continental philosophy, and contemporary Jewish narrative, he tried to orient post-Holocaust Jewish life and thought around precarious shards of moral good. The astonishing examples of Jewish and gentile resistance to the Nazi onslaught, and above all the State of Israel, were said to represent God's uneven presence in the midst of history.

In following chapters I critically examine the theological positions staked out by Rubenstein, Berkovits, and Fackenheim. I argue that post-Holocaust Jewish thought has hinged on unexamined understandings of "tradition," "reading," and "rhetoric." These hermeneutical foci lead directly to postmodern critical theory. Now obviously, Rubenstein, Berkovits, and Fackenheim display neither the same ironic self-consciousness nor sense of play shared by so many of their postmodern contemporaries. Nor (by and large) do postmodern theories show the communal solidarity or ethical urgency that dominate post-Holocaust literature. However, postmodern theories illuminate post-Holocaust thought on at least two counts. First, they provide analytical tools with which to identify and evaluate the play of difference that permeates tradition. Rather than search for uniform messages or meanings (what Martin Buber called *Botshaft*), postmodern theories allow us to critically assess the deep tensions that rend traditions. Second, postmodernism has come to shape the very same thematic horizon occupied by post-Holocaust Jewish thinkers. I refer primarily to the work of Emmanuel Levinas, Edmond Jabes, and Edith Wyschogrod. One would also include the writings of Jacques Derrida, Jean-François Lyotard, Maurice Blanchot, and Mark Taylor. Together, they have identified: [1] the unstable field that constitutes historical consciousness, [2] the experience, memory, and threat of catastrophe and rupture in the twentieth century, [3] the impotence of language and reason before this "tremendum," and [4] the potentially reorienting significance of the supplement, the trace, and the fragment. These are the postmodern topoi reflected in this study. As I see it, postmodern and post-Holocaust thinkers inhabit different sectors of style, mood, and sense within the same mental and cultural universe.

Postmodern theory also facilitates our own attempts to undo the hegemony of theodicy and "meaning" in the philosophy and sociology of religion. In chapter 1, I show how catastrophic suffering generates a vast, and heretofore unexplored, cluster of religious problems. I argue that God does not represent the sole religious figure requiring justification in the face of catastrophe. Religious thinkers must also justify social institutions and textual canons. The Holocaust has threatened the physical community of Israel, its Torah, and the motif of covenant that runs throughout its religious life. In this light, theodicy does *not* represent the privileged preoccupation in post-Holocaust Jewish thought. I argue throughout that the reconstruction of Jewish religious life and thought after the Holocaust has depended on rebuilding community and rereading texts—particularly the Hebrew Bible and rabbinic midrash. Justifying God barely enters into the equation.

In Chapter 2, I continue to explore the limits of theodicy by examining theodic and antitheodic motifs and figures in classical Jewish texts. In particular I pay close attention to the book of Deuteronomy, the book of Job, and rabbinic commentaries. Theodic texts like Deuteronomy's Song of Moses (chapter 32) depict a just, good God using painful suffering in order to punish the wicked and purify the righteous. Their authors accept suffering and urge the people to return to God and covenant. In contrast, antitheodic figures like Job depict aggrieved human parties who reject suffering and protest providence. In these texts God may appear unjust and unkind and must ultimately repent. Classical Jewish texts, I conclude, swing between a theodic center and antitheodic margins in their response to suffering. As such they provide a rich field of suggestive figure, image, and contention that Rubenstein, Berkovits, and Fackenheim reject, adopt, and transform after the Holocaust.

In Chapter 3, I examine how the phenomenon of suffering shaped the thought of Buber, Heschel, Soloveitchik, and Kaplan. I have chosen these four figures and ignore Hermann Cohen and Franz Rosenzweig for the simple fact that these latter two thinkers did not live to see the Holocaust. To be sure, Buber, Heschel, Soloveitchik, and Kaplan offered radically different understandings of God, Jewish peoplehood, mitzvah, and covenant. Yet their work betrays a surprisingly pronounced consensus surrounding the problem of evil. To be sure, none of these thinkers ever sought to formulate a systematic theodicy. Soloveitchik and Kaplan rejected such attempts out of hand. However, implicit theodic assumptions and expression permeated modern Jewish thought well into the 1950s and early 1960s. On the one hand, Buber, Heschel, Soloveitchik, and

Kaplan absolved God by blaming evil on human agents, on a callous Western civilization. At the same time, they sought to frame suffering within the larger context of spiritual catharsis and ethical good. In their view, Judaism held the same. Modern Jewish thinkers privileged the moral rigor of the prophets over Job's embittered protest. Striking a "realistic" position regarding the scope of human evil and suffering, they then sought to turn them into foundations for good. In contrast, Rubenstein, Berkovits, and Fackenheim attempted no such alchemy. Post-Holocaust thinkers, we will see, abandoned even the most modern and (self-) disguised variants of the theodic "tradition." Instead, they reconfigured tradition by appropriating antitheodic biblical and midrashic fragments and by pointedly ignoring modern-readings-of-tradition.

Having offered a more nuanced rendering of "tradition" in the first part of this book, I devote Chapters 4, 5, and 6 to Rubenstein, Berkovits, and Fackenheim, respectively. I remain deeply indebted to Steven Katz's *Post-Holocaust Dialogues*—undoubtedly the single most important example of critical scholarship in the field. In this seminal text, Katz applied a closely reasoned philosophical analysis to the claims posed by post-Holocaust thinkers. While relying on Katz, my own study includes a "literary" dimension that he left unexplored. Rhetoric simply inundates the literature. Under "rhetoric" I include hyperbolic slogans, polemical overkill, rhetorical overstatement, and gross overinterpretation expressed with the intention to shock readers, foment resistance, rally solidarity, and carve out new theological identities. Rubenstein proclaimed "the death of God" and the creation of an "insightful paganism," but he himself was neither a death of God theologian nor a pagan. Berkovits championed "authentic Judaism" by reinventing it. Fackenheim's rhetoric about the 614th commandment obscured the fact that he had reduced the content of revelation to an anxious minimum—while staking a heavy investment on highly stylized antitheodic figures for whom revelation offers little hope or consolation.

I ask my readers in advance to note the marked ambivalence with which I approach the use of rhetoric by these thinkers. I have employed both a hermeneutic of charity and a hermeneutic of suspicion. On one hand, I want to show that wild speech begets new religious expression by opening up uncharted conceptual and hermeneutical territory. As such, rhetoric proved indispensable to the formation of post-Holocaust Jewish thought. For example, I explain in Chapter 4 that Rubenstein *had no choice* but to adopt "pagan" rhetoric. His teachers at the Jewish Theological Seminary (like Heschel, Robert Gordis, Louis Finkelstein) had not provided him a Jewish vocabulary with which to formulate his own critique of theodicy. I therefore think it would be uncharitable to fault Rubenstein for not understanding the tradition as we have come to under-

stand it in the 1990s. It would also show ingratitude. I cannot but suspect that Rubenstein's blistering attacks helped prompt many thinkers
(like Berkovits and Fackenheim) to "rediscover" antitheodicy within the
tradition, if only to prove Rubenstein wrong. On the other hand, rhetoric does not always yield new insight. Indeed, we will see rhetoric missing
its mark throughout the post-Holocaust literature. In particular, Rubenstein, Berkovits, and Fackenheim respectively overstate (or rather overinterpret) their own radicalism, conservativism, or return into history. Trying to respect this ambiguity, I neither condemn nor celebrate hyperbole
and other forms of wild speech. As I see it, Rubenstein, Berkovits, and
Fackenheim demand readers who *simultaneously* endorse and distrust the
rash language that made it possible to reinvent theological and literary
origins after Auschwitz.

In the book's conclusion, I argue that the writings of Rubenstein, Berkovits, and Fackenheim coalesce into what Michel Foucault called a common "discursive formation." By this I understand Foucault to mean a
network of rules, assumptions, and expression operating anonymously
upon the individuals who speak within it. Discourse generates new discursive objects. It relies upon experts authorized to restrict its operation.
Examples of post-Holocaust discourse formation include the emergence
of privileged antitheodic subjects from the margins of tradition and attempts by an expert class to restrict theodic expression. Note too that
Rubenstein, Berkovits, and Fackenheim appeared unaware of the family
resemblance that they shared with each other. This point only confirms
Foucault's general observation that disparate authors have but an inadequate idea of the breadth of the discourse in which they themselves participate. This new post-Holocaust discursive formation bears directly on
the process of cultural transformation in modern Jewish life. Drawing on
Umberto Eco, I suggest that religious cultures prove intrinsically plastic.
In the face of historical flux, the parts that compose a tradition can always
be reconfigured into surprising new patterns. Throughout this study we
see Rubenstein, Berkovits, and Fackenheim rifling through tradition.
They abandoned what were once central ideas and texts while bringing
once-marginal themes and figures into the center of Jewish thought. In
the process they came to formulate a religious sensibility (we explain in
the conclusion: a religious aesthetic) that is unique in the history of Jewish thought.

We cannot do complete justice to the discourse without briefly explaining the relative absence of Arthur Cohen and Irving Greenberg from
this study. Cohen's *The Tremendum* may constitute the single most sophisticated piece of post-Holocaust thought written to date. Greenberg
has been among the most forceful critics of theodicy within the modern
orthodox camp. Two reasons dictate their exclusion. First, Rubenstein,

Berkovits, and Fackenheim were the first religious thinkers who systematically addressed the Holocaust. The *Tremendum* (Cohen's first and only book on the subject) appeared in 1981. As such, it owes its sophistication not only to the author's obvious brilliance but to its own belatedness. Both Cohen and Greenberg build on the discussion begun by Rubenstein, Berkovits, and Fackenheim. Like Rubenstein, Cohen does not think that God actively interferes in history; God is too impersonal a figure in his thought. Nevertheless, Cohen argues (like Fackenheim) that God maintains a trace presence within history; he likens this presence to a "filament." For his part, the specific quality of Greenberg's appeal to human dignity and sympathy echoes Berkovits's thoughts about theology and Halakha. Second, Rubenstein, Berkovits, and Fackenheim are the foci of this study because they proved to be so prolific. This allows us to trace the trajectory of their thought. In contrast, Cohen and Greenberg's writings about the Holocaust stand outside a larger post-Holocaust oeuvre. As such, they tell us less about the internal texture of an individual's intellectual development or the tensions that characterize the discourse.

Many critics of the discourse still wonder why it should have ever formed at all. This returns us to that central tenet in post-Holocaust Jewish thought concerning the Holocaust's uniqueness. One might presume that a unique evil would therefore justify unique theological and textual revisions. But, we ask again, was the Holocaust unique? Confining ourselves to Jewish history, we again note many other instances of catastrophe and mass murder. Examples include the destruction of the Temple, the Crusader massacres, the Chmelniki pogroms, and widespread massacres in the Ukraine following World War I. And even if the Holocaust was *historically* unique, does it truly represent a *theologically* unique evil? The death of thousands, tens of thousands, hundreds of thousands should also trouble religious faith. No less than the Holocaust, these events call into question the notion of a good and powerful God, acting in history, and watching over Israel with special care. The Holocaust, it would seem, does not substantially change the problem.

Indeed, I argue that the antitheodic response of Rubenstein, Berkovits, and Fackenheim to suffering does not constitute a complete novum in Jewish intellectual history. Many classical Jewish authors had already responded to the evil of their times with many of the same antitheodic positions found in post-Holocaust thought. Moreover, as David Roskies and Alan Mintz have each persuasively shown, the proponents of Yiddish and Hebrew literary modernism anticipated the rebellion of Rubenstein, Berkovits, and Fackenheim. God's absence was protested by characters in the novels of Shai Agnon and in the pogrom poetry of Peretz Markish and Hayim Nahman Bialik. Even earlier, antitheodic motifs appeared in nineteenth-century Europe—in Nietzsche's figure of the madman who declares the death of God and in Fyodor Dostoyevsky's fictional antihero Ivan Karamazov. Together, all of these writings suggest that antitheodic response to the problem of evil represents nothing new. The Holocaust has created no unique theological problem and no unique response.

Or so it seems. True, the Holocaust does not substantially change the problem of evil nor generate new types of antitheodic response, at least not in terms of strict *content*. Indeed, the exact wording of an antitheodic utterance may stay the same over time. However, the changed context in which these utterances appear after the Holocaust creates a decisive shift within the *formal* parameters of Jewish intellectual history.

Debates concerning the uniqueness of post-Holocaust Jewish thought have heretofore ignored the importance of genre. In our opinion, something new has happened within the particular field of *religious thought*. It is one thing when poets, novelists, literary figures, and philosophers challenge a God in whom they disbelieve. Take for instance the Yiddish poet Abraham Sutzkever's protest poem "Kol Nidre." Written in the Vilna Ghetto, Sutzkever drew on a long preexisting tradition. But Sutzkever never believed in the God of history! Referring to one of Sutzkever's critics, Roskies comments: "Could someone like Sutzkever carry it off? Kalmanovitsch's reaction on hearing the poem was apt: 'Whoever calls God to account [*ver es hot a din-toyre mit got*],' he argued, 'must first of all believe in God.' There was an element of posturing in a poet who in other contexts rarely invoked the name of God and whose most religious poem, written in the ghetto, 'I Feel Like Making a Prayer,' actually asserted the impossibility of prayer."[7] Kalmanovitsch addressed the irony of a nonbeliever calling God to account. Yet he may have had it backward. Modern poets and other skeptics have always found it easy to ridicule and protest a God in whom they don't believe. Theologians have exercised greater hesitation. Buber, Heschel, Soloveitchik, and Kaplan never assumed the antitheodic posture struck by poets and novelists. Antitheodicy gains a larger currency in specifically religious circles only after the Holocaust. Not just a literary trope, it has entered into the mainstream of contemporary religious thought.

We note the following structural difference. A shift between the center and margins occurs within the genre of religious thought. Although not rare, antitheodicy represented an isolated discourse in biblical and rabbinic texts. Antitheodic statements did not form together into a coherent tradition within the Hebrew Bible. In contrast, an entire historical chronicle and prophetic tradition rested on Deuteronomy's theodic discourse of rebuke and retribution. The antitheodic motifs found in the Babylonian Talmud and midrash compilations constituted suggestive counter-traditions at best. They never assumed normative status, coalesced around revered iconographic figures like the martyred R. Akiba. Nor did they enter the traditional prayer book. Antitheodicy, we safely conclude, proves more central in the writings of Rubenstein, Berkovits, and Fackenheim than in classical texts and traditions. The meaning of antitheodic expression shifts in the process of moving from the margins to the center of Jewish thought. Statements and sentiments that occupy the public center of a religious discourse carry more normative weight than they do from exoteric and literary margins where they are barely read and easily forgotten.

The broader currency and structural weight given to antitheodic discourse speak to the historical uniqueness of the Holocaust. Fackenheim has rightly observed that the Romans allowed R. Yoḥanan b. Zakkai to escape Jerusalem and establish an academy in Yavneh. The crusader massacres were marked by scattered killing. Chmelniki did not pursue a "final solution." We might say the same of the widespread massacres during the Russian Civil War. As Roskies notes, the Holocaust has become its own archetype.[8] Comparing the modern pogrom poetry of an earlier generation with the poetry written in the ghettos during the war, Roskies writes: "In all these [former cases], the scene of destruction was never more than a catalyst, a small part of the whole, and therefore its artistic representation could elicit only so much. No writer, not even Lamed Shapiro, would dwell exclusively on the meaning of Jewish catastrophe. After 1 September 1939, however, the subject of catastrophe eclipsed all others as millions of Jews suddenly found themselves standing 'at the cross roads' with nowhere to turn."[9] Catastrophe no longer represented a dissonant cloud over some distant corner of Jewish life. It engulfed the whole of Eastern and Western European Jewry, pushing the problem of evil into the center of Jewish thought. Maybe this alone does not substantively change the problem of evil. One might even hope that over time Auschwitz may no longer eclipse Jewish life and thought. But who could doubt that the record of that historical eclipse will endure in the forms of myth and memorial? Coupled with the threat of nuclear weaponry, the image of Auschwitz, I suspect, will continue to shape religious thought well into the next century. It has finally forced theologians (together with poets, novelists, and critics of religion) to consider that no promised redemption, no good, is worth the price of catastrophic suffering.

The Enlightenment as a whole has been faulted for a variety of pathologies. Social critics like Arendt, Foucault, Rubenstein, and Bauman have observed the murderous effects of rationalization and bureaucratization. Philosophers like Levinas, Derrida, and Lyotard have associated the notions of synthesis and totality with totalitarianism and terror. I do not need to rehearse these arguments but want to add the following point.

The philosopher Charles Taylor has made the counter-claim that modern men and women show heightened aversions to pain and suffering. For Taylor, modernity has come to mean sensitivity for the dignity of the individual and his or her everyday life in the here and now. This explains the response of Dostoyevsky's Ivan Karamazov for whom the suffering of even one single innocent child in this-world disrupts whatever harmony may await him in the world-to-come. Ironically, however, this very sensitivity comes at that precise historical juncture where the human person has acquired unique destructive powers. Indeed, Levinas understood how responsibilities multiply before the infinite horizon of the other's face. In my view it is technology that augments this responsibility by extending the scope of human power. At no other point in time have human beings possessed the actual power to inflict global harm. The artificially enhanced intensity of the Nazi onslaught (coupled with the precedent established at Hiroshima and Nagasaki) points to the unique responsibilities people bear today.

As such, the Holocaust points beyond itself—which is why perhaps Berkovits concluded *Faith after the Holocaust* noting the global dangers posed by poverty, environmental degradation, and atomic weaponry (a "monstrous increase in human power"). As Berkovits warned, "A much more dangerous man lives on with a soul infected by the holocaust betrayal."[10] This capacity to inflict universal harm (realized for the first time in our century) generates a unique theological problematic before which formulaic restatements of the problem of evil inevitably pale. Prior to the twentieth century, theologians offered more or less satisfactory answers as to why God would create creatures capable of murder (even mass murder) and indifference. For its part, the Book of Job ends with God's poem describing the terrible beauty that floods the world. Suffering and indifference prove ultimately unable to overshadow this theophany. Yet the force of God's response to Job wanes in the twentieth century. For the first time in history, genocidal human cultures can now turn into ash that very creation described by the author(s) of Job. This constitutes a unique theological problem. Never before have human beings had to confront the possible combination of Nazi will and American knowhow. One might very well take up the point made by Berkovits and wonder what kind of God would create such creatures.

PART I

ONE

THEODICY AND ITS OTHERS

FORMS OF RELIGIOUS RESPONSE
TO THE PROBLEM OF EVIL

A TECHNICAL TERM, *theodicy* means the "justification of God." It will be recalled that Gottfried Wilhelm Leibniz, who coined the term *theodicy*, wrote his defense of God after an earthquake devastated Lisbon in 1755. With this same event in mind, Voltaire savagely ridiculed Leibniz in his satirical novel *Candide*. Voltaire drew the comic but ill-fated figure of Dr. Pangloss in order to lampoon Leibniz's insistence that this world represents "the best of all possible worlds." I expand Leibniz's term to include any utterance whose source attempts to "justify," "explain," or "accept" as ultimately meaningful the relationship between God and evil. While theodicy constitutes a relatively recent term in the history of Western philosophy, the problems it touches upon are perennial. Like all good philosophical or theological categories, theodicy proves its worth insofar as it enables its users to identify, articulate, and schematize conceptual dilemmas and the different forms by which people address them. In our view, however, Leibniz and Voltaire saw but part of the crisis that *all* social actors (religious and secular) confront in the face of radical suffering and genuine evil.

In this chapter I show how the so-called "problem" of evil represents a cluster of interrelated problems that a one-dimensional analysis of theodicy tends to obscure. Of course, suffering undermines theological ideas surrounding God, divine attributes, and providence. But it also generates severe sociological and textual dilemmas. Religious actors defend the God whom they serve, the societies in which they live, and the constitutional documents they hold sacred. By *theodicy*, I will therefore mean only arguments used to justify God and theological belief. Although the term has enjoyed a wide currency, not every religious response to suffering constitutes a theodicy. Instead, the act of theodicy operates in tandem with what Peter Berger calls world maintenance and what has been called textual apologetics. By world maintenance, I mean the maintenance of communities and the defense of its members in the face of suffering. By apologetics, I mean upholding the relevance and value of textual canons. Acts of world maintenance and apologetics parallel the operation of theodicy insofar as they too are determined by verbs like *justify*, *explain*, and *accept*. After all, society and text (just like belief in God) suffer strain in the face of catastrophic dislocation and require social actors to come to their defense.

In the following pages, I provide what Clifford Geertz calls a "thick description" of theodicy, world maintenance, and apologetics. These three types of discourse form a "multiplicity of complex conceptual structures, many of them superimposed upon or knotted into one another, which are at once strange, irregular, and inexplicit."[1] A thick description reveals how the acts of theodicy, world maintenance, and apologetics are deeply entangled within the same semantic structure yet culturally variable. In particular, I show how the classical motif of covenant offers contemporary Jewish thinkers an idiosyncratic perspective from which to talk about God, Torah, and Israel after Auschwitz. Naturally, those who would maintain a religious system based on covenant expend great effort attending to the service of God and come to God's defense in the face of evil. But God does not represent their sole concern. After all, the theological trope of covenant is a *social* metaphor taken from the political lexicon of the ancient Near East by which vassals are bound to their suzerain.[2] In the face of suffering, proponents of covenant-theologies must also tend to the human community that joins that compact and to the written and oral contracts that bind it to their suzerain. As we are about to see, the extratheological foci of community and text circumscribe the actual exercise of theodicy and disrupt its hegemony.

At the end of this chapter, it should be clear that *antitheodicy* (the religious refusal to "justify," "explain," or "accept" the relationship between God and evil) represents an additional factor that disrupts the dominance of theodicy in religious thought. The need to uphold an endangered community may deflect religious actors from defending God or explaining evil within meaningful frameworks. The interpretation of canonical texts may authorize this turn. The presence, indeed the dominance, of theodicy in Bible and midrash remains indisputable. The book of Deuteronomy, chanted yearly in the synagogue, has contributed to the nearly hegemonic presence of theodicy in traditional Jewish thought. Witness R. Akiba who is said to have died at the hands of the Romans without complaint. In our own day, ultra-Orthodox Jews explain and accept the Holocaust as God's response to the putative sins of assimilation and Zionism. The figure of a protesting Job, however, represents a counter-tradition that has been increasingly amplified in contemporary Jewish thought. In rabbinic literature, Job-like figures protest God and providence by appealing to biblical prooftexts in their defense of a suffering community. Such antitheodic figures possess a peculiar resonance that has helped many post-Holocaust thinkers evade the scandal of theodicy.[3]

Theodicy

Historically, Judeo-Christian-Islamic religious traditions have created a profusion of theodicies meant to explain the presence of suffering in the world. These have included the denial of evil as a "real" phenomenon; dualism; just deserts; deferred compensations; divine pedagogy; free will; vicarious atonement; appeals to mystery. No matter what the response, theodicy operates on at least three levels of theoretical abstraction. At one level, theodicians try to justify divine providence and the concrete realia of historical and personal tragedy. At a second level, they explain how attributes of divine goodness and power jibe with the existence of genuine evil. Finally, theodicians try to affirm these attributes in the absolutized form of omnibenevolence and omnipotence. For their part, Jewish theologians face the additional task of trying to justify the God of Abraham, Isaac, and Jacob and the covenant with Israel.

At the most rudimentary level, the theological problem of evil is strictly one of providence. A religious believer may assume that a just, loving, and powerful deity exists but will fail to understand how a world of suffering reflects divine justice, love, and power. At this basic level of analysis, theology remains "empirical." Skeptics and believers ponder God's manifest ordering of the universe on the basis of their own personal experience or on the basis of reliable secondhand reports. Perhaps only for the sake of argument, Dostoyevsky's Ivan Karamazov admits that a supreme deity exists. However, he rebels against this God's creating a world in which children suffer torment. No final rectification, no deferred, otherworldly harmony, can justify providence. "I don't want harmony," Karamazov insists:

> From love for humanity I don't want it. I would rather be left with un-avenged suffering. I would rather remain with my unavenged suffering and unsatisfied indignation, *even if I were wrong*. Besides, too high a price is asked for harmony; it's beyond our means to pay so much to enter on it. And so I hasten to give back my entrance ticket, and if I am an honest man I am bound to give it back as soon as possible.[4]

Karamazov's rebellion builds upon long-held questions. Why did God create the world the way it is? Why does God spare the wicked? Why do the innocent suffer? Theologians have typically proffered precisely the solutions that critics like Karamazov have flatly rejected. John Hick, for example, argues that "human goodness slowly built up through personal histories of moral effort has a value in the eyes of the Creator which justifies even the long travail of the soul making."[5] To Hick, goods like freedom, compassion, and courage (along with the promise of eternal

life) lend meaning to anguish while absolving God for the actual maintenance of providence. Ultimately, such goods are said to prove to be
worth the price of blood they carry.

At a second level of theoretical abstraction, theologians and philosophers dispute God's very nature. Theodicy is now no longer about the
ordinary and extraordinary tragic realities that disrupt people's lives, but
about a "person" of transcendent power. Is God just, merciful, powerful,
or prescient? Do God's justice and mercy work in tandem? Some theologians have altered their understanding of divine attributes in order to
account for these questions. David Ray Griffin contends that "certain
assumptions about the nature of God's power that made the problem so
intractable are not necessarily inherent in the idea of perfect power."[6]
Griffin rejects the idea that God holds all power over the created world
since even the greatest possible power remains one power among others.
Griffin therefore argues that even a being with "perfect power" cannot
guarantee that other beings will avoid all genuine evil.[7] Other theologians
have revised common assumptions about God's goodness. In a critical
review of Griffin's theodicy, Philip Hefner observes that classical Jewish
and Christian texts hold God responsible for *all* acts, good and evil.
Hefner's understanding of God's nature therefore includes destructive
forces of violence and negation. For Hefner, anything less would "[miss]
the reality of tragedy and the deep-down demonic that runs through this
world's history."[8]

Historically, Western theologians have proceeded to a still higher level
of theoretical abstraction. God is not just a powerful, loving, and just
entity. Rather the very idea of God demands the notion of perfect being.
This implies omnipotence and omnibenevolence—attributes abstracted
from tangible human qualities and absolutized. Metaphysical theists like
Hick and philosophical skeptics like Anthony Flew and H. J. McCloskey
actually agree that the idea of God, whose existence they dispute, must
possess perfect power and perfect love. Any less a God is thought to
prove unworthy of worship (or at least debate). Rejecting the idea of a
finite God, Hick argues that "once our concept of God loses the firm
shape provided by an inner backbone of metaphysical ultimacy it is liable
to . . . fail to satisfy the exigencies of religion."[9] Coming from the opposite philosophical perspective, Flew admits that, logically, an omnipotent
God may retain despotic rights against human creatures. But, he argues,
"such positions are uncomfortable, particularly for those who wish also to
find in God something straightforwardly deserving praise."[10] Echoing
Hick, H. J. McCloskey also observes, "It is commonly argued that one
way of avoiding the problem of evil is to contend that God is finite,
imperfect in respect of power or goodness." However, he adds, "there

are also good reasons for believing that a finite God would not be a fitting and proper object of worship."[11]

Hick, Flew, and McCloskey agree that a God incomplete in either goodness or power would not be "worshipful." With this criterion of worshipfulness in place, they have reduced the problem of evil to a strictly logical problem. Can the concept of omnibenevolence cohere with the concept of omnipotence given the reality of genuine evil? Can God be *absolutely* good and *absolutely* powerful while permitting innocent people to suffer? If absolutely good, God would want to remove genuine evil. If omnipotent, God could remove it. This constitutes Epicurus's classical argument cited by David Hume in the *Dialogues Concerning Natural Religion*. However one decides what may be an intractable debate, the following holds true. Proponents of metaphysical theism have raised the stakes—as it were—by absolutizing the terms in dispute. In so doing, they have generated logical problems whose severity may be unique in the history of religious thought.

For their part, contemporary Jewish theologians face the same problems that beset any philosophical theist. True, the attributes of omnipotence and omnibenevolence belong less to the biblical-midrashic "God of Abraham, Isaac, and Jacob" than to the scholastic "God of Aristotle." Yet Jewish literary sources represent God as sufficiently powerful and merciful to provoke serious questions at the first and second levels of our analysis. Jewish theologians—like metaphysical theists—must wonder about the coherence of beliefs that posit the existence of a God effectively powerful or concerned with human destiny.

At the same time, Jewish thinkers face problems peculiar to Jewish traditions. Above all, they must consider the specific fate of the Jewish people and its relation with God. In this light, Jewish destiny represents a special case of providence. Both classical Jewish texts and twentieth-century Jewish thinkers have together emphasized the notion of a special and binding relation between God and His [*sic*] people—a relation described in terms of covenant. This political leitmotif complicates philosophical questions about divine existence, attributes, and providence. At the same time, it does not remain immune to historical crisis. After Auschwitz, Jewish theologians like Richard Rubenstein, Eliezer Berkovits, Emil Fackenheim, Arthur Cohen, and Irving Greenberg have come to debate God's status as Israel's covenantal partner. Does the Holocaust irreparably break the covenant between the people and its God? Does it render the very idea implausible? In contrast to a more abstract philosophical theism, the notion of covenant has forced Jewish thought into a superadded social dimension.

Covenant demands highly personified images of God—as king, father, friend, lover. Israel is said to have made a contract with a personality, not with some rarified force, power, ground, or presence. The problem of evil, however, has compelled many contemporary Jewish theologians to envision God in these more mystical, less personalist terms.[12] Theologians face two possible options if God is—as it were—"a father" who in some measure controls the world. Either that divine person inflicts or permits excruciating horror, or that divine person has so grossly neglected the governance of the world as to be effectively absent. Either option proves sufficiently grotesque to have tempted some to opt out of this dilemma by adopting less personal notions of God. Rubenstein for one could not believe in the God of History. His God reflected Paul Tillich's theological language about the "Ground of Being" and a Jewish mysticism gleaned from Gershom Scholem's monumental research in Kabbalah. Yet in abandoning personified God-talk, Rubenstein and others dilute the force of mitzvah (commandment) and community that only a personal God-idea would seem to generate. Without a personal God, covenant would seem impossible.

More traditional theologians like Berkovits and Greenberg have taken another, but equally radical, route. They maintain belief in a personal God but wonder about the future of the covenant as heretofore constituted. Does God remain sufficiently powerful, loving, good, or present to be considered reliable? A radically negative response threatens to abrogate the relationship. If the covenantal partner proves unreliable, perhaps the terms and responsibilities of the covenant need to be renegotiated. Berkovits argues that "covenant . . . not only allows but, at times, requires the Jew to contend with the divine 'Thou.'"[13] Irving Greenberg suggests that Holocaust necessitates a "voluntary covenant." For these thinkers, belief or disbelief per se are not at issue. Rather, the questions they pose concern whether and on what terms "dialogue" and relation with this God are still possible. After Auschwitz, covenant remains a theoretically plausible but potentially unbearable religious option.

Covenant lends increased, even personal pathos to post-Holocaust religious discourse. The contractual motif of covenant compounds philosophical discourse with an emotionally laden and legally binding language of rights and responsibilities. Is God a God of covenant? What were God's obligations during the systematic slaughter of His [sic] people? Where was God? Pearl Benisch, an Orthodox Jewish survivor of the Holocaust, describes how a skeptical companion told her: "You know, I always envied you your faith. I still do, more than ever, but I just cannot believe in your God. He deserted us; He deserted you. Where is He?"[14] Abstract questions about God's nature or existence reflect logical confusion and metaphysical bewilderment. Covenantal doubts concern the reliability of God and the viability of a relationship. They supplement philosophical confusion with bitter feelings of personal betrayal. In the face of this betrayal, theodicy (at least at our second and third levels of abstraction) may ultimately prove ineffective and irrelevant.

World Maintenance

In the late 1960s and early 1970s, scholars in the social sciences examined religious belief, the problem of evil, and theodicy. Combining sociological and psychological perspectives, Peter Berger has argued that theodicy is a type of social masochism that legitimates social institutions at the expense of suffering individuals. "Theodicy," he writes, "is the surrender of self to the ordering power of society."[15] According to Berger, religion demands that the suffering individual abdicate his or her private welfare before the meaning giving power of God and society. God and society constitute loci of value whose importance outweighs any single individual's personal pain. From the perspective of symbolic anthropology, Clifford Geertz contends that religious concepts provide a framework for interpreting experience in meaningful form. Sacred symbols (ideas, objects, rituals) show how a given social ethos and a cosmic nomos reflect and sustain each other.[16] According to both Geertz and Berger, religions propound a conservative message: concrete political orders reflect larger cosmic patterns and as such command reverence despite the chaos that individuals experience at liminal moments.

The key words in the sociological treatment of theodicy were *order* and *meaning*. Max Weber had already observed in his classic *Sociology of Religion* how salvation religions like Judaism and Christianity provide their members a unified worldview that lends coherent meaning to social life. According to Weber, the experience of suffering and evil disrupts meaning by unsettling the immediate correspondence between empirical reality and religious worldviews.[17] Berger and Thomas Luckmann have since developed this thesis in *The Social Construction of Reality* (1966). They describe how elaborate social mechanisms (e.g., institutionalization, legitimation, symbolic and conceptual world-maintenance, socialization, repetition) construct systems of shared meaning. Symbolic systems of legitimation are especially potent mechanisms. They order the subjective apprehension of marginal and liminal individual experience by integrating them into an overarching universe of meaning. This, it is said, promotes feelings of security and belonging. "On the level of meaning," Berger and Luckmann write, "the institutional order represents a shield against terror."[18]

Berger develops this line of argument in *The Sacred Canopy* by directly applying it to religious life. He defines religion as that human enterprise

by which cultures construct a sacred social order (cosmos) out of unruly
empirical life (chaos). Berger describes social legitimation in the terms of
theodicy. It "serves to support the swaying edifice of social order. This is
the process of legitimation. By legitimation is meant socially objectivated
'knowledge' that serves to explain and justify the social order."[19] According to Berger, religion is a particularly effective device with which to
justify social orders. It locates human experience within a noetic frame of
reference that is ultimate and universal. Religious systems combine, under one sacred canopy, an expansive host of theological, social, and textual forces. In this view theodicy remains religion's primary function.
"Evil" signifies anomalous forces that interrupt the orderly process of
world-maintenance. In response, religious actors uphold a violated social
order by justifying the relation that subsists between God and anomic
experience.[20]

Critically building on the work of Weber, Luckmann, and Berger, I
would first frame the sociological problem more baldly. Society itself
must be justified. The catastrophic suffering born of mass death and the
wholesale destruction of collective aggregates radically undermine social
and symbolic orders. War and systematic injustice provoke severe crises
under which a given social form, an entire society, may either persevere
or dissolve. Social actors wonder whether the society in which they live
contains sufficient institutional, symbolic, or moral resources with which
to survive; or whether it is so deeply implicated in either the pain that it
inflicts or the horror it suffers that nothing could possibly redeem it from
dissolution. Ideologues and intellectuals (religious or not) constantly defend social formations. They seek to show how a social formation retains
value despite the evil that it inflicts or proves powerless to prevent. In
doing so, they explain how nation-states, political parties, institutions,
holidays, leadership structures, symbols, metaphors, and discursive traditions remain worthy of devotion, respect, and care. American culture
wars over the value of the Western canon come immediately to mind as a
case in point. In these debates the canon's value is said by its defenders to
overshadow the sorry record of slavery, imperialism, sexism, and class oppression. Those who continued championing the Communist Party in
the 1950s despite revelations of the Stalinist purges represent another
example. In each case, the defenders of a social order encourage us to
accept it despite the experience or memory of evil and suffering with
which it is associated. Such attempts to explain and accept social phenomena are acts of justification—no less than theodicy, but with a clearly
different object.

So far Weber, Luckmann, and Berger's work proves particularly apt in
moving us beyond any single-minded concern with theodicy. Their research suggests that the problem of evil in religious life takes on a social

dimension that outstrips the narrow confines of theology. Ironically, however, they themselves overstate the role of symbolic orders and theodicy
in the process of world maintenance. They never indicate that religious
thinkers may try to maintain vulnerable social structures without defending God or integrating evil into a justifying universe of symbolic meaning. Even more to the point, religious thinkers may defend endangered
communities (i.e., a social ethos) by actually putting God and providence
(i.e., the sacred nomos) on trial. Weber, Luckmann, and Berger seem not
to know any religious text or tradition that include such phenomena.
Indeed, they have grossly exaggerated the psychic protection offered by
symbolic systems. They do not consider what may be the more terrifying
option—namely, rebuilding community within a symbolic system governed by an uncanny, unreliable God. At the same time, we should not
exaggerate the importance of terror as a religious motif. The everyday
(banal) structures of a self-maintaining social ethos may offer religious
actors a surprising degree of confidence and autonomy before this same
unruly *nomos*.

This of course leads us to Jewish social identity and its combination of
the prosaic and the symbolic. Since the onset of modernity, Jewish
thinkers have faced the practical question of Judaism's ability to secure its
members' continued loyalty to a corporate body. A host of modern political, economic, and ideological forces have historically worked to the det-
riment of Jewish communal bonds: social emancipation, economic integration, and universalistic ideals. The Holocaust exacerbates this process.
Today, under the triple impact of "emancipation," "enlightenment," and
genocide, Jewish theologians continue to worry about the dissolution of
the institutions, texts, and rituals that have heretofore formed the Jewish
people. This social crisis carries severe symbolic valence. A corollary to a
covenant-God are images of Israel as a people covenanted to God. The
community of Israel is said to enjoy and suffer special attention. A watch-
ful God solicits their merits and shortcomings. This attention clothes a
flesh-and-blood, social entity with a paradoxical metaphysical status that
has brought it divine love and wrath, a bright messianic promise, and
bitter martyrological experience.

Consistent adherence to democratic, universal social values, it has been
suggested, precludes the notion of exclusive social contracts. Logically,
members of particular ethnic or religious groups who would want to participate equally within a pluralistic society cannot comfortably hold that
they are more beloved by God by virtue of a special spiritual compact.[21]
The challenges posed by social inclusion and democratic ideals predate
the Holocaust. As such, the Holocaust has only intensified extant problems with the image of a covenant-people. Does God love Israel? And if
indeed God had chosen Israel (or if Israel had chosen God), why should

contemporary Jews continue to accept this designation? It is no longer
evident why a people should hold to a covenant whose terms have included recurring patterns of marginalization, vilification, persecution, exile, and (in the twentieth century) systematic genocide. As Greenberg
writes, "As the cost of faithfulness increased, the Jews might have withdrawn and cut their losses."[22] Twentieth-century history has outstripped
the modern social theories that have worked against Jewish social myths.
Catastrophic suffering may not logically preclude the image of a covenant-people, but it threatens to make the very notion unbearable.

Apologetics

Textual dilemmas generated by the problem of evil have only recently
begun to receive adequate scholarly analysis.[23] Literary canons frequently
constitute the very fabric from which cultures are constructed. A textual
tradition may depict a culture's putative origins, clarify values, envision a
future, establish observances and ritual patterns, define individual and
collective identities, and delineate institutions, lines of authority, and due
process. Almost by definition, constitutional texts become objects of special care, devotion, attention, and love. Conversely, these very same texts
(along with their faithful interpreters) invite conflict, scorn, ridicule, hurt,
hate, contempt, disgust, or apathy in the face of suffering and injustice.
As David Tracy has observed, when literate cultures suffer crisis, so too
do their books.[24]

Contemporary Christian and Jewish feminists have been among the
strongest exemplars of Tracy's point. Religious texts often trouble contemporary readers who may find no information with which to intelli-
gibly understand, accept, or resist the forces that afflict them. Judith Plaskow writes about how a single verse describing Israel's preparation
preceding God's revelation at Sinai works to exclude women from the
center of religious life. She explains: "Given the importance of this event,
there can be no verse in the Torah more disturbing to the feminist than
Moses' warning to his people in Exodus 19:15, 'Be ready for the third
day; do not go near a woman.' . . . At the central moment of Jewish
history, they are invisible. . . . It was not their experience that interested
the chronicler or that informed and shaped the Torah."[25] Any sacred text
may prove irrelevant to contemporary concerns, needs, beliefs, or tem-
pers. In this case it contains language, propositions, and images that radically contradict them. The gender inequities that characterize text and
tradition alienate feminist readers, creating a deep religious crisis. While
some (Plaskow included) struggle to reread traditional texts, many others
abandon them as irredeemably misogynist. As Mary Daly suggests, "The

women's movement [presents] a growing threat to patriarchal religion less by attacking it than by simply leaving it behind."[26]

Textual crisis occurs at three heuristically defined levels. "The text itself" is a relatively independent sequence of utterances, images, and meanings. It may include a single verse, a single chapter, a single book. Historical change may cause readers to find the isolated text outdated or pernicious. No single text, however, exists in radical isolation. The "text itself" does not exist. "Tradition" represents a second order of text and textual crisis. Any single text has always been already read in terms set by other texts. Every text represents an intertext. In this case the reader may not reject a given textual unit, but the way it is interpolated vis-à-vis other texts. "Traditional-readings-of-tradition" constitute a third order of text and textual crisis. After all, traditions are not consistent, unified, and self-enclosed units. They are diversified and densely layered. Previous readers transmit tradition in bits by selecting specific traditional texts and excluding others. In this light individuals may reject traditional-readings-of-tradition rather than individual texts or traditions.

At stake in a textual crisis is whether or not texts, canons, and the culture that defines them allow readers the power to reinterpret. Do textual traditions contain the resources with which to withstand the evil that their readers inflict on others or suffer themselves? Can people continue reading text and tradition in a traditional style or must they develop post-traditional hermeneutics? Perhaps a text or tradition remains exhausted. There are no unmined resources for particular groups of authorially intended or unintended readers to exploit. However, readers might find meanings unsuspected by authors and redactors, meanings that traditional readings ignored, obscured, or even repressed. Some readers might select certain texts from the tradition that speak to them and gradually forget those that do not. The process of textual transmission then becomes a question as to whether readers possess, take, or risk the requisite skills and authority with which to proffer strong alternative readings of the text or tradition.

In the face of evil and suffering, apologetics constitute the means by which readers justify texts, traditions, and traditional-readings-of-tradition. We identity two prevalent types: classical and revisionist. Classical apologists indiscriminately endeavor to draw other readers closer to texts, traditions, and traditional-readings-of-traditions. For them, this matrix possesses a uniform value. The entire tradition is said to be good and wholesome, despite appearances to the contrary. A case in point is the apologist who unequivocally defends texts that delineate traditional practices surrounding menstruation (*niddah* and *mikveh*). He or she might argue that the text (when properly understood) contributes to the dignity of women, moral discipline, and ethical culture. No thought is given to how such practices might work against the image and interests of women. In contrast, the proponent of a revisionist apologetic might attack a traditional-reading-of-tradition as misogynist without abandoning the text or tradition itself. For instance, the Orthodox Jewish feminist Blu Greenberg condemns misogynistic understandings of *niddah* found among medieval kabbalists while fiercely defending the tradition itself.[27] Revisionists like Greenberg reread texts and traditions. They emphasize textual meanings that traditional-readings-of-tradition had ignored, suppressed, or never even considered. In this way they explain that text and tradition hold a preponderance of value—despite traditional-readings-of-them that either provoke crisis or cannot withstand it.

From a defensive point of view, apologists of either stripe attempt to render constitutional texts unobjectionable, significantly absolved of responsibility for evil or suffering. They overlook, pacify, exorcise, or otherwise master the demons who haunt the text and the multiple layers of tradition in which it is embedded. Apologists argue that text and tradition, when viewed positively, generate narrative and practical meanings that remain worthy of transmission under proper conditions. In the end, however, apologists justify *themselves*. At all costs they must not resemble reactionary obscurants clutching a dying literature or irrelevant practice. Rather, they remain virtuous defenders of a venerable tradition or bold interpreters of a still-vital canon. In either case they defend their own devotion. Their work and thoughts retain abiding depth and significance since one can still profit from reading the texts and traditions that they champion. Apologists thereby reach this conclusion. They have wasted neither their own time nor the time of the community by poring over outdated or even dangerous books. The tradition (whether in its entirety or in part) is rendered good and wholesome despite all evidence to the contrary.

The apologetic project proves to be a mainstay in post-Holocaust thought. With Auschwitz in mind, many contemporary readers are repelled by the theodicies found in traditional Jewish sources. Both biblical and rabbinic authors depict God rewarding the righteous and punishing the wicked. In its crudest form, this leads to a just-desserts theodicy. Its proponents argue that those who suffer deserve their fate for the sins they must have committed. In this light the Holocaust has been represented as God's punishment of the Jewish people for the putative sins of assimilation and Zionism. A less punitive tradition asserts that God tests, prepares, and purifies the innocent in order to offer deferred retribution in a messianic and/or otherworldly future. Still other classical Jewish authors appeal to mystery or answer that virtue is its own reward. After the Holocaust these kinds of response are as likely to fall on deaf ears as is a just-desserts theodicy. Like God and society, "Torah" may appear unjust, unkind, and uncaring. Rubenstein has complained that in Jewish tradition, suffering people always stand in the wrong before a righteous God. From a different perspective, we saw Peter Berger arguing that "Judeo-Christian" texts demonstrate a marked masochism in the face of genuine evil. According to this line of thought, traditional texts inculcate a psychology of self-blame before a guiltless deity.

Antitheodicy

Classical Jewish texts, however, contain antitheodic sources that suggest the opposite. By antitheodicy we mean any religious response to the problem of evil whose proponents refuse to justify, explain, or accept as somehow meaningful the relationship between God and suffering. The presence of protest parables and counter lawsuit patterns within the classical canon may even provide contemporary scholars of religion sufficient warrant to look past the theodicies that saturate Jewish texts, tradition, and traditional-readings-of-tradition. Such texts suggest that religious response to the problem of suffering proves far more complicated than a one-sided analysis of theodicy would imply. Classical Jewish response to the problem of evil is overwhelmingly theodic. Nevertheless, antitheodic texts are sufficiently common to justify grouping them under a heading of their own.

In the next chapter we present a more exhaustive exposition of antitheodic texts in biblical or rabbinic literature. We suffice for now with this one example that highlights the responsibilities that fall upon the senior partner to Israel's covenant. The text does not presuppose the perfect being about whom philosophers of religion argue. Nor does it reflect the masochism that Berger suspects of traditional theistic texts. Commenting upon the fratricidal struggle between the biblical Cain and Abel, the author of one early Palestinian midrash observes with marked shock:

> It is difficult to say this thing, and the mouth cannot utter it plainly. Think of two athletes wrestling before the king; had the king wished, he could have separated them. But he did not so desire, and one overcame the other and killed him, he [the victim] crying out [before he died], "Let my cause be pleaded before the king!"[28]

This parable from Genesis Rabbah (and others like it) constitutes an antitheodic response to the problem of suffering. Its author blames neither Abel nor the wrestler. No sin is sought to vindicate God's judgment. No solace is found in the world-to-come. We find no allusions to the importance of free human will. No lessons are taught regarding virtue being its own reward. Acting like a Roman tyrant, God has failed to meet the standards of covenantal justice that are expected of Him [*sic*].

Covenant proves to be a double-edged trope. Throughout much of the biblical and rabbinic corpus, guilty human beings are hauled to court to plead their case before a divine judge. However, the notion of covenant introduces a third and unpredictable element into the relation between God and human persons. Law becomes a mediating power with its own jurisdiction. In covenant-theologies, God does not represent a distant, numinous entity. Israel and God are co-partners, a contractual agreement binding them both. As one rabbinic sage opined, "Do you know who can protest against His decree and say to Him, 'Why do you do such a thing?' He who observes the commandments."[29] Having accepted this contract, human figures use it to their own ends. They possess unique rights and language by which to press their interests *against* God. As such, theodicy does not represent the only theological response to suffering. Covenantal models of faith include an audacious language of anger and demand that expands the dialogue between heaven and earth. Indeed, sole recourse to theodicy may ultimately cripple contemporary religious discourse by forcing philosophers and theologians to defend the indefensible.

We saw above that the image of a covenant-people proves subject to serious strain in the face of suffering. However, it too creates a unique theological vantage point. The idea of covenant has both complicated and enriched theology by bringing people into the center of religious discourse. Consequently, God no longer occupies the sole or even central object of their devotion. The figure of Israel will at times actually determine contemporary Jewish religious discourse. Care for this people, its texts, and ritual patterns frames both classical and contemporary Jewish theology and dictates what Jewish thinkers say (and refuse to say) about God and evil. It explains the solidarity with the victims of suffering, a Karamazov-like rebellion on their behalf. In one rabbinic text, the rabbis depict Moses challenging God's treatment of Israel prior to the Exodus from Egypt. "R. Ishmael said: It is evident that Thou has not so far saved them. . . . Then did the Attribute of Justice seek to strike Moses, but after God saw that Moses argued thus only because of Israel, He did not allow the Attribute of Justice to strike him."[30] It is precisely this social solidarity that many contemporary critics have found lacking in philosophic theodicy—a discourse whose central pivot is God, not suffering human people.

Typically the term *apologetics* bears an unfair pejorative sense. In our view it is apologetic necessity that compels religious readers to reinvent tradition. A masterful apologist, Eliezer Berkovits draws on antitheodic traditions when formulating his own post-Holocaust thought. Compare his reading of the *akiedah* with Jacques Derrida's. Derrida has recently commented upon the silence that characterizes Kierkegaard's "knight of faith." By not speaking, this lonely Abraham bears the responsibility of being truly singular.[31] Both Derrida and Kierkegaard equate the incommensurable and incommunicable with singularity; they accept the equation even to the point of slaughtering Isaac. In stark contrast the Abraham read by Berkovits does not keep silent. This covenantal Abraham responds dialogically, "Almighty God! What You are asking of me is terrible. I do not understand you. You contradict Yourself. But I have known You, my God. You have loved me and I love You. My God, You are breaking Your word to me. What is one to think of You! Yet I trust You; I trust You."[32] Derrida's Abraham comes close to resembling the pious, resigned figure found in traditional-readings-of-tradition. His Abraham accepts a cruel command and attributes meaning to it. The command to slaughter Isaac thus turns into a good. In comparison, Berkovits's Abraham simultaneously accepts and rejects the decree—without interpreting the monstrosity as meaningful. Berkovits insists, "The monstrosity remained monstrous; the inhumanity remained foul injustice tolerated by God." And yet this antitheodic pose does not prevent Berkovits's Abraham from loving God.[33]

Sometimes a text is more important to the members of a religious culture than the God they serve. Berkovits's reading of the *akieidah* suggests how religious thinkers might decide to justify and accept the canon rather than the deity who inhabits it. In this case Berkovits can embrace a troubling figure like Abraham at Mt. Moriah because the tradition contains an antitheodic trace that reflects and contributes to his own post-Holocaust thought. He can point to doubts expressed by Abraham, Job, Habakkuk, Jeremiah, and the rabbinic maverick Elisha ben Abuyeh.[34] In so doing Berkovits becomes an apologetic rereader of the Jewish doctrine of covenant. For him Jewish texts *must* remain meaningful after the Holocaust even when God's actions prove otherwise. Artful interpretation makes it possible to read such meanings out of and into the canon.

Competing ideas about God and suffering highlight the polysemy characteristic of traditional Jewish texts. For their part, poststructuralist literary theorists (with their penchant for finding multiple and contradictory meanings) have encouraged us to detect and account for an antitheodic strain. Daniel Boyarin argues that a midrashic text represents a mosaic of interests, that rabbinic texts dialogically contest their own assertions.[35] He observes that "the heterogeneity—the multivocality of the biblical text itself, its hiatuses and gaps, creatively but not open-endedly filled in by the midrash—allows it to generate its meanings . . . in ever new social and cultural situations."[36] In this view heterogeneity, interpretation, and revision are built into the literary system of texts called Torah. Indeed, he and other poststructuralist theorists have stressed the virtually infinite power of interpretation and revision displayed by Berkovits's reading of Abraham.

These theoretical considerations will inform our own understanding of post-Holocaust Jewish theology in Part 2 of this study. Rubenstein, Berkovits, and Fackenheim inherit a historically dense body of ideas, tropes, and texts. However, this imposing inheritance does not render its readers passive. The rendering of tradition, the process of textual transmission, leaves many questions open to the free play of interpretation. Which parts of the tradition will Rubenstein, Berkovits, and Fackenheim isolate? Which will they select unreservedly? Which will they reject out of hand? Which will they transfigure? In Chapter 2 we survey theodic and antitheodic expression in Bible and midrash. This sketch will then allow us to see that Rubenstein, Berkovits, and Fackenheim refashion Jewish thought by jostling a self-contradicting literary corpus. Their work demonstrates how contemporary readers wield enormous power over theological and literary canons by manipulating textual difference.

I end this chapter with two points about the interrelationship between religious thought and reading. First, the existence of a theodic tradition, even a hegemonic one, does not preclude the presence of an antitheodic countertradition in the very same body of texts. As I show in the Chapter 2, the theological motif of covenant has generated a lawsuit pattern by which a divine judge holds guilty human parties before the bar. However, those subject to the covenant can invert the lawsuit pattern. Aggrieved human parties then successfully try their case. World maintenance, the need to maintain a suffering community and uphold the dignity of its members, may mean defending human partners to the covenant even against God. In turn, antitheodic traditions within the classical corpus authorize this move by providing textual warrants. This suggests our second conclusion. We now know that traditional texts possess a heterogeneity unsuspected by scholars in the philosophy and sociology of religion writing in the late 1960s and 1970s. Extratheological foci and antitheodic texts undermine scholarly preoccupations with theodicy, meaning, and theological categories of "worshipfulness." More importantly, they have allowed religious thinkers to sidestep philosophical assaults and counterassaults raging around belief in an omnipotent, omnibenevolent deity. As we have seen, close attention to textual difference shifts the frame of debates surrounding religion, religious thought, and the problem of evil away from any single-minded analysis of theodicy. Textual difference may also show how religious thought survives intellectual attempts to "justify," "explain," or "accept" the relationship between the God of History and catastrophic suffering. Perhaps after Auschwitz, to some degree or another, the act of loving God must remain unjustified.

TWO

ANTI/THEODICY

IN BIBLE AND MIDRASH

The continued and iterated protest against injustice, which
becomes one of the main motifs of the book, marks it as the
product of the plebeian mind. Neither Job nor his opponents
in the debate have anything in common with the Wisdom
teachers and their ideal of prudence and success, or Ben Sira
and his insistence on human freedom of choice. Widely as
these pietists disagree among themselves, thrift, diligence, and
cleverness never occur to them as ethical ideals.
(Louis Finkelstein, *The Pharisees*)

FROM THE PERSPECTIVE of biblical and rabbinic Judaism," so
writes Richard Rubenstein, "neither the justice nor the power of
God can ever be denied." Rubenstein insists that in classical Jewish texts, a just and merciful God is "the ultimate Author" responsible for
every catastrophe in Jewish history. "Before such a God," he complains,
"humanity must forever be in the wrong."[1] In contrast, Eliezer Berkovits
approaches tradition in an entirely different spirit. His treatment of Elisha
ben Abuyeh, the arch heretic of rabbinic times, represents a case in point.
The sight of suffering compels Elisha to conclude that "there is neither
judgment nor judge." Surprisingly, Berkovits (our so-called traditionalist)
refuses to condemn Elisha. Instead, he insists that Elisha "looms large in
the pages of the Talmud and forces upon the conscience of Judaism the
awareness of the seriousness of this issue."[2] Two different hermeneutical
methods are at stake here. Rubenstein finds a monolithic tradition that
permits no complaint against the magisterial God of History. For Berkovits, Judaism proves multivocal. An apostate grieved by the problem of
evil represents a legitimate voice *within* the tradition.

The contrast between Rubenstein and Berkovits illustrates how conflicts about "tradition" permeate post-Holocaust Jewish thought. One
cannot contest or champion traditional Judaism without understanding
both the range and limits that mark its treatment of a problem. Consequently, our own study of post-Holocaust Jewish theology must turn to a
close but careful reading of classical Jewish texts. By this, I mean a reading that will account for the conflicting strains that characterize a text or

tradition without overinterpreting their significance. A close reading does not overlook textual difference. But neither should it exaggerate the importance of heterogenous expression. With this in mind, I argue that loose readings of classical Jewish texts confound post-Holocaust religious thought. Rubenstein has ignored and Berkovits exaggerated the textual difference found in traditional Jewish thought. Against Rubenstein, classical Jewish texts do not always hold humanity in the wrong before the God of History. But neither does Elisha ben Abuyeh "loom large in the pages of the Talmud."

In this chapter I purposefully limit the term *tradition* to Bible and rabbinic aggadah—even though the tradition obviously contains much more. Rubenstein means the Bible when he writes, "All of the Torah is holy; all of it confronts us."[3] When he probes the "religious imagination," he only examines aggadah. Likewise, Berkovits and Fackenheim virtually ignore medieval philosophy, mysticism, and commentary in their post-Holocaust thought. Berkovits mentions medieval philosophers in only a handful of insignificant footnotes. Rubenstein and Fackenheim use Lurianic metaphors like "*ayin*," "rupture," and "*tikkun*" but do not include substantive textual analysis or even citation of kabbalistic sources. In short, when post-Holocaust theologians consider the meaning and relevance of tradition, they confine their discussion to biblical and rabbinic thought. And even then their readings prove highly selective.

Rubenstein, Berkovits, and Fackenheim faced a broad consensus among the scholarly community in the 1960s about the unity of tradition and the place of theodicy in it. Ephraim Urbach, in his classic study *The Sages*, characterized rabbinic theology in terms of "absolute theodicy." For Urbach, this meant an "unmitigated and absolute justification of God's judgment."[4] His usage conforms to our own discussion in Chapter 1. Theodicy means any attempt to justify, explain, or ascribe acceptable significance to the relation between God and evil. Prophet and sage typically taught that suffering represents just desserts or cleansing expiation. In this light they attempted to console and rally hope by salvaging God's image as loving, powerful, trustworthy, and ultimately active in human affairs. Theodicy—viewed as a dense nexus of competing images and ideas—forms a bulwark in classical Jewish thought. It dominates rabbinic exegesis and aggadah—not to mention Deuteronomy, the Deuteronomic histories spanning Joshua, Judges, Samuel, Kings, and prophetic literature. Later traditions center around the martyrological figure of R. Akiba and the victims of the Crusader massacres who willingly sacrificed their lives trusting God. Traditional Judaism seemed to offer no other type of response to the problem of suffering.

Urbach, however, grossly exaggerated the significance of classical theodicy when he called it absolute.

Exponents of current critical theory have taught us to interrogate apparently hegemonic messages. The biblical critic Mike Bal argues that coherent patterns of textual meaning are always qualified by what she calls a counter-coherence. A counter-coherence consists of disparate textual information that disrupts an otherwise monolithic message.[5] The presence of a counter-coherence does not obviate established patterns of textual meaning. Its effect is rather to "enforce an awareness of a reality that is also represented in the book."[6]

Following Bal, I will insist that classical Jewish theodicy carries its own counter-coherence, an antitheodicy, that has hitherto gone unnamed. The book of Job and rabbinic aggadah lend themselves to three basic forms of antitheodicy: complaint, solidarity, and incomprehension.

Antitheodicy mirrors theodicy in reverse but should not be confused with atheism. In both theodic and antitheodic discourse, religious believers address the relation that they see between God, providence, evil, and human suffering. However, by definition, antitheodic statements do not do what theodic statements do. They neither justify, explain, ascribe positive meaning, account for, resolve, understand, accept, or theologically rectify the presence of evil in human affairs. The authors of antitheodic statements do not assume that suffering represents a necessary or acceptable price for certain goods. Rather, they express anger, hurt, confusion. They do not try to silence suffering people. In solidarity with the community and its members, some proponents of antitheodicy protest against God and providence. Others might recognize the epistemological limits of the human mind and eschew any explanatory framework (without justifying God in the next breath!). We might have called this *anthropodicy* (the justification of "man"). Antitheodicy inverts the focus of theodicy. It represents a type of religious thought in which human persons (not God) occupy central attention. Rather than defend God or accept catastrophe, the authors of antitheodic statements justify human figures and reject suffering along with its rewards.[7]

I employ the terms *theodicy* and *antitheodicy* with extreme caution in connection with classical Jewish thought. Neither term is indigenous to that corpus. Indeed, as will become clear in this chapter's conclusion, neither points to a stable entity or fixed semantic grouping. A statement that is theodic in one context can turn antitheodic in another. The reverse also holds true. Therefore, theodicy and antitheodicy never refer to any specific semantic *content*, to any specific utterance. Like all concepts, they are *formal* indicators. We use them tentatively: to identify tensions that characterize the canon and organize its discourse under provisional headings. At the very least, the term *antitheodicy* helps us challenge attempts by theologians, scholars, or critics of religion to represent traditional religious thought as unequivocally theodic.

Classical Jewish response to suffering swings between theodic and antitheodic modes of discourse—between the Book of Deuteronomy and the
Book of Job. As evidenced below, the concluding Song of Moses in
Deuteronomy and the final chapter of Job serve as especially useful
springboards with which to further examine this tension in the Bible and,
more particularly, in rabbinic aggadah. The fact that both texts employ
a literary genre of lawsuit narrative will facilitate analysis of the tension
that subsists between theodic and antitheodic discourse. In the Song of
Moses, God calls the people to trial for abrogating the covenant. In Job a
wounded human figure contends with a God who has become mysteriously cruel. The lawsuit (*rib*) between suzerain and vassal forms a crucial juncture at which to juxtapose the interplay between theodicy and
antitheodicy in Jewish tradition. Whether the suzerain tries the vassal, or
whether vassals bring their master to court, the following holds true:
Fidelity and suffering become grave matters over which litigious subjects
dispute the often-bloodied politics of covenant in Jewish tradition.[8]

Theodicy in Bible and Midrash

At the heart of traditional Jewish theodicy lies Deuteronomy's doctrine
of reward and punishment. As a literary unit, Deuteronomy represents
the last will and testament of Moses to the Israelites before they enter the
Land of Israel. Combining law and admonition, it encodes the covenantal relationship between God and Israel that then unfolds throughout the
prophetic literature. The promises and threats described in chapter 11 are
typical of Deuteronomic discourse. If the people love and serve God with
all their heart and soul, God will provide rain in its season, food to eat,
and grass for their cattle. If they turn aside and serve other gods, He will
shut up the heavens, starve the land, and cause the people to perish.[9]
Upon delivering the law code in chapters 12–26, the rhetoric of retribution resumes with a picture of the people accepting these blessings and
curses atop Mt. Ebal and Mt. Gerizim. The text anticipates the worst but
holds out hope for the future. In chapter 30 Moses promises that God
will return an exiled Israel to its land and admonishes the people to
choose life over death. The Deuteronomist then compacts all of these
motifs into the Song of Moses—the last textual unit preceding Moses'
final blessing of the people.[10]

In the poem, occupying all of chapter 32, God summarizes Israelite
history. An eagle hovering over her nest, God has fed the people with
honey, oil, curd, milk, fat, and wheat. But "Jeshurun waxes fat and
kicks." God now threatens to hide His face from Israel. He will consume
the people, threatening them with hunger, heat, poisonous pestilence,

beasts and venom, sword and terror. Suddenly, however, God interrupts Himself. In what Gerhard von Rad has called a "soliloquy within the divine heart," God retracts His threat to scatter Israel and efface her memory.[11] With their power now dissipated, a still-faithful God promises compassion. There is none beside Him. It is He who kills and makes alive, who wounds and heals, who will avenge the blood of his servants. In the end God will graciously expiate land and people.

Alluding to Milton, G. Ernest Wright called the Song of Moses a "justification of the ways of God to Israel."[12] Indeed, this one biblical song nearly encompasses the entirety of traditional Jewish theodicy. It depicts God's kind devotions, Israelite betrayal, divine rage, and final restoration. The spectrum of reward, punishment, and expiation rests upon the idea of a morally pure God. Remembering that the Song of Moses is after all a poem, we hear the Deuteronomist sing,

> The Rock, his work is perfect;
> For all his ways are justice;
> A God of faithfulness and without iniquity,
> Just and right is he.
> Is corruption His? No, His children's is
> the blemish;
> A generation crooked and perverse.
>
> —Deut. 32:4–5

Deuteronomic theodicy is made to hinge upon the gross hyperbole expressed in these two verses. On one hand, God's ways are good and just. On the other hand, Israel stands crooked and perverse. The sins they commit precipitate the evils they suffer. In the end, however, God must overlook the moral balance between innocence and guilt. With no merit of their own, God can only turn to them in act of inexplicable grace and shower upon them blessings that they have not deserved.

The Song of Moses foreshadows almost all of the theodicies developed by the rabbis. Later rabbinic interpreters return to Deuteronomy 32:4–5, tucking their own thoughts about reward and punishment into the folds of commentary. Combining exegesis and eisegesis, the rabbis retain the biblical text in the face of historical change. This proves especially prominent in Sifre to Deuteronomy, an early tannaitic commentary. In Sifre the rabbis use Deuteronomy to interpret the disasters of their own not-so-distant past: the destruction of the Second Temple in 70 CE and the Hadrianic persecutions of 135 CE. At the same time, they outstrip Deuteronomy even as they rely upon its discourse of rewards and punishments.

Sifre chapter 307—a text commenting on Deuteronomy 32:4—contains nearly the entire range of rabbinic theodicy. The rabbis begin by counterposing the Deuteronomy 32:4 description of God as an artist with the Genesis description of God fashioning the human creature. Drawing on a philological similarity between "rock" (*Ṣur*) and "artist" (*Ṣayyar*), the text reads:

> The Rock (*ha-Ṣur*)—The Artist (*ṣayyar*), for he first designed (*ṣar*) the world and then formed man in it, as it is said, "Then the Lord God formed (*way-yiṣer*) man (Gen 2:7)—His work is Perfect (32:4): His workmanship in regard to all creatures of the world is perfect; *there can be no complaint whatsoever about His work*. None of them can look at himself and say, "If only I had three eyes, if only I had three arms, if only I had three legs, if only I walked on my head, if only my face turned the other way, how nicely it would become me!" Hence the verse [Deut 32:4] goes on to say. "For all His ways are justice"—He sits in judgment on everyone and dispenses to each that which is appropriate for him. . . . He conducts Himself uprightly with all the creatures of the world. . . . for men were created not in order to be wicked but in order to be righteous. Another interpretation: "The Rock"—the Powerful One—"His work is perfect": His actions in regard to all the creatures of the world are perfect; *there can be no complaint whatsoever about His work*. None of them can look at himself and say: "Why should the generation of the flood have been swept away by water? Why should the people of the tower (of Babel) have been scattered . . . ? Why should the people of Sodom have been swept away by fire and brimstone? Why should Aaron have assumed the priesthood? Why should David have assumed kingship? Why should Korah and his followers have been swallowed up by the earth?" Therefore the verse goes on to say "For all His ways are justice"— He sits in judgment on everyone and dispenses to each that which is appropriate for him.[13]

In this doubled interpretation of Deuteronomy 32:4–5's opening verse, the rabbis justify God on two counts. They accept the design by which the Creator formed the human creature and the way in which the Judge of history has ordered human affairs. God did not intend people to sin or suffer historical catastrophe. A just God created people for good, favors the righteous, and condemns the guilty. The text repeats itself: "There can be no complaint about his work." The repetition indicates how deeply the authors of Sifre insist on defending God, creation, and providence against the complaint of His creatures.

Deuteronomy's uneven balance between a just God and undeserving creatures saturates rabbinic thought, typically under the Hebrew rubric "*mipnei hateinu*" (literally, "on account of our sins"). This expression from the traditional festival prayer book recounts that "because of our sins we were exiled from our land." The rabbis lament their inability to perform the Temple service—a cultic service that requires a centralized place of worship in Jerusalem. This liturgical expression lamenting the *collective* punishment suffered by a guilty Israel forms part of a larger religious discourse that understands sin as causing every *individual* occurrence of suffering and death. One mishna in tractate Avot tersely relates this story about R. Hillel: "He saw a skull floating on the surface of the water. He said to it: They have drowned you because you have drowned others, and those who drowned you will themselves be drowned."[14] Violence begets violence in a reciprocal cycle. In the Babylonian Talmud, R. Ammi maintains that "there is no death without sin and there is no suffering without iniquity."[15] When pressed by his companions, he points to Moses and Aaron. Both die on account of the sin personally committed against God at Meribah.

Although his colleagues roundly dispute this radical claim, R. Ammi is not the only rabbi to link private grief to minute personal trespass. Take, for example, the rabbinic text *Avot de Rabbi Nathan*. The authors of this text describe R. Ishmael and Rabban Shimon b. Gamliel's execution during the Hadrianic persecutions. Seeking to explain why they are condemned to die like Sabbath violators, R. Ishmael finally asks Rabban Gamliel if he had ever grown haughty when teaching. Rabban Gamliel responds, "Ishmael, my brother, a person must be prepared to receive his punishment."[16] In the same text, a similar story recounts the death of a young scholar. His distressed wife visits the synagogues and study houses in search of an explanation. The text provides no answer until the sudden introduction of Elijah the prophet—a sign perhaps that the reasons for such a death lie beyond ordinary minds. Under Elijah's prolonged interrogation, the woman admits that she and her husband had once slept in the same bed during the last three days of her menstrual cycle, though she was fully clothed so as to preclude intimate contact in accordance with the law. Elijah responds, "Blessed be God who killed him, for thus is it written in the Torah, 'Also thou shall not approach unto a woman as long as she is impure by her uncleanliness.' "[17]

Both stories indicate how far the rabbis stretch the motif of retribution. R. Ishmael and Rabban Gamliel suffer political martyrdom. A young woman suffers personal tragedy. In both cases the protagonists seek some explanation that would justify the tragedy they suffer. However, neither case yields an immediate or obvious answer. Only seemingly far-fetched reasons finally explain God's decree. Momentary haughtiness and menstrual blood lend a desperate modicum of sense to their plight. In these stories the rabbis describe the causal order between sin and suffering strained to its limit—so strained that it can be maintained only by finding minute personal indiscretion to account for personal calamity. Providence does not neatly unfold in either story. Clearly, the rabbis recognize the ironic incongruence between doctrine and reality—an irony perhaps, but

one that many rabbis seriously entertain. Even though doctrines of reward and punishment become complex and attenuated, the rabbis never
reject them. Doctrines of retribution, no matter how strained, underlie
all traditional theodicy.[18]

Of course, the authors of Sifre understand that severe tensions strain
this-worldly models of retribution. As we return to Sifre, chapter 307, we
see that recourse to the future will relieve this tension. We have just seen
the text interpreting Deuteronomy's contention that the God of History
is a God of faithfulness. The text points to the distant past (the flood, the
ordination of Aaron) in order to justify the present. But, as if qualifying
itself, Sifre adds the following comment:

> Another interpretation: "The Rock"—the Powerful One—"His work is per-
> fect": The work of all creatures of the world is complete before Him, both
> the dispensing of reward to the righteous and the infliction of punishment to
> the wicked. Neither takes anything due to them in this world. . . . When do
> both of them take (that which is due to them)? "For all His ways are jus-
> tice"—in the future, when He will sit upon the throne of justice, He will sit
> in judgment on each one and give him what is appropriate for him.

> "A God of faithfulness": Just as He grants the perfectly righteous a reward in
> the world-to-come for his performance of the commandments in this world,
> so does He grant the perfectly wicked a reward in this world for any minor
> commandment performed in this world; and just as He requites the perfectly
> wicked in the world-to-come for any transgression performed in this world,
> so does He requite the perfectly righteous in this world for any minor trans-
> gression committed in this world.

Deuteronomy's rewards and punishments occupy a this-worldly, historical frame. In contrast, rabbinic theodicy plays itself out within a fantasti-
cal temporal order. The notion of a deferred retribution—messianic or
otherworldly—salvages a system of rewards and punishments within an
expanding temporal framework. Instead of understanding retribution to
operate within history, the rabbis envision it postponed until its end.
With the coming of the Messiah, the resurrection of Israel's dead, and life
in the world-to-come, the rabbis vindicate God's rule.

God's work may indeed be perfect. God may in fact reward the righteous and punish the wicked. However, our text very quickly adds, not in
this world. The authors of Sifre chapter 307 therefore point to the world-
to-come. A well-known mishna in tractate Avot iterates this otherworldli-
ness. Comparing this world to a vestibule, R. Jacob advises us to prepare
ourselves in it so that someday we may enter the banquet hall.[19] A faithful
judge, God earmarks the world-to-come—whose rewards and punishments are permanent—for the benefit of Israel and the righteous. In

contrast, God ultimately condemns the wicked even as they enjoy evanescent, worldly blessings. The rabbis are naturally aware that the deferred timing of divine retribution may astonish suffering people. In the face of shock, they counsel patience and assert that a faithful God ultimately collects His due.

The authors of Sifre, chapter 307 explain that the righteous *need* to suffer and the wicked *must* receive reward in this world. This-worldly suffering serves a crucial expiatory function.[20] In Deuteronomy's Song of Moses, God had already hinted that He will expiate His land and people. The rabbis, however, take this motif to extreme lengths. In Sifre, God afflicts the righteous in order to expiate minor transgressions committed in the here and now. God can only reward Israel in the world-to-come after cleansing them in this world. Conversely, the wicked receive reward in this world for their few good deeds so that God may punish them in the next. Suffering's expiatory power proves so powerful that the rabbis represent Abraham as anxious lest he not suffer enough. Abraham worries that he may have already exhausted his reward, leaving him insufficient credit for the world-to-come.[21]

By shifting retribution to the world-to-come, the rabbis fundamentally redefine the meaning of suffering. Unequivocally evil in Deuteronomy, suffering now assumes ambiguous value. In addition to sin and wrath, it can also signal human fidelity and devotion (*devekhut*), divine love, and spiritual perfection.[22]

While never wholly undeserved, suffering also represents the loving chastisements of a merciful God for the purpose of human betterment and salvation.[23] This revaluation assumes explicit formulation under the rubric *yisurin shel ahava* (afflictions of love). God afflicts those whom He loves in this world. In this light, suffering does not constitute an evil, but a worthy good. Interpreting the psalm "The Lord trieth the righteous, but the wicked . . . His soul hateth," R. Jonathan comments:

> A potter does not test defective vessels, because he cannot give them a single blow without breaking them. Similarly the Holy One blessed be He, does not test the wicked, but only the righteous.

Referring to a flax worker, R. Jose b. R. Ḥanina notes that the more the craftsperson beats quality flax, "the more it improves and the more it glistens."[24] God tests only that which can withstand a beating. He administers only those blows that a strong pot, good flax, and a righteous person can endure. For his part, R. Akiba therefore regards suffering as precious.[25] Afflictions of love strengthen those who suffer by cleansing them of sin. As R. Shimon b. Lakish is recorded to have said, "Sufferings wash away all the sins of a man."[26]

In light of this ambiguity regarding the meaning and value of suffering, the rabbis need to distinguish between rebuke and love. Not all instances of suffering represent afflictions of love. In most cases the rabbis mean by the latter simple physical ailments that affect the individual. According to R. Jacob b. Idi, afflictions of love do not include a pain that might keep a scholar from study. According to R. Aha b. Ḥanina they do not involve the interruption of prayer.[27] However, Sifre reflects the degree to which some rabbis accept even the most terrible suffering. Still interpreting the opening stanza of Deuteronomy 32:4, our text tells this story of R. Ḥanina b. Teradion and his family:

> Another interpretation "The Rock, His work is perfect": When they apprehended R. Ḥanina b. Teradion, he was condemned to be burned together with his Torah Scroll. When he was told of it, he recited the verse, "The Rock His work is perfect." When his wife was told, "Your husband has been condemned to be burned, and you to be executed," she recited the verse, "a God of faithfulness and without iniquity." And when his daughter was told, "Your father has been condemned to be burned, your mother to be executed, and you yourself to be assigned to (disgraceful) work," she recited the verse, "Great in counsel, and mighty in work, whose eyes are open" (upon all the ways of the sons of men to give every one according to his ways) (Jer 32:19).
>
> Rabbi Judah (the Prince) said: How great were these righteous persons, in that at the time of their trouble they invoked three verses justifying (God's) judgment, which are unequaled in Scripture. The three directed their hearts (towards God) and accepted the justice of God's judgment.

This martyrological account differs from the story about R. Ishmael and Rabban Gamliel in the following respect: R. Ḥanina b. Teradion and his family neither search for nor discover any mitigating sin that could explain why they suffer. They eschew any explanatory scheme based on thisworldly or otherworldly retribution. They simply justify God, accepting death and degradation.

R. Ḥanina b. Teradion and his family exemplify the rabbinic virtue of serving God solely for its own sake. They justify God's decree without recourse to worldly or otherworldly salvation. We find an oft-cited expression of this theme in Pirkei Avot. Antignos of Soho cites Shimon the Righteous who counseled his students not to act like servants who serve their master on the condition of receiving a reward. Rather, one should serve one's master without considering reward.[28] According to R. Meir, those who occupy themselves with the Torah for its own sake are beloved by God.[29] In a similar vein, Ben Azzai claims that ulterior goods do not constitute the true reward for the performance of a mitzvah. A mitzvah's reward is another mitzvah just as more sin represents sin's true dessert.[30]

Martyrdom (*kiddush ha-Shem*) provides the ultimate opportunity to perform mitzvot for their own sake since martyrs demonstrate selfless devotion to God. R. Akiba's martyrdom embodies Deuteronomy's exhortation to "love the Lord your God with all your heart, and all your soul and all your might."[31] In a well-known aggadah, the Talmud relates how it became time to recite the *Shema* just as the Romans were flaying R. Akiba's flesh with iron combs. As he fulfills the command of reciting the prayer, his astonished disciples ask, "Our teacher, even to this point?" R. Akiba responds:

> All my days I have been troubled by the verse "with all they soul," [which I interpret,] "even if he takes thy soul." I said: When shall I have the opportunity of fulfilling this? Now that I have the opportunity shall I not fulfill it?

R. Akiba performs a mitzvah, ignoring even the most extreme extenuating circumstances that might have kept him from it. He selflessly performs the mitzvah in this world for its own sake. But our text points to his reward in the world-to-come. A heavenly voice (*bat kol*) proclaims: "Happy art thou Akiba, that thy soul has departed with the word *eḥad* (one)! . . . Happy art thou Akiba that thou art destined for the life of the world to come."[32]

The authors of this text must have recognized the irony of R. Akiba's death concluding on such a happy note. His students express incredulity when they ask, "Even to this point?" Should not devotion to God and Torah have at least this limit? In a purely this-worldly framework, the account of R. Akiba's death should have ended sadly. Even the angels ask, "Such a Torah, and such a reward?" But the text turns tragedy into triumph by pointing to the world-to-come. This is not the only rabbinic text that describes R. Akiba leaving his companions bewildered. More than once his response to tragedy appears wildly counter-intuitive. One aggadah in Sifre tells how the sages rend their garments at the sight of the destroyed Temple. When they see a fox running out of the ruined Holy of Holies, they begin to weep. But R. Akiba laughs. "Akiba," his colleagues respond, "You never cease to astonish us." Pressed to justify himself, R. Akiba explains that since the prophecy regarding the Temple's destruction has been fulfilled, so too will prophecies regarding its restoration.[33] Explaining the difference between R. Akiba and his companions, Alan Mintz has observed that R. Akiba sees the whole process of sin, punishment, and restoration whereas they see only the tragic moment.[34] Reference to the future renders R. Akiba strangely happy before national and personal catastrophe.

R. Akiba's example provides a useful context within which to evaluate Sifre's remarkable depiction of R. Ḥanina b. Teradion and his family. Faith in the future allows R. Akiba to counter-interpret present catastrophe as a disguised good. In contrast R. Ḥaninah b. Teradion and his family take Deuteronomy to its ultimate limit. Enmeshed in the present, their frame of reference belongs solely to this-world. They do not refer to messianic redress. No heavenly voice proclaims their reward in the hereafter. R. Ḥaninah b. Teradion and his family do not rejoice like R. Akiba. Indeed, they outdo R. Akiba by justifying God's decree without recourse to interpretive stratagems. Ultimately, R. Akiba accepts the cost of what he understands to be a painful good. In contrast, R. Ḥaninah b. Teradion and his family accept without hope or promise a divine judgment that has condemned them.

In sum, Sifre, chapter 307 provides a concentrated compendium of rabbinic theodicy. It contains the doctrines of *mipnei hateinu* (just deserts), *yisurin shel ahava* (afflictions of love), the promise of otherworldly rewards, and exemplars of selfless devotion. Interpreting the Deuteronomist's central assertion of divine faithfulness, the rabbis have produced an intensive theodic message. Read together, the individual utterances that comprise it can be arranged into a coherent pattern that reads as follows:

> God rewards the righteous on the basis of accrued merit and punishes the wicked on the basis of accumulated sin. Although this retributive order is not necessarily revealed in our particular historical framework or even in this-world, God will faithfully dispense proportionate retribution in the messianic future and in the world-to-come. Indeed suffering often represents the means by which God purges Israel for its few sins in this-world so as to accrue merit for messianic and other-worldly futures. In the meantime, Israel must trust God and accept suffering. God is a loving father and a just judge whose mitzvot Israel should observe solely out of love—without any thought of the reward that is often dispensed in this world and that is surely to come in the future.

In Chapter 1 we saw how theodicy includes a cluster of functions. Theodicians justify, explain, and accept the relationship that subsists between God and evil. The response in Sifre, chapter 307 fits this pattern. The rabbis *justify* God's government of the world and Israel's affairs. They *explain* the purpose of suffering. When circumstances push the problem to its outermost limit, the rabbis can only commend virtue, *accept* suffering, and trust God.

Above all, traditional theodic figures like Rabban Gamliel, R. Ishmael, R. Akiba, R. Ḥaninah b. Teradion and his family do not complain. They exercise all the noble virtues: courage, patience, honesty, trust, hope, humility, and devotion. At the same time, we find perhaps two discordant elements in Sifre's overwhelmingly theodic commentary to Deuteronomy 32:4–5. First, our author resorts to sarcasm. The text mimics those who would prefer to have been born with three eyes or three legs or who whine about the generation of the flood. Second, our author argues not once, but twice that "there can be no complaint whatsoever about his work. . . . He sits in judgment on everyone and dispenses to each that which is appropriate for him." Both the sarcastic impatience and the word-for-word repetition suggest that perhaps our author protests too much. Perhaps his contemporaries have wondered whether God really distributes to all that which is appropriate for them. Perhaps doubts have led the unlearned or incautious astray. Or even more to the point: perhaps the author of *Sifre*, chapter 307 repeats himself precisely because impertinent expressions of complaint, solidarity with suffering people, and bewildered incomprehension occupy a remarkable place *within* the very canon of classical Judaism.

Antitheodicy in Bible and Midrash

As G. E. Wright observes, the Song of Moses takes the form of a divine lawsuit (*rib*). In this literary genre, the prophet calls heaven and earth to witness against Israel. The heavenly lawsuit implies a suzerain who claims authority over all the earth. It implies a covenant that this suzerain grants a vassal—one that the vassal has broken.[35] There exists, however, another type of lawsuit pattern in which the vassal takes his master to court. Most significantly, Norman Habel and Bruce Zuckerman have separately noted the presence of litigation (*rib*) in the dialogues of the book of Job.[36] In the view of one scholar, "The book not only abounds in judicial phraseology, but formally cannot be understood better than as the record of the proceedings of a *rib* [lawsuit] between Job and God Almighty in which Job is the plaintiff and prosecutor, the friends . . . are witnesses as well as co-defendants and judges, while God is the accused and defendant, but in the background and finally the ultimate judge of both Job and his friends."[37] Job's litigation inverts Deuteronomy's heavenly lawsuit by radically reversing the roles of prosecutor and defendant. Job censures God throughout the dialogues that constitute the major portion of the text. He calls God to account in order to uphold his own innocence. So far, the protesting Job who appears in the dialogues represents the archetype of what we now call antitheodicy.

At the end of the book of Job, the text's redactor ultimately seems to turn against the protagonist in order to defend God. In a marvelous display of divine power, God finally tells Job that he has no right to condemn Him. As Zuckerman notes, the theophany explodes the carefully constructed semblance of judicial process. Not an impartial court proceeding, but the colossal force of God's creation decides the case. Far from antitheodicy, the book of Job wrests judgment in God's favor.[38] In spite of his efforts, Job must terminate his suit before the majesty of a Creation that only God can control. It appears then that the redactor had included Job's angry litigation only to intensify reverence for God, creation, and providence.

Or does it?

Identifying the book of Job's theodic or antitheodic significance hinges on a proper interpretation of what may or may not be the retraction of Job's protest in 42:6. According to the Jewish Publication Society's translation (1917), Job repents. Following God's theophany, Job concludes, "Wherefore I abhor (*'em'as*) my words, and repent (*nihamti*), seeing I am dust and ashes." According to Edwin Good, this verse constitutes nothing less than the "punchline" of the entire book.[39] If Job repents, the book ends on the strong theodic note that most critics have heretofore observed. But if Job never retracts his complaint, the protest stands and the book remains consistently antitheodic to the very end.

I can think of no other case in which the interpretation of an entire text hangs on one such punchline, on the precise interpretation of two words. Does the Hebrew word *'em'as* mean "retract" or "despise"? Why does Job despise? Of what does he recant? The word *nihamti* is also unclear. Does it mean that Job "repents"? Or does *nihamti* reflect a turn of mind? And if the former, how does he repent? With contrition? Reluctantly? Of what does he repent? Does Job despise his own complaint? Or has he come to hate dust and ash? A brief look at a number of possible translations shows that the meaning of this verse proves notoriously unclear.

'al ken 'em'as we-nihamti 'al 'aphar wa 'epher

Job 42:6,

Wherefore I abhor my words; and repent,
Seeing I am dust and ashes.

JPS (1917)

Therefore, I recant and relent,
Being but dust and ashes

JPS (1985)

Therefore I retract
And repent of dust and ashes.

Habel

Therefore I despise and repent
of dust and ashes.

Good

According to the 1917 JPS translation, Job "repents" *in* dust and ashes. He now abhors his former complaint and piously retracts. Habel's Job behaves quite differently. According to Habel, the Hebrew word *niḥamti* (repent) reflects a change of mind. First, Job retracts (*'em'as*). That is, he forsakes litigation. However, he repents *of* dust and ashes. That is, Job picks himself up, forsakes lamentations, forswears remorse, and returns to normal life.[40] Good takes Habel's Job one step further. He notes that no direct object immediately follows the word *'em'as* (abhor) in the Hebrew text. That is, Job does not abhor or retract his complaint! According to Good, the verbs "despise" and "repent" share a single direct object: "dust and ashes." Good has Job actively come to despise the religion and rituals of mortification and self-abnegation.[41]

To be sure, biblical critics before Habel and Good pointed to the contrast between the Job depicted in the dialogues and the Job in the prologue and epilogue. The source critics could not resolve antitheodic complaint with what seemed to be the book's theodic finale. This perceived difference supported the theory that at least two authors (one pious, one impious) wrote what came to be known as the Book of Job. Habel and Good effectively resolve this tension. In their view we have no theodic conclusion to contradict Job's protest. According to both Habel and Good, the book of Job does not end with remorse. Habel has Job abandon litigation while preserving the claim to his own innocence. The struggle ends, with neither side of the dispute having persuaded the other. According to Good, Job does not even relent. One need not accept in its entirety either Habel or Good's version of the story's ending. Yet they have persuasively shown that the language of Job 42:6 does not necessarily permit us to resolve Job's protest into a more refined theodicy than the ones offered by his companions.

The possibility that Job does not retract his complaint may have been recognized in rabbinic sources. Compare the response of two rabbis with a Christian reading of Job. In the New Testament's epistle of James, the apostle observes, "Ye have heard of the patience of Job, and have seen the end of the Lord; that the Lord is very pitiful and tender of mercy."[42] James suggests that Job repents, having now witnessed God's tender mercies over creation. In contrast, rabbinic response proves less sympathetic. The rabbis do not make a penitent of Job. To the contrary! The rabbinic sage Raba interprets the seemingly pious verse "In all this Job did not sin with his lips" (2:10) to mean that Job had already sinned in the supposedly pious prologue—not with words, but in his heart. Raba accuses him of seeking to "turn the dish upside down" by declaring God's works worthless. Joining the conversation, Rab declares repeatedly, "Dust should have been put in the mouth of Job!" Unlike the apostle James, Raba and Rab are either unmoved by Job's retraction or unable to

find one. The only difference between Rab and Raba is whether to rebuke or pity. Somewhat mitigating Rab's stern retort, Raba suggests that
"a man is not held responsible for what he says when in distress."[43]

Raba and Rab's criticism notwithstanding, Job's complaint repeats itself in rabbinic literature. As we have seen, R. Ishmael, Rabban Gamliel,
R. Akiba, R. Ḥanina b. Teradion, and his family accept their own torment. But like Job, other rabbis express complaint with the way God
orders the world against the righteous. Of course, differences distinguish
the rabbis from Job. Unlike Job, the rabbis seldom protest on the basis of
personal torment or even in their own voice. They enlist biblical personae
to justify a suffering community before God. In Israel's defense, reim-
agined biblical figures try God for His performance as Judge of History.
God is once again put on trial on account of the innocent. And remarkably, God accepts their judgment and repents!

This rabbinic counter-lawsuit pattern is epitomized in Lamentations
Rabbah—a commentary to the biblical book that laments the destruction
of Jerusalem by the Babylonians in 587 BCE. In the rabbinic commentary,
the rabbis counterpose the Babylonian destruction with the Roman dev-
astation of Jerusalem and the Temple in the year 70 CE. As Mintz has
noted, the rabbis hyperbolically saturate Lamentations Rabbah with stories relating Israel's guilt.[44] Over and over, the text recounts the sins on
which account God destroys the Temple and Jerusalem this second time.
Sin—that is, gross infidelity—explains ensuing catastrophe. The rabbis
recount Israel's rejection of God, Torah and its teachers, and numerous
ethical and cultic violations.

However, in the midst of these accusations, R. Samuel bar Naḥmani
describes a heavenly trial scene.[45] Following the pattern established in the
Song of Moses, God calls a suffering Israel to court. But in a twinkling,
Israel's advocates turn the trial on its head. As Mintz observes, the author's sympathy suddenly turns away from God and toward the suffering
community.[46] A lamenting Abraham demands to know why God has sin-
gled out his children. Even the angels grieve over the broken covenant.
Now on the defensive, God blames Israel for transgressing the entire
Torah and assembles the letters of the Hebrew alphabet to testify against
the people. The trial, however, has already turned into a fiasco. Abraham
shames the letters of the Torah into silence, reminding them how Israel
had zealously received the Torah at Sinai. Abraham, Jacob, and Moses
recount the troubles they had personally suffered in this world. On the
basis of ancestral merit (*zekhut avot*), the patriarchs and Moses turn on
God in order to defend their children.

In the face of catastrophe, the rabbis have turned the lawsuit pattern
against God, the Creator and Judge of Heaven and Earth. The trial crests
as Moses and Rachel begin to testify. Reviewing the torments suffered by

Israel at the hands of the Babylonians, Moses refers God to His own
Torah. In a highly imaginative retelling of her own struggle with her
sister Leah, Rachel reminds God of her own mercy and forbearance. We
cite in brief their testimony,

> Moses again lifted up his voice, saying, "O captors, I charge you, if you kill,
> do not kill with a cruel death; do not make a complete extermination; do not
> slay a son in the presence of his father nor a daughter in the presence of her
> mother. . . ." But the wicked Chaldeans refused to comply with his request,
> and they brought a son into the presence of his mother, and said to his
> father, "Arise, slay him!" His mother wept and her tears fell upon him, and
> his father hung his head. [Moses] further spoke before [God]: "Sovereign of
> the Universe, Thou hast written in Thy Torah, 'whether it be a cow or a
> ewe, ye shall not kill it and its young both in one day' (Lev 22:28); but have
> they not killed many, many mothers and sons, and Thou art silent!"

> At that moment, the matriarch Rachel broke forth into speech before the
> Holy One . . . and said, "Sovereign of the Universe, it is revealed before
> Thee that Thy servant Jacob loved me exceedingly and toiled for my father
> on my behalf seven years. When those seven years were completed . . . my
> father planned to substitute [Leah] for me to wed my husband. . . . I re-
> lented, suppressed my desire, and had pity on my sister that she should not
> be exposed to shame. . . . And if I, a creature of flesh and blood, formed of
> dust and ashes, was not envious of my rival and did not expose her to shame
> and contempt, why shouldest Thou, a King who liveth eternally and art mer-
> ciful, be jealous of idolatry in which there is no reality and exile my children
> and let them be slain by the sword, and their enemies have done with them
> as they wished!"

> Forthwith, the mercy of the Holy One, blessed be He, was stirred, and He
> said, "For thy sake Rachel, I will restore Israel to their place."[47]

These testimonies are hermeneutically sophisticated and theologically
complimentary. The rabbis have Moses bring a passage from the ritual
law of Leviticus in order to defend Israel. Slaughtered Israelites take the
place of cattle, sheep, and their young wrongfully slaughtered on the
same day. For her part, the rabbis have Rachel shaming God with her
own example of compassion. She rereads her own bitter struggle with her
sister Leah and turns herself into a figure of sisterly affection. Theologically, one appeals to God's own sense of justice, the other to God's
own mercy. In both cases ancestral figures reread the biblical record in
order to criticize God for failing Israel. According to this text, God's
conduct has been neither just nor merciful.

Max Kadushin, in his thoughtful study of rabbinic value-concepts,
notes how the Hebrew terms *din* and *raḥamim* respectively designate

"divine justice" and "love." Their presence provides the media through which "the rabbinic mind" experiences God.[48] Our trial scene, however, makes the obverse point: people may experience God through the *absence* of these attributes. Moses points to the absent attribute of *din*. Rachel points to the absence of *raḥamim*. God's justice and mercy lie in remission. Moses must therefore work to reactivate God's dormant justice. Rachel regenerates God's sense of mercy. The clarity of this scene is so unlike the biblical Book of Job, with its ambiguous conclusion. There we had been left to wonder if Job retracts his complaint before the God who appears to him out of the whirlwind. Has he won or lost his suit? We find no such confusion in the rabbinic midrash. Here it is God who must withdraw his complaint against Israel and repent before Rachel!

God's response reassuringly suggests that Rachel ultimately succeeds in stirring divine mercy. David Roskies has even suggested that God's response to Rachel returns the reader to a "more benign universe [where] the harsh sentence of history promised to come to an end."[49] I am not so sure. After all, does God remain a God of justice and mercy by promising to restore Rachel's children? Is that all it takes? Is all well that ends well? To be sure, the text's messianic promise comforts. In this sense, this antitheodic narrative contains a theodic counter-coherence. However, the universe that Israel continues to inhabit in Lamentations Rabbah's account of this-world is far from benign. Moreover, other rabbinic texts show images of God that prove far more disturbing than the one of a God who does not live up to His own standards of justice and goodness. These depict God as perennially silent and absent, unjust and even cruel.

The motif of an absent God who hides His face is not uncommon in either biblical or rabbinic literature. God threatens to hide from Israel in the Song of Moses.[50] "The Lord saw and was vexed and spurned His sons and daughters. He said: I will hide my countenance from them and see how they fare."[51] The psalmist pleads, "Awake, why sleepest Thou, O Lord? Arouse Thyself, cast not off for ever. Wherefore hidest Thou Thy face and forgettest our affliction and our oppression?"[52] R. Meir takes up this trope in Genesis Rabbah. He likens God to "a judge before whom a curtain is spread, so that he does not know what is happening without." His companions quickly warn him, "Let that suffice thee, Meir."[53] According to Louis Finkelstein, R. Meir does not protest divine absence. He merely follows Greek philosophers in assuming that divine providence does not protect specific individuals.[54] But in Chapter 1 of this study, we quoted another aggadah from the same text. In this legend, R. Shimon bar Yoḥai presents an even starker picture. Here God appears in the guise of a Roman tyrant who does not interfere as Cain stands poised to murder Abel. Having the power to stop the fight, God is made to assume responsibility for Abel's death.[55] Neither R. Meir nor R. Shimon

b. Yoḥai think that absence constitutes a necessary divine attribute. R. Meir seems to fault God for remaining behind a curtain. In R. Shimon b. Yoḥai's parable, the king is physically present, but morally absent. Both R. Meir and R. Shimon b. Yoḥai accuse God of failing to act in circumstances that require the active mediation of mercy and power on behalf of suffering people.

Authors of other aggadot go further still and depict divine *malevolence*. Exodus Rabbah contains a remarkable story comparing Job to a drunken palace guard rashly cursing the Governor and His justice. In the Bible God silences Job by pointing to Creation's grandeur and mysterious terror. In the midrash, Job begs for forgiveness upon witnessing God imprison Miriam, banish Moses, blind Isaac, sentence Abraham, and cripple Jacob.[56] While rare, the motif of a violent God is not isolated to this retelling of Job. Inverting the kindly paternalism more common to classical Jewish sources, some rabbis depict God as a violent *pater familias*—a wife-beater, an abusive parent, and a child killer.

> Her best friends ask God, "How long will you go on beating her? If your desire is to drive her out, then go on beating her till she dies; but if you do not wish her [to die], then why do you keep on beating her?"[57]

> I shall let her go free, in keeping with the ordinance. . . . "and if a man smite the eyes of his bondman, or the eye of his bondwoman . . . he shall let him go free" (Ex. 21:26). Since I have smitten both eyes of my children . . . is it not right therefore that they go forth into freedom?[58]

> R. Yoḥanan said, "The matter may be compared to the case of a king who had two sons. He got mad at the first and took a staff and beat him and sent him away. . . . He got mad at the second and took a staff and beat him and sent him away. He said, "I am the one whose way of bringing up sons is all wrong. . . . " R. Shimon b. Laqish [*sic*] said, "The matter may be compared to the case of a king who had two sons. He got mad at the first and took a staff and beat him, and he gasped and died. . . . He got mad at the second and took a staff and beat him and he gasped and died."[59]

The explicit moral of these stories varies. The story about Job the palace guard warns its readers to watch their words and accept divine judgment without rash complaint. What could be more pious? The latter stories promise that in the end God will neither divorce nor disinherit His people Israel. What could be more comforting? At the same time, perhaps regardless of intent, the authors of these stories present a disturbing picture of God gone berserk.

Despite the boldness of these texts, rabbinic authors do not complain against God lightly. Their challenges must meet proper conditions. Torah constitutes one crucial criterion. In the Lamentations Rabbah trial scene,

Moses holds God to His own law. Elsewhere in the same text, R. Berekiah depicts the community accusing God for failing to give Israel a burial—in contrast to the Torah which obligates burying the dead.[60] In both cases human figures try God before the law. But God can only be tried before the law by those who champion it. The author of one midrash clearly makes this point when he asks:

> Do you know who can protest against His decree and say to Him, "Why do you do such a thing?" He who observes the commandments. . . . Who is there who can say to Him, "Why should you do this to your creatures? Act with them in accordance with your Attribute of Mercy!" It is the man who observes the commandments.[61]

In contrast, Fyodor Dostoyevsky has Ivan Karamazov's principled complaint degenerate into patricide and insanity. Karamazov's protest is antinomian, unprotected by the ordering frames of faith and law. In contrast, rabbinic complaint cannot be isolated from questions of authority, right, and intent. Only authorized persons are entitled to complain—and only for the right reason. Torah and fidelity to both it and the community provide the necessary warrants with which to challenge God.

Communal solidarity constitutes a connected factor governing rabbinic protest. In the stories we have so far seen, rabbinic complaint is fundamentally communitarian. In the midrash, Moses and Rachel do not protest their own personal disappointments. They are only advocates for the plaintiff Israel. R. Berekiah does not present his own complaint, but the community's. We find this communal solidarity baldly stated in the following midrash from Exodus Rabbah. In this text Moses protests God's treatment of Israel three different times. Each time, the midrash recounts, "Then did the Attribute of Justice seek to strike Moses, but after God saw that Moses argued thus only because of Israel, He did not allow the Attribute of Justice to strike him."[62] In this text the dignity of the community actually outweighs the dignity of God.

As David Hartman has observed, rabbinic response to evil belongs more to religious anthropology than to philosophical theology.[63] It entails as much a social etiquette as a theological project. This etiquette includes instances of individual suffering as well as that of the community. When R. Ḥiyya b. Abba falls ill, R. Yoḥanan visits him and asks whether his sufferings are welcome to him. R. Ḥiyya responds, "Neither they nor their reward." At this point, instead of contesting his colleague, R. Yoḥanan gives him his hand and "[raises] him up." The text continues as R. Yoḥanan in turn falls ill. He, too, welcomes neither his suffering nor its reward. At this point R. Ḥanina offers him his hand and "lifts him up." The story then describes R. Eleazar falling ill and crying. R. Yoḥanan asks why R. Eleazar weeps. He assures R. Eleazar that merit receives reward and tells him of his own sufferings. But R. Eleazar explains that he weeps for "this beauty" (his body) that is destined to rot in the earth. He is afraid of dying. At this point both Eleazar and his visitor weep. Eleazar then says that he welcomes neither his sufferings nor their reward, at which his visitor gives him his hand in order to "raise him."[64] Instead of tormenting each other with theodicy, the rabbis grieve together. God, just desserts, the world-to-come are simply irrelevant in this axis of response. Castigating Job's friends, the rabbis warn in an unrelated gemara, "If suffering and sickness befall anyone, or if his children die, one must not say to him as Job's friends said to Job, 'Whoever perished being innocent? Is not thy piety thy confidence?' "[65]

Religious thinkers (including biblical and rabbinic authors) often try to couch suffering and death in terms of spiritual goods and ethical virtues. In contrast, classical Jewish texts contain antitheodic strains according to which suffering and death remain less a spiritual opportunity than a sad mystery. In the Book of Job, God points to creation and to Job's fundamental ignorance of its workings. According to some critics, the text leaves unclear whether God's response satisfies Job. For their part, many rabbis seem saddened by the mystery of suffering. Upon reading the Book of Job, R. Yohanan would habitually conclude: "The end of man is to die and the end of a beast is to be slaughtered and all are doomed to die. Happy is he who was brought up in the Torah . . . and has given pleasure to his Creator."[66] R. Yohanan evokes the melancholy of Ecclesiastes when reading the Book of Job. He acknowledges the common fate of both the righteous and wicked while affirming the importance of Torah and pleasing God. He denies neither the problem of disproportionate suffering nor the value of living according to the mitzvot. However, he does not address theological questions. He blames neither God nor Job.

Why this silence? We find in rabbinic texts vivid accounts describing the heavenly court, God's attributes, and divine intent. Yet a certain epistemological modesty will often characterize rabbinic response to suffering—as if the rabbis prefer picturing the unseen while remaining reticent about the suffering they witness every day. R. Yannai is reported to have said, "We cannot account for the tranquility of the wicked or the afflictions of the righteous."[67] The mystery of suffering scandalizes other rabbis. Referring to God's collaboration with the Satan in the prologue of the book of Job, R. Yohanan exclaims: "Were it not expressly stated in scripture, we would not dare say it. [God is made to appear] like a man who allows himself to be persuaded against his better judgment."[68] The expression "were it not expressly stated . . . we would not dare say it" suggests nothing but horrified confusion. It conveys the same shock registered by R. Shimon Bar Yohai's response to God's abandoning Abel, "It

is difficult to say this thing and the mouth cannot utter it plainly." Both
R. Yoḥanan and R. Shimon b. Yoḥai express surprise and shock. Suffering
has broken the ability to speak, to wield words, to understand.

Classical Jewish authors typically warn against pursuing hidden mysteries—be they metaphysical or moral in character. In the book of Job, God
tries to overpower and stifle human reason before the awesome depths of
creation. Job is given no explanation for what has happened to him. To
be sure, rabbinic authors give human (halakhic) reason enormous sway.
But God silences rabbinic figures perplexed by the fate of the righteous.
In another well-known aggadah, God silences Moses who has just witnessed both R. Akiba's erudition and torture at the hand of the Romans.

> When Moses ascended on high he found the Holy One . . . engaged in
> affixing coronets to the letters. Said Moses, "Lord of the Universe, Who
> stays Thy hand?" He answered, "There will arise a man at the end of many
> generations, Akiba ben Joseph by name, who will expound upon each title
> heaps and heaps of laws." "Lord of the Universe," said Moses, "permit me
> to see him." He replied, "Turn thee round." Moses went and sat down
> behind eight rows [and listened to the discourses upon the law]. Not being
> able to follow their arguments he was ill at ease, but when they came to a
> certain subject and the disciples said to the master "Whence do you know
> it?" and the latter replied "It is a law given unto Moses at Sinai" he was
> comforted. Thereupon [Moses] returned to the holy one . . . and said,
> "Lord of the Universe, Thou hast such a man and Thou givest the Torah by
> me!" He replied, "Be silent for such is my decree."
>
> Then said Moses, "Lord of the Universe, Thou hast shown me his Torah,
> show me his reward." "Turn thee round," said he; and Moses turned round
> and saw them weighing out his flesh at the market-stalls. "Lord of the Universe," cried Moses, "such Torah, and such a reward!" He replied, "Be silent
> for such is my decree."[69]

In this midrash God has silenced Moses not once but twice as if to say
that for good or evil, God's decrees remain impervious to human reason.
The rabbis in a similar aggadah record God silencing Saul. Saul asks God
why he must slaughter Amalekite women, children, and cattle. At this
point, a heavenly voice cites the book of Ecclesiastes to warn him, "Be
not righteous overmuch."[70] These two aggadot share a common formal
structure. God decrees death upon innocent people. A human witness,
Moses or Saul, interrogates the justice of this act. God ends the interrogation. Like the biblical Job, the midrashic Saul and Moses receive no
explanation.

According to Urbach and Fishbane, the midrashic account of God's
response to Saul and Moses constitutes a theodicy. Urbach argues that

the rabbis "had no answer except the justification of the Divine judgment. . . . " Fishbane calls God's response to Moses a brusque theodicy.[71]
But neither text records any such justification. God only tells Moses and
Saul to remain silent. But why does God remain silent?! The author
could have easily had God justify the judgment against the Amalekites by
recounting their iniquity. God could have assured Moses of Akiba's reward in the world-to-come. Nor does the text indicate how Moses or
Saul respond. Do they accept God's decree? Are they bitter? Are they
assured or confused? We have no way of knowing. The story ends as the
dialogue breaks down. In contrast, *Sifre*, chapter 307 presents Rabbi
Judah's gloss following the story of R. Ḥanina bar Teradion and his
family. "How great," he exclaims, "were these righteous persons, in
that at the time of their trouble they invoked three verses justifying
(God's) judgment . . . and accepted the justice of God's judgment."
No such gloss provides a theodic context with which to interpret the
silence of Moses and Saul. Both texts end abruptly, leaving their protagonists mute. These stories remain ambiguous at best, and as such,
deeply discomforting.

Between Theodicy and Antitheodicy

With their deeply ambiguous conclusions, the stories about Job, Saul,
and Moses highlight the difficulty of assigning clear significance to any
religious response to suffering. In this spirit, I conclude this chapter with
hesitation. Any given utterance by which a religious thinker responds to
suffering can constitute a theodicy in one semantic context and an antitheodicy in another. Only the location of the utterance within a field of other
statements determines its theodic or antitheodic significance. Avowals
of mystery in one context may serve to assure us that God understands
even when we cannot. The sentence "I don't understand" is followed by
statements that effectively affirm: "Therefore I dare not judge God. I
should trust God and accept the sufferings that afflict myself or others."
However, the admission of human ignorance can also become antitheodic. Expressions of astonishment, pain, outrage, and disappointment
can follow the utterance, "I do not understand." Last, the admission of
ignorance can be followed by an open silence, as in the story of Saul and
Moses. Left to dangle in silence, this avowal of mystery remains a deeply
ambiguous statement, its theodic or antitheodic identity indeterminate.

The significance of a religious utterance may, in fact, prove double-
edged. The author of an apparently antitheodic statement may ultimately
use it to reassert theodicy. In temporal or semantic isolation, the attempt
to accuse God clearly constitutes an antitheodic response to tragic suffer-

ing. However, within an expanded temporal framework such protests may ultimately justify God. After all, good kings and understanding parents respect the sound judgment and even the anger of their subjects or children. Children return to God, having argued their case. In the case of the lawsuit in Lamentations Rabbah, God may accept their claim and actually repent. On the other hand, apparently theodic accounts of deferred retribution may contain unintended antitheodic significance. Do the world and human affairs follow a well-planned, well-ordered, progressive purpose? Recourse to a messianic or otherworldly future might imply that divine providence cannot be justified at the present moment. We therefore conclude that theodicy and antitheodicy do not represent stable entities. Instead, they constitute interpretive boundaries between which religious discourse plays back and forth. To determine the actual theodic or antitheodic significance of a given statement requires semantic and temporal context.

The question of context brings us to the following point. Please understand that I do not want to overemphasize the importance of antitheodicy in classical Jewish texts. Against both Rubenstein and Berkovits, I would argue that its place lies somewhere *between* the margins and the center of classical Jewish thought. Antitheodic expression does not occur as rarely as Rubenstein suggests. It appears throughout the corpus of biblical and rabbinic literature. But neither do antitheodic figures loom large within the center of tradition as claimed by Berkovits. They do not enter into the liturgy. In the history of Jewish iconography, no antitheodic figure shares the stature afforded to Abraham at the *akeidah* or to R. Akiba sanctifying the name of God unto his very own death—that is, not until recent times. Antitheodic sources come to dominate the center of Jewish thought only in the post-Holocaust literature. As such, post-Holocaust antitheodicy might resemble traditional antitheodicy in terms of strict *content*. The Job who complains in the Bible offers the same complaint as the Job who appears in the writings of an Eliezer Berkovits. Yet the *formal* arrangement of this and other antitheodic sources undergoes a radical transformation. They now belong to the privileged center of a religious discourse. They carry normative weight. This transformed status consequently bears on the meaning of propositions in which they appear. Statements like "Elisha b. Abuyeh looms large in the pages of the Talmud" obviously intend something different than statements like "Dust should be put in the mouth of Job."

Traditional antitheodicy and post-Holocaust antitheodicy will appear closely related yet radically disconnected—depending on whether one looks to content or form. However, at the very least, our own reading of biblical and rabbinic antitheodicy suggests two minimal conclusions about traditional Jewish thought. First, contemporary readers must exercise care when assigning unequivocally theodic significance to ancient texts. The very fact that rich textual traditions carry contradictory messages precludes simple, unequivocal readings. Second, contemporary readers need to rethink the relation between tradition and theodicy. Attempts by theologians, scholars, and critics of religion to conflate tradition and theodicy do not help us understand the full range of discourse that has historically characterized religious life and thought. We have seen that a traditional religious response to suffering need not justify, explain, or accept the relation between God and evil. In the face of suffering, religious thinkers have been seen to exercise a skeptical spirit and admit with the philosopher Voltaire that "this is not clear."[72]

In our view, any reading of classical Jewish texts should at the very least recognize this tension. The modern thinkers whom we examine in Chapter 3 failed to meet this standard. Martin Buber, Abraham Joshua Heschel, Joseph Soloveitchik, and Mordecai Kaplan sought to make sense of suffering. They defended God against the callous culture of modernity, attributed positive moral and spiritual significance to suffering, and counseled patient hope. In their eyes, catastrophe signified an affliction that elevates the soul. Seeking classical prooftexts, they employed entirely theodic traditions. In their thought, the rigor of the prophets and the patience of the suffering servant overwhelmed the figure of Job. Modern Jewish theologians approached Scripture, midrash, and other Jewish texts with considerable ingenuity. However, their reading of tradition and theodicy has not weathered well. Current critical scholarship has taught contemporary readers to identify the polysemy structuring traditional text. Critical readers no longer accept unified teachings, what Buber called *Botshaft*. Instead, they now seek to analyze the strains and stress that run throughout the text. We will see that modern readings of traditional theodicy and antitheodicy ultimately prove flat in light of contemporary hermeneutics and post-Holocaust manipulations of the textual difference explored in this chapter.

THREE

THEODICIES

IN MODERN JEWISH THOUGHT

Since I love suffering as a power but shudder
with horror when I encounter it as a fact . . .
(Stefan Zweig, in letter to Martin Buber)

"EVERY ACTUAL theoretical engagement with the question of theodicy," Eliezer Schweid has recently written, "is a perspective engagement with the problem via its history."[1] Sometimes, however, circumstances compel theologians to abandon immediate historical moorings. Richard Rubenstein barely mentions Abraham Joshua Heschel, though he must have had him in mind when he argues that "regrettably most attempts at formulating a Jewish theology since World War II seem to have been written as if the two most decisive events of our time for Jews, the death camps and the birth of the State of Israel, had not taken place."[2] In another essay, challenging the theological tenets of Reconstructionism, Rubenstein fails to mention Mordecai Kaplan—the intellectual founder of the movement! For his part, Emil Fackenheim relies heavily on Martin Buber's understanding of revelation. But Fackenheim faults Buber for having "had a lifelong difficulty with the recognition of evil."[3] In turn, Eliezer Berkovits ignores completely the preeminent Orthodox Jewish thinker Joseph Soloveitchik—even in his critical study of modern Jewish philosophy! Taken together, these veiled references, attacks, and omissions raise the obvious question, Why do post-Holocaust theologians dismiss or ignore four of the most important Jewish thinkers of the twentieth century?

In this chapter I examine the response of Buber, Heschel, Soloveitchik, and Kaplan to the problem of evil. We know, of course, that vast differences separated these four thinkers from each other. Buber's I-Thou philosophy was purposefully antinomian in its rejection of formal religious practice. In contrast, Heschel sought to show how Jewish observance transports the pious Jew into a realm of wonder. Soloveitchik cared less about wonder than about Halakha which he described phenomenologically. Kaplan viewed Judaism through the lens of Durkheimian sociology and American pragmatism. And yet despite these differences, we find a surprising consensus. The problem of suffering deeply exercised the work of all four thinkers before and especially after the war. Although it did not come to eclipse their thought, the problem of suffering deeply colored their understandings of the world, the human condition, and the nature of God. Indeed, implicit theodic expression permeated modern Jewish theology well into the 1950s and early 1960s. Buber, Heschel, Soloveitchik, and Kaplan sought to integrate evil and suffering into a larger pattern of spiritual and ethical meaning, purpose, and value. They seemed incapable of imagining that such patterns might break before Auschwitz and its memory.

These four thinkers each professed what they claimed to be a "realistic" attitude toward the problem of suffering. Soloveitchik and Kaplan even claimed that they rejected theodicy. Indeed, a definite but ultimately limited realism characterized the writings of all four thinkers. As a response to evil and suffering, a realistic worldview is one that accounts for the ubiquity of suffering. A religious worldview that does not recognize how evil and suffering saturate existence remains unrealistic. Arguments (like those advanced by medieval philosophers) that seek to deny the ultimate reality of genuine evil fail to meet this standard of realism. In this respect Buber, Heschel, Soloveitchik, and Kaplan never ignored, much less tried to deny, the ubiquitous presence of evil. But realists must meet a second standard and follow the law of noncontradiction. According to this rule, a thing cannot be one thing and its opposite. In our case this means that evil cannot be both evil and good at the same time. For their part Buber, Heschel, Soloveitchik, and Kaplan violated this standard by attributing meaningful, superordinate significance to genuine evil. In their writings evil ceased being *merely* evil and suffering ceased being *simply* suffering. These writings show religious thinkers forcing evil and suffering into an overarching framework of good—even when their authors ostensibly reject the very project of theodicy. Rubenstein, Berkovits, and Fackenheim, later chapters show, approach the problem of suffering with far greater realism. They at least refuse to turn evil into either a good or a foundation of good.

The problem of Auschwitz, if not Auschwitz itself, constitutes a caesura in the theological and readerly canons of twentieth century Jewish thought. Buber, Heschel, Soloveitchik, and Kaplan's absence from the post-Holocaust theological literature illustrates the fundamental ruptures that characterize any process of cultural definition, continuity, and change. In his groundbreaking essay "Revelation and Tradition as Religious Categories in Judaism," Gershom Scholem had already identified the dynamic aspect of cultural transmission. Scholem sought to show how the given and the spontaneous—that which newly flows into the stream of tradition—are combined in passing on the patrimony of each generation to the next.[4] According to Scholem, tradition reflects neither a unified discourse nor the simple, sum total of a cultural patrimony, but instead, always, a specific and partial selection from that inheritance. Scholem's insight proves especially prescient for our study of post-Holocaust Jewish thought and its break with tradition and modern-readings-of-tradition. In classical Jewish lore, Moses received a dual Torah at Sinai. He in turn transmitted this dual Torah to elders, prophets, and to the members of the Great Assembly. Post-Holocaust theologians received their Torah (written and oral) from Breslau, Berlin, Frankfurt, and New York—and found it wanting.

Martin Buber

More than almost any other modern Jewish thinker, Martin Buber has been accused of underestimating the scope of evil and suffering in the world. In large part the criticism is undeserved. To be sure, an almost gentle optimism pervaded Martin Buber's writings on relation and dialogue. In his classic *I and Thou*, a loving description of a house cat occupied as much attention as the demonic figure of Napoleon. To many of his critics, Buber had ignored how power, hierarchy, and violence undermine the open spirit of deference and reciprocity that marked his own writings. He had seemed to ignore the limits to and the underside of relation. Scholem caustically noted, "Buber could have pointed out—I often wonder why he never did—that the first dialogue among human beings mentioned in the Bible, the one between Cain and Abel, also leads to the first murder."[5] Scholem's critique of Buber suggests that the life of dialogue remains subject to systemic violence and convulsive destruction—an account of human relation far from Buber's kind enthusiasm. But Buber was not so naive. He knew no less than Scholem that not all relationships are mutual, that violent discord permeates what he called the I-It mode of human existence. The "naïveté" of Buber's response to evil lay not so much in his failure to identify the problem, but in his interpretation of it. In this, Buber was neither more nor less "realistic" than his contemporaries.

Scholars have generally turned to Buber's *The Eclipse of God* (1952) in order to evaluate his response to the Holocaust. Chronologically this makes a certain amount of sense. It was Buber's first major text written after the war in which he addressed the moral crisis of the times. Strangely, however, the Holocaust and the problem of suffering hardly figured as explicit thematic foci in this text. I therefore follow Steven Kepnes who has used *Buber's Prophetic Faith* (1949) as his basis for discussing Buber's understanding of catastrophic suffering.[6] Ostensibly written about Israelite religion, *The Prophetic Faith* provided a vehicle for

Buber's own theological reflections. As Kepnes observes, the relation between reading and religious thought governed Buber's "hermeneutic theology."[7] Buber spun his own worldview into and out of the ancient text. Always returning to the themes of dialogue and relation, Buber sought to uncover what he considered Scripture's deep, unified thematic core: the relation between God and Israel.[8] Ironically, Buber's description of the prophets shed more light on his own response to suffering than does the philosophical analysis provided in the more contemporary *Eclipse of God*.

One cannot but suspect that the theodicies recapitulated in the final chapter of *The Prophetic Faith* were Buber's own. Those biblical positions that he himself rejected received critical censure. Perhaps surprisingly then, Buber did not condemn out of hand the Deuteronomic idea of collective reward and punishment. Why, for instance, does the righteous King Josiah die after purifying the Temple cult from idolatry? Why has the land once again fallen under foreign yoke, when it had enjoyed strength and independence under the idolater-king Manasseh? Buber explained that Josiah's death serves the good purpose of undermining "religion." After all, God desires a human people, not a cult. Echoing the rhetoric of rebuke established in Deuteronomy, Buber wrote, "Opposite the self-reliant, spirit-forsaken civilization religion there stands here for all to see God's ancient instruction of the nomad tribes."[9] In an earlier essay Buber had applied a prophetic social ethic to the story of Babel's destruction. After Babel, Buber taught, the nations must bind themselves together into a single humanity in order to realize God's dominion upon the earth. Chaos and catastrophe occur when people fail to establish a just and loving common life.[10]

Buber, of course, did not think that God literally punishes Josiah measure for measure. Instead, retribution was said to signify a process that is collective and impersonal. Buber explicitly rejected any notion that God directly rewards individual merit and punishes individual sin. In fact, he bitterly opposed the prophet Ezekiel for individualizing the doctrine of reward and punishment. According to Buber, Ezekiel "set up man as a creature serving in the world 'for the sake of receiving a reward.' "[11] At the same time, motifs drawn from Deuteronomy figured in his own more subtle analysis. Buber knew that no calculus could divine the precise effect of every individual sin. But people suffer when the community sins, when its members turn away from and against each other. God does not directly make sinners suffer. These are the *indirect* consequences that ultimately follow upon disrupted interpersonal orders. Suffering represents an immanent historical effect, a natural consequence. In Buber's thought, collective sin and collective suffering resembled karmic phenomena. One follows the other independent of direct divine intention.

Recognizing that sin and suffering are often incommensurable, Buber used other biblical models to interpret the personal disasters suffered by individuals. He rejected the advice and rebukes of Job's friends, who remain convinced of the justice underlying God's judgment of Job. Buber agreed with Job that it is "no longer possible for one who has been smitten with such sufferings to think God just." And yet he ultimately understood Job's misfortune in terms of spiritual catharsis and religious illumination. Buber wrote: "Job knows that the friends, who side with God, do not contend for the true God. He has recognized before this the true God as the near and intimate God. Now he only experiences Him through suffering and contradiction, but even in this way he does experience God."[12] In this view the book of Job is less about the suffering of an innocent man than about the conditions underlying religious encounter. According to Buber, Job's tale narrates "the man of suffering, who by his suffering attained the vision of God."[13] Perhaps unconsciously, Buber had echoed the rabbinic notion of afflictions of love. In Chapter 2 we saw the analogy of a craftsperson who cannot refine a piece of flax without beating it. For Buber, Job does not encounter God without "suffering and contradiction." Although Buber did not deny Job's agony, he attributed meaningful, cathartic significance to it.

Job represented but the penultimate figure in Buber's recapitulation of biblical theodicy. According to Buber, God loves those who suffer willingly.[14] Buber therefore turned to the Suffering Servant in Deutero-Isaiah in order to symbolize the willful acceptance of affliction. This iconographic figure had long been popular in modern Jewish readings of the Bible. In his magisterial *Religion of Reason* (1919), Hermann Cohen had linked Israel's election to vicarious suffering. To Cohen, Israel represented the archetype of suffering Humanity.[15] Jewish history formed a continuous chain of tribulation.[16] For Buber, in contrast, the servant symbolized the prophet who upholds the relation between God and His people by bearing affliction. For both Cohen and Buber, however, the servant was a messianic figure patiently awaiting ultimate redress. Until then, suffering and exile constituted constant and defining (*essential*) parts of Jewish life. As if echoing Cohen, Buber described exile as "the essential form of the people . . . endowed with the mystery of suffering as with the promise of the God of sufferers."[17]

The critique of modern life expressed in *The Eclipse of God* formed a practically seamless outgrowth from Buber's earlier biblical exegesis. As its title suggested, Buber saw the twentieth century as a time of religious and moral "eclipse." Buber warned that the turn away from God results in death and desolation. Without a radically transcendent other, people were said to possess no absolute moral guidelines with which to ground interhuman relations. Buber argued that people enter into relation with the transcendent, absolute other by generating luminous but subjective images of it. Once upon a time, the ancient peoples of the Far and Near East were said to have possessed such images: pallid, crude, "altogether false and yet true," fleeting and dreamlike. One could call upon them in order to resist "the deception of the voices" that threaten to draw people into the mania of convulsive destruction.[18] In contrast, the image-making power of the modern human heart was said to have declined. Buber accused modern philosophy (represented by Martin Heidegger, Jean Paul Sartre, and Carl Jung) of dissolving the bond between a transcendent absolute and ethics. In Buber's view, "philosophy holds that we lack today . . . the spiritual orientation which can make possible a reappearance of 'God and the gods,' a new procession of sublime images." Instead, philosophers had sought to discover within immanent intellectual structures the power to decode the mystery of existence—resulting in a terrifying reign of false absolutes and moral eclipse.

Buber's critique of modern life and thought did not, however, leave him hopeless. Buber resisted the notion that the contemporary eclipse of God represented a permanent human condition. On the contrary he maintained that such a crisis might generate a great spiritual catharsis. The person of faith in modern times may lack the image-making powers possessed in previous ages. But Buber encouraged modern men and women to remain open to the "fear of God." Buber knew from the Bible that religious fear becomes especially pronounced during periods of despair and crisis. It represents that stage in earthly life during which "all security is shattered. . . . Through this dark gate (which is only a gate and not, as some theologians believe, a dwelling) the believing man steps forth into the everyday which is henceforth hallowed as the place in which he has to live with the mystery."[19] Building on the discussion of Job in *The Prophetic Faith*, Buber based the encounter with God on personal anguish. In fact, Buber had long understood God to constitute an uncanny and even dangerous presence. An essay entitled "In the Midst of History" (1933) represents a case in point. Buber had professed that he could find no way to objectively understand Israel's historical plight. He intoned, "Ah, I do not long to know why I suffer, but only if it is for your sake that I am to suffer."[20] In "Imitatio Dei" (1926) Buber painted an unsettling image of divine destructiveness: "Only when the secret no longer stands over our tent, but breaks it, do we learn to know God's intercourse with us."[21]

Buber's metaphor of "eclipse" has left his post-Holocaust critics dissatisfied. Fackenheim maintains that Auschwitz calls into question the very possibility of any significant speech, much less dialogue.[22] Indeed, Fackenheim understands the impermanence of an eclipse as a hopeful image.[23] As Buber hoped, no eclipse lasts forever. Rubenstein rejects the image of

eclipse for the same reason. Instead, he employs the Christian metaphor
of God's death in order to evoke the complete absence of divine-human
encounter in a radically secular age.[24] According to both Fackenheim
and Rubenstein, Buber's formulation failed to meet the enormity of
Auschwitz.

In his defense, we might point out how Buber had actually approxi-
mated Rubenstein and Fackenheim's own post-Holocaust sensibilities.
Buber's most significant discussion of Auschwitz appeared in an essay
entitled "The Dialogue between Heaven and Earth" (1952). At first
glance this brief essay held little in common with either Fackenheim or
Rubenstein's thought. Buber began by noting that the Bible is "full of a
dialogue between heaven and earth. It tells how again and again God
addresses man and is addressed by him. . . . "[25] Such a view, Buber realized, no longer seems plausible. Nowadays even believers do not insist
that God communes with human figures. Biblical dialogues remain but
instructive, mythical figments from the ancient past. Nevertheless, Buber
left open the possibility of renewed dialogue. The faithful reader of Scripture "must endorse the view he has learned from it: what happened once
happens now and always, and the fact of its happening to us is a guarantee of its having happened."[26]

However, Buber assumed an antitheodic tone as the essay continued
to unfold. He described the psalmist with understated pathos: "For one
who believes in the living God. . . . and is fated to spend his life in a time
of His hiddenness, it is very difficult to live."[27] In Buber's reading, the
situation of the psalmist evoked the late-twentieth century. Turning then
to Job, Buber explicitly transposed the biblical Job into a post-Holocaust
world. We quote extensively:

> How is a life with God still possible in a time in which there is an Auschwitz?
> The estrangement has become too cruel, the hiddenness too deep. One can
> still "believe" in the God who allowed those things to happen, but can one
> still speak to Him? . . . Dare we recommend to the survivors of Auschwitz,
> the Job of the gas chambers: "Give thanks unto the Lord, for He is good; for
> His mercy endureth forever"?
>
> But how about Job himself? He not only laments, but he charges that . . .
> the judge of all the earth acts against justice. And he receives an answer from
> God. But what God says to him does not answer the charge; it does not even
> touch upon it. The true answer that Job receives is God's appearance only.
> . . . Nothing is explained, nothing adjusted; wrong has not become right,
> nor cruelty kindness. Nothing has happened but that man again hears God's
> address. . . .
>
> And we?

We—by this is meant all those who have not got over what happened and will not get over it. Do we stand overcome before the hidden face of God . . . ? No, rather even now we contend, we too, with God, even with Him. . . . We do not put up with earthly being; we struggle for its redemption, and struggling we appeal to the help of the Lord, who is again still a hiding one. In such a state we await His voice. . . . Though His coming appearance resemble no earlier one, we shall recognize again our cruel and merciful Lord.[28]

In contrast to *The Prophetic Faith* and *The Eclipse of God*, this short text contained a pronounced antitheodic strain. We no longer see the paradigmatic "man of faith" in the moralizing prophet, but in a suffering servant who rejects affliction and contends with God. Buber used the figure of Job to unleash an untypical tide of disappointed anger with Gods's hiding. At least in this short text, God possessed a cruelty that Buber refused to justify, explain, or accept.

Buber, however, tempered the antitheodic thrust underlying even this late essay. He continued to believe that God appears to people only through catharsis. Even with no wrong righted, Job was once again said to encounter God. Even now after the Holocaust, Buber appealed to the help of God and awaited God's voice. The antitheodic element in "The Dialogue between Heaven and Earth" only intensified an older line of thought. "Doom becomes more oppressive in every new eon, and the return more explosive." These were the concluding words of *I and Thou* (1923). There Buber had written: "History is a mysterious approach to closeness. Every spiral of its path leads us into deeper corruption and at the same time into more fundamental return. But the God-side of the event whose world-side is called return is called redemption.[29]" In light of these remarks, Scholem's critique of Buber's optimism proves to have been unfair—but only to a point. Buber had always recognized the power of evil and its destructive reach. But Buber never stopped trying to reframe the existence of genuine evil in terms of catharsis, return, and redemption. This theodic interpretation sustained his faith in religious dialogue throughout the contemporary eclipse of God. He had difficulty imagining that Auschwitz remains unredeemable, without meaning, a black hole forever disrupting the dialogue between heaven and earth.

Abraham Joshua Heschel

Edward Kaplan has argued that Abraham Joshua Heschel employed an often-enigmatic religious rhetoric in order to transform his readers' consciousness of reality. Language helped evoke the astonished sense of the ineffable by which spiritually sensitive people intuit the mystery of existence.[30] However, the lyrical quality of Heschel's thought obscured a pronounced pessimism that characterized nearly the entirety of his literary career. In his posthumously published *A Passion for Truth*, Heschel turned to Reb Menahem Mendl of Kotzk (the Kotzker). Compared to the Baal Shem Tov's joyous piety, the Kotzker's deeply contentious faith seemed paradigmatic for a post-Holocaust world. Under the Kotzker's spell, Heschel began to wonder if "distress at God's predicament may be a more powerful witness than tacit acceptance of evil as inevitable." Heschel favored "the outcry of anguish" to religious callousness or flattery.[31] "Underneath the [Kotzker's] reverence," Heschel wrote, "was dissent and contentiousness, a sense of outrage at the depth of falsehood afflicting the world. . . . For who was responsible that we hurried about in a world of phantoms? Was only man to blame?"[32]

Heschel, however, could not sustain this antitheodic line of thought. Upon comparing the Kotzker with Job, he immediately retracted his own religious protest. Turning against Job, Heschel argued that "the most fiery accusations could sound like gibberish when articulated."[33] Heschel seemed to suggest that words could never unlock the mystery of suffering. But he insisted that meaning transcends the absurdity people confront in this world. Human creatures are partners in God's battle with chaotic forces. Their task: to reduce distress and advance redemption. Facing human violence, Heschel defended God. He asked, "In a world where God is denied . . . compassion sloughed, violence applauded, in a world where God is left without allies—is it meaningful for man to court-martial Him?"[34] Mortified at the sight of modern violence, Heschel expressed compassion for God. His chapter on "The Kotzker and Job" concluded with this apocryphal story. Soon after the war, a Jewish functionary from the United States meets a Holocaust survivor on a train in Europe. At first the survivor will not pray because of Auschwitz. But, upon viewing the American at prayer, the survivor relents. He explains, "It suddenly dawned upon me to think how lonely God must be; look with whom He is left. I felt sorry for Him."[35] The story is not a little precious. But it highlights Heschel's general approach to the problem of evil. An abandoned God called forth the compassion of His [*sic*] suffering servant.

A Passion for Truth did not typify the corpus of Heschel's writings. Published posthumously in 1973, it represented a relatively late addition to the theological discussion already inaugurated by Rubenstein, Berkovits, and Fackenheim. It was one of the few times that Heschel explicitly referred to the Holocaust and employed antitheodic protest. Yet even in this unusual text, Heschel could not criticize God without retracting at once. He pitied God more than Job.

The ambivalence expressed in this late text had already marked the chapter on evil in *Man Is Not Alone* (1951)—Heschel's first programmatic theological statement. Heschel began the chapter by hurling contentious questions before God. History, he began to argue, had come to resemble "a stage for the dance of might and evil—with man's wits too feeble to separate the two and God either directing the play or indifferent to it." Heschel, however, immediately dispelled these angry words. Echoing the authors of Deuteronomy, he maintained, "the major folly of this view seems to lie in its shifting responsibility for man's plight from man to God, in accusing the Invisible though iniquity is ours."[36] According to medieval free-will theodicies, God leaves people free to do good or wreak havoc. For his part Heschel refused to blame the God of History when the immediate responsibility for evil lay with human beings. In particular, "modern man" assumed the central focus of his rage. The initial voice of anger directed toward God represented nothing more significant than an effective strategic device—one also employed by Soloveitchik and Kaplan. Heschel rhetorically challenged God in order to answer more forcefully the charge in God's defense against the culture of modernity.[37]

In his book detailing "the making of the modern self," the contemporary philosopher Charles Taylor has argued that deep moral sources ground modern standards of good. Taylor maintains that a heightened intolerance for suffering marks the modern period. Moral horrors continue to exist, to be sure, but "they are now seen as shocking aberrations, which have to be hidden."[38] Taylor, of course, recognizes that modernity represents a "unique combination of greatness and danger, of *grandeur et misère*." But his text contains only scattered, impressionistic references to "our own savagery in this century," to Hitler, the Kharkov famine, Cambodian Killing Fields, and other "moral evasions." In stark contrast to this almost sanguine view, Heschel emphatically denounced the moral poverty that characterizes the modern West. He bemoaned, "With a capacity to hurt boundless and unchecked, with the immense expansion of power and the rapid decay of compassion, life has, indeed, become a synonym for peril."[39] Practically the entire corpus of Heschel's writings articulated a deep distrust of contemporary civilization. Consistently taking the side of God, he considered "modern man" to be selfish, callous, and above all vicious. In one 1944 essay, Heschel pointed to the conflagration raging throughout Europe and lamented, "There has never been more reason for man to be ashamed than now."[40]

Heschel's rebuke of "modern man" echoed the deuteronomist and the prophets. But much like Buber and many of the rabbis, Heschel ultimately understood suffering as a spiritual discipline. In *Man Is Not Alone*, Heschel described Judaism as a pattern of living that could catapult the observant Jew into the realm of light and wonder. The *tzadik* (in hasidic thought, a righteous, holy rebbe) represented Judaism's ideal religious virtuoso. Heschel described the *tzadik*'s power of vision as follows: "in the roughened, soiled hands of devoted parents, or in the maimed bodies and bruised faces of those who have been persecuted but have kept faith with God, he may detect the last great light on earth."[41] Heschel described the *tzadik* at peace with life. The *tzadik* acquiesces in life's vicissitudes, glimpsing potential meanings. "Every experience opens the door into a temple of new light, although the vestibule may be dark and dismal."[42] Heschel was to develop the trope of "light" in *God in Search of Man*. There he argued that some people may indeed sense God's presence in moments of joy. But, he urged, "there are those who sense the ultimate question in moments of horror. . . . The world is in flames, consumed by evil. Is it possible that there is no one who cares?" For Heschel, both joy and misery point to God, the ultimate owner of this burning world.[43]

The great light in the eye of the *tzadik* reflected a world caught between horror and beauty, fear and hope. Combining the faith of the Baal Shem Tov and the Kotzker's, Heschel's own thought oscillated between wonder and dread. Through it all, he remained confident in the meaning that even the encounter with evil can generate. Heschel returned with particular effect to the motifs of light and fire in *A Passion for Truth*. This time Heschel had the "palace" symbolize an incandescent world. Commenting on a midrashic parable about Abraham's vision of a luminous castle, Heschel wrote: "In the original Hebrew the phrase describing the palace, *birah doleket*, is ambiguous. It could mean a 'palace full of light' or a 'palace in flames.'"[44] By using the motifs of light and fire, Heschel showed how the opposite impressions of beauty and horror both generate religious astonishment. This same ambiguity shaped his understanding of the Holocaust, the establishment of the State of Israel, and the Six Day War. In *Israel: An Echo in Eternity* (1967), Heschel wrote: "This is what the prophets discovered. History is a nightmare. There are more scandals, more acts of corruption, than are dreamed of in philosophy. . . . [But] together with condemnation, the prophets offer a promise. . . . The end of days will be the end of fear, the end of war; idolatry will disappear, knowledge of God will prevail."[45] In effect, Heschel had the prophets mediate the Kotzker's caustic bitterness and the Baal Shem Tov's hopeful confidence.

Like Buber, Heschel did not reject out of hand the deuteronomistic-prophetic leitmotif of retribution. Heschel also used the doctrine of retribution to upbraid the human person and human communities. Indeed, for both Buber and Heschel, God could manifest a dangerous presence. However, in contrast to Heschel, Buber had less to say about God and God's nature. A sublime figure, Buber's "Eternal Thou" escaped predicative definition. Heschel took more theological liberties (at least in his early work). In *The Prophets*, Heschel described how divine rage can fill the cosmos. Rejecting the tenets of medieval theology, Heschel considered affect integral to Godhead. In his reading of the prophets, wrath constituted a justifiable aspect of divine pathos. "Pathos includes love," Heschel wrote, "but goes beyond it. God's relation to man is not an indiscriminate outpouring of goodness, oblivious to the condition and merit of the recipient."[46]

Heschel, however, refused to bring the twinned motifs of wrath and retribution into his own interpretation of contemporary Jewish history. In *Israel: An Echo of Eternity*, he expressed deep despair before the memory of Auschwitz. It would be blasphemy, he knew, to accept the establishment of the State in 1948 and its military victory in 1967 as a "compensation." And yet Heschel experienced the rebirth of a Jewish State after the Holocaust as nothing less than a resurrection. Its existence, he argued, "makes life less unendurable."[47] Its rebirth calls for a renewal of trust in the God of History and holds out hope in the messianic promise that alone could make life meaningful. "Instances of God's care in history," Heschel wrote, "come about in seeming disarray, in scattered fashion—we must seek to comprehend the unity of the seemingly disconnected chords. . . . Exceedingly intricate are His ways."[48] The establishment of the State enabled Heschel to trust God's scattered providence—even after Auschwitz.

Heschel's thought continuously oscillated between despair and hope, but always to the same spiritual purpose. Heschel may have rejected Buber's antinomianism, but they were of one mind when it came to interpreting the phenomena of evil and suffering. Both recognized the ubiquity of suffering while attributing to it an overriding religious significance. For his part, Edward Kaplan has since described the cathartic function of despair and suffering in Heschel's writings. Dread prepares the encounter with God. Kaplan quotes Heschel, "We must first peer through the darkness, feel strangled and entombed in the hopelessness of living without God, before we are ready to feel the presence of His living light."[49] The combination of suffering and despair constitutes a potent spiritual opportunity. As Kaplan concludes, "Heschel's mysticism is an active wager that despair is the birth, not the grave, of a significant, and perhaps sacred, lifetime."[50] Kaplan has noted the pervasiveness of despair in Heschel's thought without, however, wondering how Heschel's spiritual itinerary might have foundered upon it. Does the price of Heschel's wager remain too high? What does spiritual perfection have to do with the death of millions? Can Auschwitz and its memory really generate mystical illumination? For many, the Holocaust might not represent a way-station but rather a terminus for any religious confidence or meaning.

Joseph Soloveitchik

Before turning to Joseph Soloveitchik, we note that Buber and Heschel had abandoned the formal task of logically reconciling abstract attributes like divine omnipotence and omnibenevolence with the existence of evil. Unlike some medieval philosophers, they did not describe evil as a mere negation or lack of being in order to justify God's creation. In fact, a professed hostility to theodicy characterized modern Jewish thought. Few would have disagreed with Soloveitchik when he wrote:

> Judaism, with its realistic approach to man and his place in the world, understood that evil cannot be blurred or camouflaged and that any attempt to downplay the extent of the contradiction and fragmentation to be found in reality will neither endow man with tranquility nor enable him to grasp the existential mystery. Whoever wishes to delude himself by diverting his attention from the deep fissure in reality . . . is nought but a fool and fantast. It is impossible to overcome the hideousness of evil though philosophico-speculative thought.[51]

Buber and Heschel, had sought to recreate a modern variant of Hasidic spirituality. One might have expected a more thoroughgoing realism from Soloveitchik, a scion of Lithuanian rationalism. For Soloveitchik, Judaism opposed any philosophical or theological attempt to overlook tragedy or tranquilize pain. The Judaism he epitomized encouraged neither foolishness nor fantasy. According to Soloveitchik, the observant Jew realistically confronts human existence and tragedy. Ironically, however, Soloveitchik resorted to the same theodicies that he ostensibly rejected.

Soloveitchik's most important treatment of the problem appeared in an essay entitled "The Voice of My Beloved Knocks" ("Kol Dodi Dofek," 1956). In this essay Soloveitchik distinguished two modes of human existence. On the one hand all people (even "halakhic men") live in the mechanistic and meaningless dimension of fate (*goral*). Soloveitchik described fate as "an existence of compulsion . . . , one link in a mechanical chain, devoid of meaning, direction, purpose, [and] subject to the forces of the environment into which the individual has been cast by providence, without any prior consultation." Victims of dumb happenstance, people suffer for no apparent cause or meaning. In Soloveitchik's words, their afflictions appear "shadowy and murky, like satanic forces, the offspring of the chaos and the void which pollute the cosmos." The world of fate, the world in which we all live, lacks any superordinate, spiritual significance. Perplexed and panicked, the person of fate desperately seeks fruitless metaphysical explanations with which to accommodate or obscure the evil they suffer or witness.[52]

In contrast to the determined realm of fated phenomena, Soloveitchik recognized a second dimension of human existence in which people become free and active creators by turning fate (*goral*) into purpose or destiny (*yeud*). Soloveitchik followed Kant by establishing a binary opposition between a mechanistic, phenomenal order and a noumenal realm of freedom and moral value. "Man," Soloveitchik wrote, "is born like an object, dies like an object, but possesses the ability to live like a subject . . . who can impress his own individual seal upon his life and can extricate himself from a mechanical type of existence and enter into a creative, active mode of being."[53] In this second dimension, the dimension of purpose (*yeud*), the problem of suffering receives new form. The halakhic Jew does not deny the reality of evil. A good Kantian, Soloveitchik knew that no metaphysical answer can resolve the riddle of human anguish. Instead, observant Jews pragmatically investigate their halakhic, ethical obligations. What is one to do? How is one to act? What obligations does suffering impose? At the level of destiny, halakhic Jews do not concern themselves with the reason or purpose of evil. Rejecting theodicy, they try instead to sublimate it.[54]

This rejection of theodicy ultimately proved disingenuous. While claiming to jettison metaphysical theodicies, Soloveitchik surreptitiously adopted theodic themes to his own ends. Nor did Soloveitchik himself shy from metaphysical speculation. After all, he too was a man of fate. Interpreting the first chapter of Genesis, Soloveitchik upheld its testimony that the cosmos is very good. "However," he warned, "this affirmation may only be made from the infinite perspective of the Creator." Although the *finite* human mind finds itself enmeshed in a fate it cannot understand, the Bible points to a beautiful tapestry of exquisite design. Soloveitchik argued that "as long as man's apprehension is limited and distorted, as long as he perceives only isolated fragments of the cosmic drama and the mighty epic of history, he remains unable to penetrate into the secret lair of suffering and evil. . . . We alas view the world from its reverse side. We are therefore, unable to grasp the all encompassing framework of being."[55] Despite all claims to the contrary, Soloveitchik here came close to denying the reality of evil. He dismissed the problem of evil's theoretical cogency by highlighting the faulty character of human perception. Soloveitchik thus denied the human ability to solve the mystery of suffering while remaining confident that, from God's perspective, the world exhibits a meaningful and beautiful design. But by his own standards, Soloveitchik had no right to talk about "encompassing frameworks" beyond the limits of his understanding. Violating the strictures of Kantian epistemological critique, Soloveitchik's turned to the medieval metaphysical speculations that he himself rejected.

Soloveitchik's ambiguous rejection of speculative theodicy did not preclude him from developing a different form of theodicy, a "halakhic" one. For Buber and Heschel, suffering had signified a spiritual possibility. In contrast, Soloveitchik seemed to frame the problem of evil in strictly human terms. Suffering signified a moral promise that one was halakhically bound to uphold. In an argument resembling the rabbinic notion of afflictions of love, Soloveitchik wrote: "Affliction comes to elevate a person, to purify and sanctify his spirit, to cleanse and purge it of the dross of superficiality and vulgarity, to refine his soul and to broaden his horizons. In a word, the function of suffering is to mend that which is flawed in an individual's personality. The halakha teaches that the sufferer commits a grave sin if he allows his troubles to go to waste and remain without meaning or purpose."[56]We have already seen throughout this study that theodicy constitutes a complex phenomenon combining acts of justification, explanation, and acceptance. We have seen that different types of theodicy provide radically divergent assessments of suffering. Soloveitchik, we now see, had only said that it was impossible to overcome the problem of evil through *speculative* thought. Indeed, the source and purpose of evil remained immune to human explanation. However, Soloveitchik never denied that a *halakhic* approach could redeem it. He accepted suffering as a divine pedagogy capable of building moral character.

Soloveitchik's halakhic response to suffering precluded Job-like complaints directed against God. Indeed, traditional theodic themes governed all of Soloveitchik's reading of biblical texts in "Kol Dodi Dofek." In the opening sentence of the essay, Moses bangs upon the walls of Heaven, demanding to know the secret of suffering.[57] However, Soloveitchik turned against Job and his complaint. His critique of Job relied on midrashim that account for Job's suffering by inventing sins unmentioned by the biblical text. According to Soloveitchik, Job never really identifies with the suffering of his people. He abandons Jacob struggling with Esau, Laban, and the mysterious stranger at Jabbok. He fails to protest Pharaoh's decrees against the Israelites. He refrains from helping Ezra and Nehemiah rebuild the land of Israel. With all his former wealth, Job remains deaf to his people, caring only for himself and his house. Following the rabbis, Soloveitchik ignored the opening phraseology of the Book of Job, "There was a man in the land of Uz, whose name was Job; and that man was whole-hearted and upright."[58] According to Soloveitchik, Job is not an innocent man, but a selfish egoist. But in the end, and this is Soloveitchik's point, Job prays for his friends, having learned through suffering the secrets of sympathy, community, and solidarity.[59] Job's suffering had acquired moral significance.

One might want to argue that this attempt to redeem suffering does not itself necessarily constitute a theodicy (even if it lends itself to that suggestion). As an antitheodicy, we might read Soloveitchik's interpretation of Job far more charitably. The significance of suffering has nothing to do with God or defending God. The meaning of suffering (or rather, the meaning that practical reason lends it) is human. Job redeems suffering. He affords it purpose and value by turning it into a foundation for good, into moral opportunity. Job admirably makes the best of a bad situation, as must we all. By the end of the story, he has learned sympathy, community, and solidarity; he does not justify God, seek future redress, explore metaphysical questions, or explain the working of providence. To be sure, this represents a strong possible reading of Soloveitchik. However, it misses the following point. Soloveitchik could have turned Job into the antitheodic figure that our possible reading suggests. His Job might have been an innocent person (a suffering servant) who does not deserve to suffer, but redeems it nonetheless. Soloveitchik could have blessed Job. Why then does Soloveitchik preclude Job's complaint? Why does he blame Job and call him an egoist? And why does he justify God in the next sentence?

In Chapter 2 we saw how traditional Jewish thought swings between Deuteronomy and the figure of Job. Soloveitchik's own reading of this tradition proved less fluid. By condemning Job, Soloveitchik implicitly justified a God and providence whose operations he himself could not explain. And not just implicitly! Rejecting Job's complaint, he suggested a halakhic response to the Holocaust that turned upon the phraseology of Deuteronomy and rabbinic formulations of *tziduk ha-din* (the justification of the decree). He wrote: "When the impulse of intellectual curiosity seizes hold of a person, he ought to do nought but find strength and encouragement in his faith in the creator, vindicate God's judgment, and acknowledge the perfection of his work. "The Rock His work is perfect; for all His ways are justice."[60] The fact that Soloveitchik openly eschewed speculative theodicy in the opening pages of "Kol Dodi Dofek" might have lead some of his readers to think he rejected theodicy in toto. Yet Soloveitchik's response to the Holocaust was, in the end, no less theodic than the philosophical theodicies that he ostensibly opposed. Against the intellectual and emotional anguish propelling the author of Job, Soloveitchik justified divine judgments by drawing upon the virtue of faith and invoking Deuteronomy 32:4–5.

The justification of God and providence was especially pronounced in Soloveitchik's interpretation of the Song of Songs, where he defended God against the most unlikely human aggressor. Soloveitchik followed the rabbis by reading the biblical love song as a parable for the relationship between God and Israel. In Soloveitchik's retelling of the biblical love song, God suffers because the beloved Shulamite delays but a moment in responding to a midnight call. She had searched in vain, longing for her lover. And suddenly God appears, repeatedly knocking at her door. But, to Soloveitchik, the human heart is crooked. The Shulamite momentarily refrains from leaving the comfort of her bed for the door. By then, however, it is too late. God has left. According to Soloveitchik, God has been patient with the Shulamite.[61] Soloveitchik never wondered why the Lover departs so quickly, never to return, leaving the beloved Shulamite abject. Throughout nearly the entirety of his reading, Soloveitchik failed to sympathize with a broken human heart. By defending God's absence, he laid the fault entirely on the shoulders of the Shulamite.

Soloveitchik's response might seem a little less severe once we notice that Job and the Shulamite did not represent actual suffering people. Instead, Soloveitchik used these biblical figures to illuminate the historical shortcomings of his own community. Job's failing to protest "Pharaoh" or help "Nehemiah" symbolized the failure of American Orthodox Judaism to protest Hitler or to support the establishment of the State of Israel. Like the Shulamite, the orthodox establishment in the United States had tarried before God's urgent historical call. After the absolute concealment represented by the Holocaust, God suddenly manifested God's self, knocking at the despondent lover's door. The United Nations declaration supporting Jewish statehood in 1947 was said to be nothing less than an act of God in history. Soloveitchik counted further occurrences of God's voice urgently beckoning from the gates of heaven: defending the State of Israel, battling Christian triumphalism, and stemming Jewish assimilation.

Soloveitchik had never meant to blame the Jews of Europe for lingering like the Shulamite. He had only tried to link contemporary suffering into a unified narrative pattern. But history confused this pattern. Unknowingly, I think, two Shulamites had slipped into Soloveitchik's thought: the Shulamite of Auschwitz and the Shulamite of the United States. Soloveitchik used two disparate pictures of the Shulamite in order to represent the Jewish people during World War Two. Compare these two separate renditions of the young woman upon her bed:

[I] "God who conceals Himself in dazzling hiddenness" suddenly manifested Himself and began to knock at the tent of His despondent, disconsolate love, twisting convulsively on her bed, suffering the pains of hell.[62]

[II] What was our reaction to the voice of the Beloved that knocketh, to God's bounteous kindnesses and wonders? Did we descend from our couches and immediately open the door? Or did we, like the Shulamite maiden, continue to rest and tarry rather than descend from our beds?[63]

In the first picture, Soloveitchik depicted the Shulamite of Auschwitz writhing in pain upon her bed. But rather than address her plight, he condemned the Shulamite painted in his second picture. The Shulamite of America represented a spoiled princess. The Shulamite of Auschwitz agonized in hell while the American Shulamite rested in comfort. Trying to justify God's judgment, Soloveitchik could only blame the American Shulamite. But in the process, he seemed to avert his gaze from the Shulamite of Auschwitz.

A fundamental tension characterized Soloveitchik's vindication of God. On the one hand, his analysis remained within the limits of reason set by Kant. He admitted that all attempts to explain the source and purpose of suffering ultimately fail. He claimed no objective view of any "larger perspective." Instead, suffering constituted an ethical challenge before which selfish egoists like Job and the American Shulamite were obligated to prove and purify themselves. At this level, Soloveitchik advanced a "practical theodicy" (one that reflects the operation of what Kant called practical reason). This response, some may have thought, even bordered antitheodicy. On the other hand, we do not forget the treatment of Job and the Shulamite and the recapitulation of Deuteronomy 32:4–5. Moreover, Soloveitchik confidently stepped beyond the limits of reason set by Kant. He pointed to a larger metaphysical framework, came close to denying the reality of evil, and described the establishment of the State of Israel in metahistorical terms. In short, Soloveitchik simultaneously maintained and violated the canons of Kantian rationalism. This tension served the creative purpose of bolstering faith in divine justice. One way or the other, Soloveitchik managed to justify God's judgment against suffering human figures.

Mordecai Kaplan

A similar irony pervades Mordecai Kaplan's response to the problem of evil and suffering. According to Kaplan, the founder of Reconstructionism, Judaism was a religious civilization whose basic theological tenets required fundamental revisions in the modern age. In particular, Kaplan challenged the Jewish tradition of "supernaturalism." He firmly believed in human progress and held an optimistic faith in life's ultimate goodness. Nevertheless, he rejected philosophical solutions to the problem of evil.[64] The attempt to deny the reality of evil, he thought, was "just so much wasted breath, because to the extent that anything is evil . . . it is evil and nothing else."[65] Kaplan, it had seemed, would approach the problem of evil with the realism of an American pragmatist. Yet, like Soloveitchik, Kaplan abandoned theodicy at the surface level while surreptitiously reproducing his own version of it.

Kaplan's response to the problem of evil rested on two prongs: one theological, the other anthropological. At the metaphysical level, Kaplan radically rethought the notion of divine personhood and the concept of

omnipotence. This meant rejecting the idea that God created all things
(good and evil). It also meant rejecting any thought that God plans every
twinge of pain, cruel act, and human sin. "It is sufficient," he wrote,
"that God should mean to us the sum of the animating, organizing
forces and relationships which are forever making a cosmos out of
chaos."[66] According to Kaplan, the idea of God represented a hypostasis
of positive forces that govern the world. God was said to be the totality
of forces that makes life worthwhile, the creative life of the universe, not
its omnipotent overlord. Evil was simply that "phase of the universe" that
had not yet been penetrated by godhood."[67]

By relieving theology of certain logical problems, Kaplan hoped to salvage an intellectually credible image of God as the ultimate force for
good in the universe. However, as Eliezer Berkovits notes, Kaplan's "enthusiasm for living" in a post-Holocaust age involved no less a leap of
faith than the one performed by proponents of supernatural theology.
Berkovits savagely criticized Kaplan's optimism.[68] Unlike Kaplan, Berkovits found no moral progress within the natural realm. Nature revealed
only manifold disharmony.[69] Indeed, Kaplan had failed to consider the
dialectic by which the forces that make life worthwhile inseparably min-
gle with negating destructive powers. By this light, his religious natural-
ism proved no less problematic than the supernatural theism it was intended to replace.

Kaplan was a better moralist than speculative theologian. Seeking to
redirect human consciousness, he argued against morbid proclivities that
fix human attention onto evil. For Kaplan, they could only provide a
distorted, dismal view of the world. People should instead attribute
worthwhile significance to the phenomenon of evil. Distress serves a positive function, just as pain warns the human body and keeps it from danger. Having compared moral evil to a biological reflex, Kaplan went on
to talk about the importance of "meaning." He argued that the Jewish
people has always turned the experience of catastrophe into messianic
hope. Israel survived catastrophic upheavals because the Jewish people
found meaning in them. For Kaplan, Judaism "helps us discern in the
very suffering that proceeds from our shortcomings the evidence of a
divine law which shows us the way to overcome them."[70] Once again, we
see a modern Jewish thinker confidently combining realism with interpretive speculation. Kaplan recognized the far reach of evil but thought that
imposing a meaningful framework transforms it into good.

Unlike Heschel, Kaplan allowed no room in his thought for despair.
His understanding of justice and injustice represents a case in point. Kaplan preached the virtue of courage with great assurance because he was
confident in the eventual triumph of the former. True, he acknowledged
that a sensitive soul might echo Job's cry.[71] But Kaplan hedged his sympathy for Job by pointing to the anarchist martyr Bartolomeo Vanzetti.

Wrongly executed by the State of Massachusetts in 1927, Vanzetti had abiding faith in justice and humanity, which proved to Kaplan that even victims of gross injustice can and should remain hopeful. He argued, "If the very victim of the orderly violence that makes our economic system can testify to a growing sense of justice, then surely Job is proved wrong, and we have no right to feel God-forsaken."[72] This use of Job was typical in modern Jewish theology. Like Heschel and Soloveitchik, Kaplan had placed questions about divine justice into the mouth of a biblical figure and then proceeded to supply him answers. Sensitive souls might momentarily sympathize with Job but then were told not to cry. In Kaplan's moral and theological understanding of the world, people have no right to feel God-forsaken. God is not a person capable of saving human beings. Therefore God cannot forsake them. According to Kaplan, Job does not understand that it is the very human demand for justice that manifests divinity in the social world.

Kaplan's understanding of God's goodness followed suit. While preaching patience and resolve, Kaplan did not ignore the emotional predicaments that suffering people face. He knew that innocent people, especially children, suffer in a still-imperfect world. Is then God not good? Kaplan's theology again absolved God of responsibility. By definition, only goodness manifests godhood. According to this theology, God does not exercise external control over the evil that mars human life. It therefore makes no sense to blame God for permitting it to happen. When asked how he would address a child with polio, Kaplan answered,

> God did not make polio. God is always helping us humans to make this a better world, but the world cannot at once become the kind of world He would like it to be. . . . When the doctor relieves your pain . . . it is with the intelligence that God gives him. . . . Do not feel that God does not care for you. He is helping you now in many ways, and He will continue to help you. Maybe some day you will be restored by His help to perfect health. But if that does not happen, it is not because God does not love you. If He does not grant you all that you pray for, He will find other ways of enabling you to enjoy life. Be thankful to God for all the love and care that people show toward you, since all of that is part of God's love."[73]

Admittedly, these constitute hypothetical words delivered to a child. They are simple and unsophisticated. And yet they encapsulate the decency of Kaplan's response to the problem of suffering. He minimized neither the presence of disease nor the shock that afflicts those who suffer it. He blamed neither the child nor the child's parents. He did not even promise that God could succeed in overcoming the child's affliction. Instead, Kaplan pointed to the love present in the concern that doctors and family bestow upon the child. This love was said to manifest divinity.

Now granted, one may have to put on a brave face for children. There can be no doubt as to Kaplan's sympathy for the children and families who suffer this predicament. But one wonders why he answered the question in the way that he did. After all, Kaplan could have simply said that God simply lacks the power to alleviate this suffering. Why even mention divine love? In the last chapter, we saw how the rabbis in the midrash and Talmud also try to console and heal each other. We saw an aggadah in which R. Ḥiyya bar Abba, R. Yoḥanan, and R. Eleazar each in turn fall ill. Upon being asked, they each repeat that they welcome neither suffering nor its rewards. Their colleagues who have come to comfort do not accuse. In this Kaplan followed in their footsteps. But neither do the rabbis try to absolve, explain, or find meaning in disease. They exercise greater discretion. No one counsels thankfulness. Unlike Kaplan, the rabbis do not point to divine love when it is not clearly manifest. Instead, they have the sense not even to mention God.

We began this section noting how Kaplan rejected traditional theodicy, only to find that he surreptitiously introduced theodic themes into his own thought. First, Kaplan absolved God by relieving "Him" of omnipotence. A God who does not control cannot be blamed. But even though he said he wouldn't do it, Kaplan ultimately denied the reality of evil. As Berkovits notes, Kaplan saw evil as a mere negation of good with no independent reality of its own.[74] For Kaplan, "religion should indicate to us some way whereby we can transform the evils of the world, if they are within our control, and transcend them, if they are beyond our control. If we heed the creative impulse within us which beats in rhythm with the creative impulse of the cosmos, we can always find some way of making our adjustment to evil productive of good."[75] In the end, Kaplan did not consider evil to constitute an integral part of the world. As such, he came to resemble the medieval theologians whose theodicies he rejected. He himself actually claimed that evil was ultimately a product of "mere negation, chance, or accident which is inevitable only in the logical and passive sense that darkness is the inevitable concomitant of light."[76] These are Kaplan's own words! Since evil only constitutes privation, he held out hope that we might one day transform it into something else. Although Kaplan rejected theodicy, the theodic dimension of this conclusion proved overwhelming.

Conclusions

I understand that readers may hardly recognize the work of Buber, Heschel, Soloveitchik, and Kaplan as theodicy. They offered no formal arguments justifying providence; they did not seek to explain how attributes like mercy and power cohere in the face of evil; they did not blame suffering people; they did not openly declare the preciousness of suffering; they did not appeal to messianic or otherworldly compensations, they tried (not always successfully) to eschew metaphysical speculation. Yet we have identified a theodic impulse (to defend God and redeem suffering) running throughout their thought. Buber, Heschel, Soloveitchik, and Kaplan gave theodicy as good a name as it may ever get. Their response to the problem of evil stayed (more or less) within the parameters of a religious humanism. That is, they showed how human persons might extract a modicum of spiritual or moral good out of suffering. Rather than remain subject to evil, they sought to overcome it. In doing so, Buber, Heschel, Soloveitchik, and Kaplan spoke to the power of religious thought to transform moral experience by framing the phenomena of evil and suffering into broad interpretive schemes. This said, I would not want to overlook the following point. The degree to which the figure of redemption applies to catastrophic events like the Holocaust, the full extent to which moral phenomena prove open to interpretation, are subject to serious suspicion.

The success of any theodicy rests largely on a theologian's ability to reinterpret the phenomenon of suffering. Such an exercise requires no small amount of artistry. In an aphorism entitled "What One Should Learn from Artists," Friedrich Nietzsche has suggested that the value or meaning of any experience depend on how a willful human being crafts it into a larger pattern. Nietzsche's lifelong interest in aesthetics bears on our own preoccupation with the problem of evil and suffering. He asks:

> How can we make things beautiful, attractive, and desirable for us when they are not? And I rather think that in themselves they never are. Here we could learn something from physicians, when for example they dilute what is bitter or add wine and sugar to a mixture—but even more from artists. . . . Moving away from things until there is a good deal that one no longer sees . . . or seeing things around a corner and as cut out and framed; or to place them so that they partially conceal each other . . . ; or looking at them through tinted glass or in the light of the sunset; or giving them a surface and skin that is not fully transparent—all this we should learn from artists while being wiser than they are in other matters.

As understood by Nietzsche, artists reframe and conceal the ugly. They look at the grotesque through tinted glass and transform it into something lovely. Nietzsche does not, of course, limit his remarks to artists. He concludes this aphorism evoking the poetry of everyday life. "We want to be the poets of our life—first of all in the smallest, most everyday matters."[77]

In the beginning of this chapter, I argued that "realists" never interpret genuine evil in terms of good. Evil remains evil. Ultimately, however, the phenomena of suffering and destruction prove subject (although not fully captive) to the same play between interpretation and counterinterpretation suggested by Nietzsche. According to Nietzsche, nothing is ever "in itself" beautiful or attractive. He thinks the same of evil. In *Beyond Good and Evil*, he writes, "There are no moral phenomena at all, only a moral interpretation of phenomena."[78] I know of no religious thinker who could ever share such a position—at least not explicitly! Indeed, in the last chapter we read a rabbinic aggadah about the destruction of the Temple in the year 70 CE that illustrates Nietzsche's point. R. Akiba laughs while his colleagues mourn the Temple's loss. He explains: the prophet Jeremiah records Uriah the priest who foresees the ruin of Jerusalem. The prophet Zechariah, on the other hand, envisions Jerusalem's rebirth. R. Akiba concludes, "I rejoice therefore that in the end the words of Uriah have been fulfilled, because this means that so will the words of Zechariah."[79] Forcing the destruction of Jerusalem into a larger temporal pattern, R. Akiba interprets an ostensible evil in terms of good. Religious thinkers, like Nietzsche's imagined artist, implicitly craft the experience of suffering and loss into larger patterns of signification. Neither the destruction of the Temple nor the phenomenon of evil are good or bad outside the interpretations that give them moral shape.

Buber, Heschel, Soloveitchik, and Kaplan (like R. Akiba) surreptitiously preferred "art" to realism when responding to suffering. One might even support them for this. Of course, they would have bitterly resisted linking them with Nietzsche's re-evaluation of values, his insinuation that there are no moral phenomena in and of themselves. As theologians, they sought to ground ethics within a framework of absolute value. Yet Nietzsche could have been describing modern Jewish theodic response to the problem of suffering when he writes: "We know quite well how to drip sweetness upon our bitterness, especially the bitterness of the soul; we find remedies in our courage and sublimity as well as the nobler deliria of submission and resignation. A loss is only a loss for barely one hour; somehow it also brings us some gift from heaven—new strength, for example, or at least a new opportunity for strength."[80] Nietzsche is more radical, certainly more perverse than Buber, Heschel, Soloveitchik, and Kaplan. With no small sense of irony, he approaches the cruelties that horrify bourgeois moralists and calls them good. But modern Jewish thinkers had also sought "gifts from heaven," a core of meaning and value in evil. Buber and Heschel found spiritual catharsis. For Soloveitchik and Kaplan, suffering constituted a school of moral discipline, inculcating virtues of patience, compassion, and courage. Like alchemists turning lead into gold, all four thinkers tried to fashion evil and suffering into a foundation for new spiritual strength.

Within definite limits, neither religious thinkers in search of meaning nor even poststructuralist critics could possibly object to this goal of turning evil into good. Poststructuralism in particular has taught us to see the enormous powers of human interpretation. One might even use it to re-evaluate the much maligned figure of theodicy. No signifier, including the signs that mark suffering and evil, possesses a stable significance, pre-established referent, or self-identical essence. If every "text" points to every other "text," if every sign points beyond itself to still other signs, there is no reason why Auschwitz should point only to Auschwitz. Auschwitz can point (or be forced to point) toward its polar opposite, the resurrection of the Jewish people and the redemption of the world. Death can point to life. Nietzsche in particular was sensitive to the way in which good can become evil and evil good through an infinite play of deferral and difference. Indeed, from a moral point of view, why shouldn't one violate "the nature" of evil and turn it into a "foundation" for good? Why shouldn't one try to extract a modicum of meaning out of catastrophic circumstance? In this light, theodicy need not be "true" in the sense of reflecting an existing state of affairs. Theodicy represents the power of art and fantasy to reshape the world, to reconfigure human experience, to redeem suffering, through creative acts of interpretative intervention. According to this reading, theodicy provides an important tool with which contemporary religious thinkers can put poststructuralist theories regarding the free play of signifiers to good moral purpose. This includes refashioning chaos into cosmos, meaninglessness into meaning, despair into hope.

This works only to a point.

Some evils remain radically resistant to any frame of good. Nietzsche never considers the possibility that an artist might actually fail to turn something ugly into something beautiful. For Nietzsche in the nineteenth century, there seemed to be no limits to the will to power. Perhaps the power of interpretation still seems limitless in our own age of digital imaging and other cybernetic modes of information-manipulation. Dare we, however, refract Auschwitz through the tinted glass described by Nietzsche? Can we turn it into good or into an occasion for good? Following Nietzsche's lead, many poststructuralist critics will argue the obvious point that no single perspective is ever absolute. This may be true without obviating the suspicion that some kinds of interpretation fall short—especially theological attempts to render catastrophic suffering "meaningful." Long before the Holocaust, Ivan Karamazov rejected the scandal of fashioning virtue and value on the backs of suffering children. There are epistemic and moral limits to the act of philosophical, theological, or artistic representation at which any act of murder or violence, much less Auschwitz, resists its strongest interpreters.

In the introduction to this study, I pointed to discursive factors in order to explain why so little direct reference to the Holocaust appears in modern Jewish thought throughout the 1950s. The Holocaust lay at the limit of interpretation for Buber, Heschel, Soloveitchik, and Kaplan. I do not think critics should blame them for not yet having at their disposal the riveting memoirs of Elie Wiesel, Primo Levi, Jean Amery, or Bruno Bettelheim. Eichmann was not tried in Jerusalem until 1963. Auschwitz itself had not yet turned into the distinctly resonant trope that it has since become. Modern Jewish thinkers simply lacked the historical, literary, and iconographic tools with which to grasp in full the Holocaust's impact on religious thought. This recognition lay just a few short years beyond the horizon of their religious imaginations. In contrast, Rubenstein, Berkovits, and Fackenheim crossed that epistemic limit. They explore the theological dimensions of Auschwitz with the help of novelists, poets, historians, and social scientists. In the process, their thought becomes "post-Holocaust" in a far deeper sense than chronological coincidence.

A chasm opened up by Auschwitz separates Rubenstein, Berkovits, and Fackenheim from the writings of Buber, Heschel, Soloveitchik, and Kaplan. We must note, however, one important continuity between modern and post-Holocaust Jewish thought. Steven Katz has observed how Heschel polemicized against medieval notions of divine perfection.[81] The same insight applies to all modern Jewish theologians. Medieval philosophers had cast God in absolute terms, perfect in power, unchanging in nature, and immune from human machinations. Knowingly or unknowingly, modern Jewish theologians began to change this picture. For Kaplan, God was not perfect in power. Buber described God as an uncanny, even destructive agent. In Heschel's thought, God required human others and suffered at their hands. For Soloveitchik, God remained vulnerable to the Shulamite's betrayal. Post-Holocaust theologians have in turn radicalized this shift away from the tenets of medieval theology. They show exactly how imperfect God appears in the harsh light of Auschwitz. In the following chapters I argue that Rubenstein, Berkovits, and Fackenheim reject the tradition of theodicy that modern Jewish theologians had bequeathed them. They refuse to speak of suffering in terms of spiritual catharsis or moral education, much less human guilt. Instead, they turn against theodicy in all its mutant forms and support Job's complaint against the God of History.

PART II

FOUR

"HITLER'S ACCOMPLICE"?!

REVISIONING RICHARD RUBENSTEIN

> After all, a misunderstanding is often nothing but the
> paradoxical abbreviation of an original line of thought. And it
> is precisely such a misunderstanding which has frequently
> become productive of new ideas in the mystical sphere.
> (Gershom Scholem, *Major Trends in Jewish Mysticism*)

RICHARD RUBENSTEIN'S seminal *After Auschwitz* marks a milestone distinguishing modern Jewish theology from contemporary Jewish thought. Published in 1966, it offered the first theological reflections in which the Holocaust was a driving preoccupation. The very word *Auschwitz* in its title immediately riveted readers' attention to the Holocaust. The word *after* suggested that Jewish life and thought can never be the same. Abraham Joshua Heschel, Martin Buber, Joseph Soloveitchik, and Mordecai Kaplan—among the great interpreters of Judaism in the twentieth century—had touched on the Holocaust only briefly. None confronted the problem of evil as relentlessly or as radically as did Rubenstein. He attacked belief in the God of History, the notions of covenant and election, the hallowed texts of Jewish tradition, and the scandal of theodicy. Rubenstein's argument was simple: to posit a just and omnipotent God covenanted to Israel *and active in its affairs* could only mean that God justly willed the murder of six million Jewish people. Rubenstein therefore proclaimed "the death of God" and turned to what he called "the tragic fatalities of the God of nature."[1] No Jewish theologian had ever attacked the God and tradition of covenant and election with such categorical rage.

In this chapter I revise a standard scholarly view of Rubenstein recklessly abandoning traditional Jewish sancta. With the passing of time, his earlier radicalism waned. Rubenstein's confrontational self-presentation had involved as much style as substance. In more recent works—including the recently published second edition of *After Auschwitz*—he no longer talks about "radical theology" or "the death of God." Even Rubenstein's earliest writings prove less radical today than they appeared in the 1960s and 1970s. Indeed, he had never rejected God, Torah, or Israel in the first place. He had only cast them under a strange, different light. Rubenstein, I argue, was less a revolutionary than a revisionist who began the inevitably awkward process of remolding Jewish theological and textual traditions in light of the Holocaust. At the same time I also argue that he never produced what the literary critic Harold Bloom might have called a truly "strong" counter-tradition. That is, Rubenstein failed to force the Hebrew Bible and rabbinic midrash to speak compellingly in his own post-Holocaust voice.

The overwhelmingly hostile reception accorded Rubenstein is a nadir in modern Jewish intellectual etiquette, with but few exceptions marked by mischaracterization, simplification, and trivialization. Critics have regularly dismissed the relevance of Rubenstein's writings to Judaism and its theological and communal cultures. They have accused him of being uncritically captive to passing trends in Protestant and psychoanalytic circles. Rubenstein's critics have even exploited his own autobiographical admissions to impugn his good sense and sanity. In the most egregious case, one critic called Rubenstein an accomplice to Hitler. Respectful critics (much less, enthusiastic disciples) have been few and far between. And even they frequently miss the complex belief, the ambivalent commitment to Jewish texts, and the deep concern for the Jewish people that distinguished Rubenstein's early thought.[2]

In 1974 the contemporary theologian Arthur Green recounted his first response to *After Auschwitz*. Green described an initial excitement among his fellow rabbinical students at the Jewish Theological Seminary. He recalled, "Here was someone finally dealing with the issues—someone finally raising the questions we had been afraid to raise except to ourselves and perhaps to our closest friends."[3] Not without his own criticism, Green remembered this book with respect and even enthusiasm. However, most of the passions Rubenstein provoked at the time were hostile. In one of the first written responses, the eminent Bible scholar Robert Gordis defended the tradition so vigorously attacked in *After Auschwitz*. Gordis urged his readers to "discover that a viable faith in the Biblical God operating in history is still possible—that it is, in fact, far superior to the newly packaged religions that 'celebrate' the 'absurdity' of human existence."[4]

The vehemence of Gordis's response should have surprised no one. As Steven Katz explains, "close perusal reveals that [Rubenstein] is . . . guilty of using evocative and emotional language to obfuscate rather than clarify, to arouse rather than illuminate."[5] At the same time, an inattention to style and rhetoric frustrated a proper understanding of Rubenstein's work from the very start. This too was Rubenstein's fault. His very language, his choice of words and terminology, was as if purposefully intended to repel Jewish readers. Imagine the reaction of his teachers at the Jewish Theological Seminary, encountering a melange of images like "the death of God," "paganism," "earth divinities," "cannibal mothers," "Dionysus and Apollo," "Nature," "eros," "immanence," "tragedy," "absurdity," "a cold, heartless, indifferent universe," "radical theology," and "rupture." How Greek must Rubenstein have appeared to an establishment whose own religious rhetoric invoked transcendence, ethics, covenant, history, and continuity! To his teachers, Athens defined the border separating sacred from profane, Israelite from pagan, Jew from gentile.[6]

Rubenstein gave his critics every reason to dismiss him, perhaps even still today. Nevertheless, I strongly contend that his thought requires readers who both value and look past slogans and rhetoric. The picture of Rubenstein that I present will not jibe with the figure pilloried by his critics. Nor (for that matter) was Rubenstein the petulant radical he himself often pretended to be. He was rather and always a loyal son of Israel, a neomystic, and an imaginative reader of traditional Jewish texts. As Jacob Neusner notes, "The abuse to which [Rubenstein] has been subjected [is] the highest possible tribute to the compelling importance of his contribution."[7] Indeed, Rubenstein's theological and textual revisions have had a profound but unrecognized impact on contemporary Jewish thinkers—even on those who were to deny his influence.

Tragic Theology

The Problem of Evil after Auschwitz

Katz was not the only critic to have wondered why Rubenstein insists that the Holocaust provokes such a radical and *unique* challenge to faith in God. "Did belief in God ever make sense?" Katz asks. Katz points to a tragic litany of Jewish history, the rabbinic heretic traditional Elisha ben Abuyeh, and Dostoyevsky's fictional antihero Ivan Karamazov.[8] Of course, philosophical debates about God and the problem of evil are nothing new. Citing Epicurus, David Hume maintained, [1] if God cannot prevent evil, then God is not omnipotent; [2] if God is not willing to prevent evil, then God is not omnibenevolent; and [3] there would be no genuine evil if God is able and willing to prevent it.[9] In fact, Rubenstein's own critique of traditional theism resembles (if only in part) the ones posed by skeptical philosophers and secular critics of religion long before the Holocaust. Consciously echoing Ivan Karamazov, Rubenstein concludes that "a God who tolerates the suffering of even one innocent child is either infinitely cruel or hopelessly indifferent."[10] According to his own argument, the death of one innocent person represents as serious a challenge to belief in an omnipotent and omnibenevolent God as the death of six million. Why insist then that the Holocaust constitutes a unique theological challenge?

Katz's point holds insofar as the discussion reflects upon the philosophical coherence of purely theological propositions. However, we have already seen that extraphilosophical factors complicate religious thought. In chapter 1 of this study, I argued that the problem of catastrophic suffering, mass death and the wholesale slaughter of entire communities, provokes a host of social and textual problems that a one-dimensional theological or philosophical analysis obscures. Rubenstein proves no exception. Abstract arguments guide, but do not ultimately govern Rubenstein's theological project. Three extraphilosophical factors distinguish Rubenstein's argument from the ones made by skeptical philosophers— factors that uniquely apply to Jewish tradition and the Holocaust's impact on it. For Rubenstein, the problem of evil revolves around the traditional motif of a *collective* covenant between the God of History and the Jewish people, the question of numbers, and the ominous presence of Christian antisemitism.

The particular welfare of the Jewish community dictates nearly every theological choice that Rubenstein has ever made. Following the example of Mordecai Kaplan, Rubenstein vociferously rejects the traditional doctrines of election and chosenness. But unlike Kaplan, humanistic and democratic ideals do not motivate his negation. Nor does he abandon the idea of covenant in order to abandon the community. Rather Rubenstein tries to relieve the Jewish people of extraordinary moral and psychological burdens while protecting them from Christian antisemitism. He argues: "The tendency of the Church to regard the Jews in magic and theological terms encourages the view that the vicissitudes of Jewish history are God's will. If we accept [this theological premise], there is no way of avoiding . . . [the conclusion that] God sent Hitler. But how can we ask Christians to give up these premises if we continue to regard ourselves in this light?"[11] Why should the welfare of the Jewish community or Christian antisemitism dictate Rubenstein's rejection of covenant? Rubenstein explains that Israel's fate bears grave import for theological traditions rooted in the Hebrew Bible. Scripture itself depicts God choosing the community as the special object of divine preoccupation. It holds beliefs and hopes concerning this particular national *collective*. "From the perspectives of both Judaism and Christianity," Rubenstein writes, "the Holocaust can hardly be considered a random occurrence since it was inflicted upon the community which the Bible asserts to be God's chosen people."[12]

When social factors like community and covenant distinguish religious thought, the number of people killed and traumatized by mass death exacerbate the problem of evil. Brute numbers and raw statistics ultimately hold theological significance. Theologians and philosophers with sufficient ingenuity may find it possible to absorb personal tragedies into larger patterns of symbolic meaning and social organization. However, overarching worldviews require social legitimation, what the sociologist of religion Peter Berger called a plausibility structure. As Berger argues, the plausibility of any symbolic order depends upon social structures in which this reality is taken for granted.[13] The unjust death of a single individual will usually fail to render an entire symbolic system implausible—not like the relatively sudden death of entire populations. Individual and collective tragedy present different orders of crisis. There is, Rubenstein claims, "a profound difference between a situation in which some persons suffer and perish unjustly but the group survives and one in which an entire group . . . is obliterated."[14] In the best of cases, the suffering individual can rely on broad social networks of sympathy and support. In contrast, catastrophe and cataclysm rip apart those networks. Simply put, individual suffering (even large scale massacre) does not provoke the same order of crisis as genocide.

The role played by potentially hostile outsiders constitutes the last extra-philosophical factor distinguishing Rubenstein's discussion. It is impossible to underestimate the impact of Christian thinkers on Rubenstein's thought. They provide a negative foil for his own Jewish ruminations. Rubenstein's encounter with a German pastor named Heinrich Gruber is a case in point. Gruber was a theologian who had been incarcerated in Dachau for his opposition to the Nazis. After the war he testified against Eichmann and worked to reconcile German Christians and Jews. Yet Rubenstein is horrified to hear this otherwise sympathetic Christian describe the Holocaust as God's will and Hitler as God's instrument. He suspects that Gruber, despite his proven goodwill, holds the Jewish people guilty for the putative sin of rejecting Jesus.[15] The fact that Gruber was German intensifies the significance of the encounter. Rubenstein has since wondered "whether his own views on God and the Holocaust would have changed as much . . . had a non-German member of the clergy . . . offered him the same interpretation of the Holocaust." When he left Gruber's home, "something in him had changed permanently and decisively."[16]

This disturbing exchange constitutes an important, yet curious source of Rubenstein's radical program. It suggests that the objective coherence of religious propositions does not concern Rubenstein nearly as much as how others subjectively manipulate them. Traditional assertions about God, covenant, and suffering are not intrinsically problematic. They become problematic only insofar as they engender crippling feelings of collective guilt. In particular, they trouble Rubenstein when Christians, even sympathetic Christians, exploit them in order to fault the Jewish people.

In this case, Rubenstein has not rebelled against Judaism, but against a Christian pastor who had himself survived Dachau. Neither Heschel nor Buber, but rather Gruber "dramatized the consequences of accepting the normative Judeo-Christian theology of history in light of the camps."[17]

Another example of the negative impact of Christian thinkers can be found in an important essay entitled "God's Omnipotence in Rabbinic Judaism." In this piece, Rubenstein attacks "traditional Jewish belief" in divine omnipotence. The essay appears in *The Religious Imagination* (1968)—a text devoted to exploring the interface between psychoanalytic theory and rabbinic aggadah. Rubenstein draws on a rich body of rabbinic lore in order to argue that, in Jewish tradition, the disaster befalling Korah in the biblical book of Numbers conclusively proves him in the wrong before God. The catastrophe suffered by Korah's band is said to indicate divine displeasure. But at the end of this essay on rabbinic lore, Rubenstein cites how Justin Martyr used the rabbis' assertion of divine omnipotence against the Jewish people.[18] Rubenstein's interest in Justin Martyr is not simply comparative. The presence of Justin Martyr in this essay suggests that Christian readings of traditional Jewish doctrines shape his discussion of the problem of evil. Rubenstein has rejected what he perceives to have been a traditional Jewish doctrine on the basis of how Christians wield it against Jews.

The "Death of God"

Rubenstein's critics complained about his embracing "the death of God." The phrase, coined by Nietzsche, had been popularized by radical Protestant theologians writing in the 1960s under the influence of Paul Tillich. But what could Rubenstein have possibly meant by this misleading slogan? Was Rubenstein an atheist? When all is said and done, the slogan refers only to the "God of History." Like Tillich, Rubenstein attacks belief in the God of classical theism. According to Rubenstein, the God of History represents the perfect, immutable Creator who remains outside of and apart from the world and its history in a stance of omnipotent control and judgment. In the introduction to "The Dean and The Chosen People," he writes, "If I believed in God as the omnipotent author of the historical drama and Israel as His Chosen People, I had to accept Dean Gruber's conclusion that it was God's will that Hitler committed six million Jews to slaughter."[19] Like a mantra, Rubenstein repeatedly refers to this image of God as the "the ultimate actor in history." In an act of gross caricature, he never stops insisting that this was the God whom traditional Jewish texts depict. Again, in *Morality and Eros* (1970), the God of History is said to represent the "perfect, unchanging Creator and Lawgiver who stands in isolated splendor outside of his creation."[20] As we will see, this image represents a clear but crude negative standard that orients Rubenstein's post-Holocaust thought.

"The ultimate actor in history" appears as the chief villain in the aforementioned essay "God's Omnipotence in Rabbinic Judaism." In the Bible, Korah chafes against Moses and Aaron's political and priestly prerogatives. An omnipotent God ultimately arbitrates the conflict between Korah and Moses with a deadly show of force. Korah's arguments, represented by the rabbis as highly reasonable, are reduced to nought before a destructive display of divine power. Rubenstein argues: "The overwhelming power of God is the ultimate source of religious authority in the Korah legends. The point of the legends is that the sign was given to Moses rather than to Korah. This alone settled the matter. Korah's disaster is the final proof of the fallacious character of his claims."[21] According to Rubenstein, the text represents God's power in absolute terms. Divine power is "overwhelming," "final." It alone determines right from wrong. Rubenstein, however, overstates his case. He argues that God's irresistible power constitutes the paramount source of legitimate authority in rabbinic/Jewish theology writ large.

Rubenstein has relied on rabbinic literary sources to prove his point about traditional theology. But did "Judaism" really understand divine power in the way that Rubenstein insists it did? After all, Korah represents a poor example with which to compare the respective authority of God and human persons in classical Jewish theology. Indeed, the rabbis frequently depict legitimate human authorities whose status and power often equal and sometimes outweigh God's own. In the famous aggadah about the oven at Aknai, the rabbis argue about its ritual purity. The sages disagree with R. Eliezer, who calls on a host of divine interventions to prove his case. But a majority of sage opinion overrides God in this halakhic dispute! This does not represent an isolated aggadah. It forms part of a larger religious tradition that recurrently portrays human decisors as God's partners. Stories of God deferring to human authorities frequent rabbinic literature. In the Talmud and midrash, Moses argues with God about the Golden Calf. A midrashic Jacob, Moses, Elijah, and Samuel invert the order of creation. Elisha and Elijah were said by the rabbis to execute the very same miracles performed by God. At least in these rabbinic legends, God and righteous men are said to share the very same power. The omnipotent "ultimate actor of History" caricatured by Rubenstein hardly represents the normative God-idea found in Jewish texts.

At the same time, one should not cavalierly dismiss Rubenstein's rendition of traditional theology. As Eliezer Schweid notes, most ultra-Orthodox Jewish thinkers have resisted any attempt to disassociate historical events like the Holocaust from direct divine intervention. For them, the

Holocaust was a sign of wrath and salvation. God used Hitler to punish secular Jews (Reform Jews in Western Europe, Zionists in Eastern Europe) and to try the righteous in order to prepare them for the messianic age.[22] Even after Auschwitz, most ultra-Orthodox Jews would accept at face value the Deuteronomist's hyperbolic description: "The rock, His work is perfect, for all His ways are justice; a God of faithfulness without iniquity, righteousness and upright is He. The corruption is not His; it is that of his children, the spot is theirs."[23] These words do not necessarily mean that the finite human mind can understand the reasons why God orders providence the way God does. They only demand trust that God remains a God of faithfulness. For his part, Rubenstein resists these verses from Deuteronomy. Read in light of the Holocaust, they imply that those who died in the ghettoes and camps were guilty and corrupt. They imply that God is righteous and providence perfect. In light of the Holocaust, this image of God effectively dies.

But what does this mean? Most of Rubenstein's Jewish critics never tried to ascertain the use to which he put the "death of God." They were offended by Nietzsche's image then current among radical Protestant theologians. In contrast, we begin by noting that the very essay in *After Auschwitz* in which Rubenstein accepts the "death of God" moniker contains a radical critique of Thomas Altizer and William Hamilton—two important Protestant death-of-God theologians.[24] Note too his trenchant criticism of Harvey Cox, another radical Protestant theologian. In both cases Rubenstein rejects their optimistic vision of untrammeled freedom in the modern world. The "death of God" does not signal liberation, but tragedy and upheaval. The phrase was not meant by Rubenstein to be a *literal* description about God. Instead, it describes the human condition in the twentieth century. He used this Christian image to radicalize Buber's metaphor of divine eclipse. God's "death" points to the total non-existence of divine-human encounter in a radically secular age.[25] Rubenstein has since drawn an even greater distance between himself and his Protestant counterparts. In the second edition of *After Auschwitz*, he explains that "over the years the first edition has come to be seen less as an expression of death-of-God theology than as the initial expression of contemporary Jewish Holocaust theology."[26] Clearly, Rubenstein had chosen a metaphor, not a theological identity!

God after the Death of God

Amazingly, few of Rubenstein's critics bothered to note that God survives the "death of God." Rubenstein implicitly makes this point in a chapter of *After Auschwitz* entitled "The Rebirth of Israel in Contemporary Jewish Theology." Instead of theism, we now see a new theology derived from a loose amalgam of Greek tragedy and myth, archaic and mystical Jewish traditions, Hegelian philosophy, Tillichian theology, and a protofeminist theological vocabulary. Rubenstein calls it "insightful paganism."[27] In his view Zionism signifies the Jewish return to pagan origins, to the old gods of the land, and to the primordial powers of earth and fatality that they represent. Rubenstein celebrates this renewed contact with the powers of life and death in the Land of Israel and even associates it with Canaanite gods and goddesses. He writes, "Increasingly, Israel's return to the earth elicits a return to the archaic earth-religion of Israel. This does not mean that tomorrow worship of Baal and Astarte will supplant the worship of Yahweh; it does mean that earth's fruitfulness, its vicissitudes, and its engendering power will once again be central spiritual realities of Jewish life, at least in Israel."[28]

This "insightful paganism" proves deeply gendered. Reference to Astarte and other feminine images shape Rubenstein's radical project. God no longer represents what later feminist theorists might have called a phallocentric figure who towers over creation in a stance of omnipotent judgment. Godhood no longer stands outside of nature's vicissitudes in a state of static, solitary perfection. Rubenstein proclaims: "No more will God be seen as the transcendent Lord of nature, controlling it as if it were a marionette at the end of a string. God will be seen as the source and life of nature, the being of the beings which ephemerally and epiphenomenally are nature's self-expression.[29] God is a womb, the mother who "participates" in the life of the creaturely world. Rubenstein has opted for a more "feminine" set of religious metaphor. He prefers ostensibly maternal images of "ground," "source," "abyss," "matrix," and "sacred womb" to more patriarchical images of distance and control. This gendered shift in religious expression defines Rubenstein's putative "paganism" and the resistance it evoked. As Judith Plaskow has since observed, "Anxieties about polytheism, sensuousness, female imagery, and goddesses tend to get lumped together both with each other and the general opprobrium the term paganism arouses."[30]

In our view Rubenstein's thought does not prove as pagan as his rhetoric suggests. He is not a pantheist, much less a polytheist. Rubenstein is a "panentheist"—a theologian who sees the world constituting the life of a divinity that transcends it. As the unitary source of life, death, and the natural wheel, God remains ontologically distinct from nature. Revealed in nature, Godhood unfolds in the world while constituting the primordial origin to which all lives ultimately return. In an important essay from *Morality and Eros* entitled "God After the Death of God," Rubenstein explains: "God is the ocean and we are the waves. In some sense each wave has its moment in which it is distinguishable as a somewhat separate entity. Nevertheless, no wave is entirely distinct from the ocean which is its substantial ground."[31] Appropriating Hegel's distinction between Spirit and nature, Rubenstein writes, "Beyond the empirical world of dichotomous oppositions and discrete, isolated entities, there is, according to Hegel, a unified totality that can be rationally and conceptually grasped."[32] In Rubenstein's thought, nature is like a wave that forms a momentarily discrete and separate entity and yet remains integrally connected to the ocean surging through it. God is an all-encompassing plenum that differentiates itself in time and manifests itself through the world, but with no explicit or redemptive purpose. Ultimately Godhood returns to reestablish a long-lost primordial totality out of its own archaic self.

As we see it, paganism provided Rubenstein a vocabulary with which to articulate a nontheistic theology—years before feminist and kabbalistic tropes began to enter the mainstream of contemporary Jewish religious thought! Writing the first edition of *After Auschwitz* in the 1960s, Rubenstein had no other language. In the second edition (published in 1992), he can explicitly drop the first edition's pagan references and rhetoric. He admits that "one of the most debatable aspects of the first edition was its affirmation of a form of Jewish paganism. . . . " However, he continues, "Although this position is modified in the current edition, I continue to emphasize the immanence rather than the radical transcendence of God."[33] Still later in the text, he writes, "The dialectical mystical elements in my thinking have endured; the pagan element has proven less durable."[34] Paganism proves to have been nothing more than a trope, a way in which to describe God as an immanent force within the world. Like the often misunderstood "death of God," this figurative allusion does not indicate a determinate pagan identity.

Critics have typically overlooked the ethical dimension to this putative, early "paganism." Katz, for instance, devotes a considerable amount of critical analysis explicating the deficiencies of nature paganism but remains puzzled by the concluding remark to the first essay of *After Auschwitz*. In this essay, Rubenstein describes Nazism as a psychotic affair, a movement drunk with power, in love with death, and contemptuous of restraint. He cryptically concludes, "There is more realistic pleasure in the disciplines and norms of the Living God than in all the freedoms of the death of God."[35] Katz can only call this statement "a curious self-contradiction."[36] In fact, Rubenstein expends considerable effort explaining that all things are *not* permissible after the "death of God." The world according to Rubenstein runs according to the iron law of hubris and nemesis. Instead of a religious ethics founded upon the moral categories of "good and evil," he has proposed an unfamiliar ethics of limit and excess. In Greek thought, "Hubris never signified complete and total lawlessness. . . . It was followed, as night follows day, by inevitable nemesis, which righted wrong and restored nature's disturbed equilibrium. Good and evil were rooted in the very nature of the cosmos itself."[37]

With a little hermeneutical charity, one might see that Rubenstein's panentheism represents a type of monotheism with roots in Jewish and western mysticism. The pagan, polytheistic figures that appear in Rubenstein's theological writings function as a set of hypostatized images with which he clarifies different attributes of a single God. Following Nietzsche in *The Birth of Tragedy*, Rubenstein has "Apollo" represent measure, order, and limit. "Dionysus" is said to represent excess and flux. But rather than separate divinities they "are in reality masks of the God who abides after the death of God. That God is not the perfect, unchanging Creator and Lawgiver. . . . He manifests himself (so to speak) in the dynamic, ever-changing structures of reality itself. Above all, God manifests himself in and through Mother Earth and the material cosmos."[38] Apollo and Dionysus form into a unity. Like the frequently hypostatized attributes of *din* (justice) and *ḥesed* (mercy) in rabbinic thought, they constitute relatively independent forces linked within an overarching divine matrix. They represent different attributes of a single God. For Rubenstein, the holiness of God stands beyond any attribute or representation, beyond the maleness of Yahweh or the femaleness of Canaanite goddesses. The Hebrew Bible's God and the pagan deities of Canaan express the same basic phenomenon. He writes, "The commanding Father God, the King who lovingly guided His regal son, and the thunder-god dwelling in his heavenly abode, are all manifold aspects for the same faceless Abyss."[39]

Paul Tillich, with whom Rubenstein studied at Harvard, called this primordial and ultimate reality the "Ground of Being." Tillich writes that "in mystical language the depth of the divine life, its inexhaustible and ineffable character, is called 'Abyss.'"[40] Rubenstein calls this primordial ground the "God of Holy Nothingness." The term signifies neither religious nihilism nor atheism. It only evokes God's mystery and namelessness. In *Morality and Eros*, Rubenstein explains:

To speak of God as the Holy Nothingness is not to suggest that he is a void. On the contrary, he is an indivisible plenum so rich that all existence derives from his very essence. God as the Nothing is not absence of being but a superfluity of being.

Why then use the term Nothingness? Use of the term rests in part upon a very ancient observation that all definition of finite entities involves negation. The infinite God, the ground of all finite beings, cannot be defined. The infinite God is therefore in no sense a thing bearing any resemblance to the finite beings of the empirical world.[41]

These themes run throughout all of Rubenstein's theological writings. The Infinite God is a no-thing whose existence remains distinct from any measure, quality, or character. In *After Auschwitz*, God's Holy Nothingness constitutes a majesty that stands over against human finitude.[42] "Why is there something rather than nothing?" In the wake of this unanswerable question comes a sense of the mysterious plenum into which human persons are "absurdly" thrown. Before this terrifying abyss, mystics intuit God's incommensurability with all measurement, logic, and relation.[43]

The God of Nature is neither a calming nor a loving presence. Standing beyond all categories, the God of Holy Nothingness is an amoral power that transcends human categories of good and evil. Rubenstein understands God's presence as numinous and threatening. Indeed, God has a patently demonic side. Rubenstein criticizes liberal Jewish theologians for refusing to consider the dangerous qualities of the divine *mysterium*. According to Rubenstein, they wanted a moral God because they lacked the courage of the absurd and tragic. In contrast, he appreciates how archaic strata of the Bible represented the Holy eviscerating those who approach improperly. Alluding to the narratives of Nadav and Abihu in Leviticus and the story of Uzzah in Second Samuel, Rubenstein concludes that, even in the Bible, "God in His holiness is more than a moral force."[44]

Rubenstein's theological vision is profoundly tragic. The terrifying source of life and death, the God of Holy Nothingness does not redeem her children. No ethical act of turning (*tshuva*) or magical act of theurgy can ransom human persons from death and vicissitude.[45] In this view, life constitutes a constraining system of needs and wants. Rubenstein argues: "There is only one Messiah who redeems us from the irony, the travail, and the limitations of human existence. Surely he will come. He is the Angel of Death. Death is the true Messiah and the land of the dead the place of God's true Kingdom."[46] Rubenstein expresses the sad conviction that death remains the only ultimate redemption from uncertainty and trial. In this theological economy, death and unredeemed existence are simply the price we pay for life, love, and joy. Tragedy obviates the theodic tradition of rewards and punishments. Death and suffering represent the impersonal swing of fate, not intentional and justified punishment.

The ironic critical conclusion is that Rubenstein's own theology rests upon a weak theodic foundation. In the first chapter of this study, I argued that the act of "acceptance" constitutes a key component of theodicy. That is, theodicians accept the presence of genuine evil in a God-governed (or God-filled) world. Rubenstein, of course, rejects traditional theodicies that posit providence, just deserts, and deferred compensations. However, a rhetoric of acceptance surreptitiously slips into his own theology. In "God After the Death of God," he states that "all the joys and sorrows of the creative drama of life [represent] the deepest expression of divine life."[47] He concludes the essay suggesting that "we must forsake the quest for redemption and *accept* life with its limitations and ironies. . . . All we have is this world. Let us endure its wounds and celebrate its joys in undeceived lucidity."[48] In *After Auschwitz* Rubenstein envisions "a world content to *accept* the joyful sorrow of what-is."[49]

The affirmation sounded by Rubenstein self-consciously echoes Nietzsche (along with Herbert Marcuse and Norman O. Brown). As Walter Kaufmann has observed, Nietzsche's thought displayed a "Dionysian faith" of radical yes-saying. Kaufmann quotes Nietzsche in *Ecce Homo*, "My formula for the greatness of a human being is *amor fati*: that one wants nothing to be different—not forward, not backward, not in all eternity. Not merely bear what is necessary, still less conceal it . . . but love it."[50] One of Nietzsche's most famous formulations of this idea appears in the myth of the eternal recurrence. In an important aphorism in the *Gay Science*, Nietzsche envisioned a demon asking: "Do you want this [life] once more and innumerable times more?" Only the most well disposed person, could crave nothing more fervently and respond "never have I heard anything more divine!"[51] Nietzsche was in no way unaware of evil. However, as we suggested in the conclusion of the previous chapter, evil remained subject to an artist's transvaluation. Suffering was absorbed by this yes-saying logic.

Rubenstein, however, can only mimic Nietzsche imperfectly. After Auschwitz, any Dionysian faith must ultimately fall short. How do Nazis constitute "deep expressions of divine life"? Can one really "accept the joyful sorrow" of extermination camps? Reflecting back on history, could Rubenstein have said in good faith, "Never have I heard anything more divine!" and will its eternal return? I don't think so. The problem of evil and suffering ultimately threatens to scuttle Rubenstein's Dionysian faith, just as it threatens traditional faith in the God of History.

In a very critical sense, Rubenstein's Dionysian faith requires *even greater* justification than the faith advanced by thinkers like Buber, Heschel, Soloveitchik, and Kaplan. They, unlike Rubenstein, never accepted the empirical and suffering "what-is." Instead, they privileged a redeemed future over a vicious present. Their God is frequently absent, standing at a further remove from the scandal of history. In contrast, the God of Nature directly participates in mayhem. The God of Holy Nothingness is "omnipresent," although not in the usual sense meant by theologians. This God resides within destruction. The Holy Nothingness gen-

erates this-world and its vicissitudes from out of its own fecund plenitude. Yet, a God so involved in the world and its attendant suffering
becomes deeply complicit and can only invite the wrath and enmity of
her aggrieved children.

This quandary assumes an air of mounting crisis as we examine Rubenstein's discussion of religious love, language, and shared experience. Despite a Nietzschean rhetoric of *amor fati*, Rubenstein confesses that he
cannot love the God of Nature. He admits in the first edition of *After
Auschwitz* that "we are enjoined to love God 'with all thy heart, with all
thy soul and will all thy might.' But I cannot. I am aware of His holiness.
I am struck with wonder and terror before His Nothingness, but I cannot
love Him. I am affrighted before Him. Perhaps, in the end, all I have is
silence."[52] In the second edition of *After Auschwitz*, Rubenstein describes
how he remains mute in synagogue. A desire to celebrate sacred times
and seasons with the community draws him to its sacred space. But once
inside, "we are struck dumb by words we can no longer honestly utter.
All that we can offer is our reverent and attentive silence before the Divine."[53] This admission, I think, contributes to an intimate portrayal of
deep religious sensitivity. However, it reflects a sensitivity that allows no
liturgical praise, petition, or protest, no hallowed love or hate, no voice,
no language, and hence no shared religious experience with which to
divine post-Holocaust Jewish existence.

To his credit, Rubenstein realizes that his theological vision is not
trouble-free. He acknowledges that "by virtue of His, or Its, all-encompassing nature, the God who is the Source and Ground of Being is as
much a God-who-acts-in-history as the transcendent Creator God of the
Bible." He admits that he has found no solution to the problem of evil.
But Rubenstein argues that at the very least, his own theological position
does not force him to interpret the Holocaust within the framework of
just or delayed deserts. Jewish suffering represents only tragic misfortune.
He observes, "creative destruction and even destruction transcending the
categories of good and evil may be inherent in the life of Divinity, but
not punitive destruction."[54] Punishment at the hands of an infinitely just
and powerful God must entail guilt or reward. Ultimately, theists must
therefore blame the victims of suffering or interpret evil in terms of catharsis and redemption. Instead, Rubenstein's own theological vision
folds back into an overriding solidarity with the Jewish people. While still
subject to a crisis of theodicy, his theology saves him from blaming suffering people or upholding them to impossible spiritual or ethical demands.
Rubenstein can faithfully defend Israel from theological calumny while
unequivocally rejecting the notion that catastrophe bears any disguised
good.

Textual Revision after Auschwitz

In the introduction to this chapter, we saw how Robert Gordis attacked this "newly packaged" Dionysian faith. Gordis considered it to be a completely foreign implant, alien to the true spirit of Jewish tradition. But did Rubenstein ever reject the Jewish textual tradition in its entirety? In our view Rubenstein couples a strategic misreading with a revaluation of Jewish textual traditions. Rubenstein's early rhetorical radicalism obscures how his thought has swung between the rejection and revision of Jewish literary sources. Rubenstein, I argue, began the inevitably awkward process of remolding Jewish theological and textual traditions in light of the Holocaust. In the early 1960s tradition was thought to espouse a univocal theodic message to the problem of suffering. Ephraim Urbach called rabbinic response to suffering an "absolute theodicy." Rubenstein's fight against theodicy, we suggest, necessitated profoundly bitter misreadings of Jewish literary texts. At the same time, he never produced what the literary critic Harold Bloom might have called a truly "strong" misreading. That is, Rubenstein failed to force the authors of the Hebrew Bible and rabbinic midrash to speak compellingly in his own post-Holocaust voice.

The Religious Imagination epitomizes the ambivalence about tradition that typifies Rubenstein's writings. He uses Freudian theory to explicate rabbinic texts, while mining them for psychoanalytic insight. Katz has accused Rubenstein of submitting traditional narrative to a privileged but foreign psychoanalytic interpretive frame.[55] True enough, terms like guilt, anality, castration anxiety, sublimation filter Rubenstein's analysis of rabbinic aggadah. On closer examination, however, the relation between Freud and Jewish literary tradition does not appear so unbalanced. According to Rubenstein, "Freud has demonstrated that religious rite is more than gross and deceived superstition, and that it is, in fact, rooted in the deepest ironies of the human condition."[56] Rubenstein even uses Freud to defend Jewish Law. The rabbis were not hopeless neurotics enslaved to an arbitrary law and a tyrannical deity. They stressed the realistic freedoms that only Law can guarantee. For the rabbis, "creation meant limit; existence could only be partial. Nevertheless the reality of human freedom was never in question."[57]

The Religious Imagination represents, at the same time, a eulogy. Rubenstein commends the rabbis for having effectively coped with political catastrophe, the torments of the unconscious, and life's inherent limits. He writes, "Of all the gifts the Aggadah bestowed upon the rabbinic Jew, it is likely that none was as precious as the gift of meaning."[58] The rabbis, according to Rubenstein, made tragic misfortune meaningful by interpreting it as punishment and by imbuing it with redemptive significance.[59] He nevertheless argues that rabbinic response to disaster is no longer viable in the late twentieth century. The modern critical methods employed by the social sciences have robbed tradition of the noetic quality and sacred status without which it cannot effectively function. The rich world of aggadah, Rubenstein sadly concludes, is "an irretrievably lost haven of human truth."[60]

Rubenstein recognizes Van Harvey's point that historical method demands canons of critical judgment that fundamentally threaten traditional faith claims.[61] Obviously, modern readers can no longer read Bible and midrash in the way premodern readers once read them. However, Rubenstein's particular hermeneutical method involves hopelessly problematic assumptions of their own. Relying on Louis Ginzburg's monumental *Legends of the Jews*, Rubenstein has tried to reconstruct a representative "psychological image of the Jewish people as a whole." Although he claims that rabbinic aggadah does not constitute a monolith, he finds only uniform rabbinic teachings. He dismisses textual heterogeneity as "surface variety" that embellishes a normative "religious, and cultural, and psychological mainstream."[62] With this assumption in place, Rubenstein, as it were, reads only "half" of any given traditional text. That is, he consistently ignores half of the text in order to condemn the psychological implications of the half he has read. Yet his approach to these very texts proves inconsistent. His own use of classical texts undermines his own rhetoric of irretrievable rupture and his own misreading of tradition.

Misreading Tradition

A telling (if not typical) instance of Rubenstein reading only half a text appears in an almost incidental passage of *The Religious Imagination*. We saw in Chapter Two, above, how the talmudic tractate Shabbat records two contrasting opinions about sin and death. R. Ammi, we remember, asserts that "there is no death without sin and there is no suffering without iniquity." According to R. Ammi, the reason why people suffer and die is that they sin. His colleagues protest. R. Samuel b. Nahman actually defends Jacob's eldest son Reuben, the sons of Eli and Samuel, and a host of other characters whom the Bible records as having sinned. In fact, he claims, they were innocent. R. Samuel b. Nahman argues, "Whoever maintains that [so and so] sinned is merely making an error." They did not die because of sin. In the end, this talmudic text rejects R. Ammi's position with a strongly worded refutation.[63] As David Kraemer notes, "Remarkably, [the author of this text] is not even willing to consider the possible enduring merit of the traditional position. In his eyes, suffering and justice are two separate discussions."[64]

According to Rubenstein, however, "Rabbi Ammi states the rabbinic view of sin and death."[65] He presents R. Ammi's opinion as normative without mentioning the remainder of the text—thus reducing the sequence of opinion and counter-opinion to the one voice that he himself vociferously rejects. Indeed, Rubenstein repeatedly obfuscates the heterogeneity of opinion found in traditional Jewish thought. His understanding of the tradition ruptured by the Holocaust remains partial at best. Incredibly, in the case of Shabbat 55a, Rubenstein has *literally* cited only half of the traditional *sugya*!

Rubenstein has consistently argued that the theodicies found in Jewish literary sources inculcate a psychology of self-blame. In his essay "God's Omnipotence in Rabbinic Judaism," he points to the theodic expression permeating the rabbinic text Lamentations Rabbah. He observes how the rabbis repeat, "Since they sinned, they were exiled" and concludes, "The details vary but the thought is everywhere the same. There is apparently no other explanation of national misfortune in rabbinic literature."[66] Rubenstein acknowledges expression of protest in rabbinic aggadah but dismisses them as "muted and inferential." He suggests that the rabbis cannot openly complain but are forced to express themselves through heretical figures like Korah, Dathan, and Amiram.[67] Rubenstein ends this essay assailing the traditional response of self-blame, self-punishment, and heightened guilt. He hopes that a more "realistic" response to tragedy might bring "a diminution of Israel's pathetic and often disastrous need to blame itself for all its misfortunes. Before God, man may not be entirely in the wrong."[68]

Rubenstein, to be sure, does not mention the trial scene from Lamentations Rabbah that we discussed above in Chapter 2, an occasion when God is in the wrong and must repent before the matriarch Rachel! He may not have known of its existence. But what about Job? Even this classical reservoir of antitheodic protest against the God of History remains only dimly palpable in *After Auschwitz*. In one passage Rubenstein alludes to Job as a figure of guilt before the magisterial God of "traditional theism."[69] In another passage he remarks briefly that the testing of Job cannot be likened to the agony of European Jewry. To see any purpose in the death camps means interpreting the Holocaust as a meaningful expression of divine will.[70] This treatment of Job repeats itself in *The Religious Imagination*. In a brief paragraph in the introduction, Rubenstein calls Job an inadequate model for post-Holocaust theology. Job is said to have maintained a faith in God's "ultimate beneficence." And once again, Rubenstein observes the obvious fact that Auschwitz dwarfed the suffering of Job (an individual who in the end survives his ordeal).[71]

Why does the discussion of Job in *After Auschwitz* and *The Religious Imagination* remain so incidental, even superficial? Neither text offered the detailed analysis of the biblical text that one might have expected from a Jewish theologian writing after the Holocaust. We have already seen in Chapter 3 how Martin Buber made compelling use of Job in his "Dialogue Between Heaven and Earth." While still rejecting the modern-day relevance of this biblical figure, Rubenstein would soon provide a closer reading in an essay entitled "Job and Auschwitz" (1970). Rubenstein admits that *historically*, the book of Job once provided a powerful response to the problem of suffering. It helped people speak truthfully about suffering without compromising faith in the biblical God.[72] Job is now said to represent a border figure who refused to reject God or regard all suffering as punitive.[73] However, here too, Rubenstein precludes the figure of Job from having any *contemporary* relevance. First, the biblical Job maintained his dignity and self-respect throughout his trial. In contrast, Rubenstein argues that those subjected to the total and unprecedented assault of life in the camps suffered complete psychological collapse.[74] Belief in meaningful order and the God of theism who presides over it becomes nonsensical in the absurdly "psychedelic world" of modern, bureaucratic, technological civilization and the forms of mass death it generates.[75]

In our view, this more nuanced reading of Job follows a uniquely contorted logic. Rubenstein first admits the presence of an antitheodic figure in the Bible who refuses to justify the God of History. Then he insists that it cannot make sense of the Holocaust and proceeds to define traditional response to suffering as punitive in nature. In fact, Rubenstein continued to describe "traditional" Jewish interpretation of catastrophe as *essentially* punitive as late as 1983! He has thus effectively marginalized any antitheodic counter-tradition that might have qualified his own reading of the Bible—in order to represent "The Tradition" as the theodic monolith that he must reject after the Holocaust.[76]

Unfortunately, Rubenstein's critics have used these misreadings of Jewish tradition to dismiss Rubenstein's project in toto. In our view, his misreading of traditional Jewish texts, his inability to read tradition's other "half," is not without a certain heuristic value. Rubenstein rivets our attention on the theodic strands of traditional Jewish thought in order to highlight (in as gross a form as possible) the unacceptable implications of applying them to the Holocaust. However (and here we agree with the critics), this penchant for highlighting the presence of classical theodicy creates a critical blind spot. It leaves Rubenstein with a neat, but ultimately skewed, portrait—one that excludes heterogeneity from the fabric of traditional thought.

But, Rubenstein was not the only one who overlooked the presence of antitheodicy in Jewish literary sources. No modern Jewish theologian, rabbi, or scholar in the 1960s barely considered, much less used, classical antitheodic motifs. To the great majority, God was a figure of love, wisdom, or power. Turbulence and rage directed against God were not recognized expressions of faith and piety. Instead, scholars sought uniform, theodic teachings. Methods of reading multiple, complex, and self-contradictory meanings in texts—a staple of current hermeneutics—were barely even imagined at the time. The ability to negotiate and tolerate inconsistency had not yet become a scholarly virtue. Indeed, the early 1960s and its ideas about religious piety and textuality are in many ways as lost today as the ancient texts that Rubenstein tries to bury.

Creating a Counter-Tradition

Ironically, Rubenstein's own implicit turn to traditional texts undermines his explicit hermeneutical assumptions. In this respect, Rubenstein's thought comes to resemble what David Biale has called a "counter-history." According to Biale, the advocates of counter-histories transvalue old facts and texts. They believe that "the vital force [of history] lies in a secret tradition" that has hitherto gone unnoticed.[77] Buber and Scholem (the subject of Biale's study) were two of the most influential Jewish counter-historians of the twentieth century. Representing Jewish variants of late romanticism and early modernism, Buber and Scholem sought to reappropriate the expressive (and ultimately redemptive) power of Eastern and archaic traditions. Each reappraised textual traditions that nineteenth-century Jewish liberalism had sought to bury. Buber disinterred Hasidism, Scholem the Kabbalah, in order to renew Judaism in the twentieth century. Rubenstein's own work belongs to this modernist tradition of renewing marginalized textual sources over against liberal religious mores. Like Buber and Scholem, Rubenstein also tries to initiate a major textual paradigm shift—one based on language loosely drawn from Scholem's researches in Lurianic Kabbalah and from the book of Leviticus.

Rubenstein was the first Jewish theologian to have integrated Lurianic metaphor openly and self-consciously into his own thought. Allusions to Lurianic doctrines of the Ein Sof, creation, catastrophe, and repair appear throughout his earliest writings. This one from *After Auschwitz* is typical: "In Luria's myth, *creatio ex nihilo* is taken to mean creation out of the 'no thing' which is the primordial Godhead. The primordial ground is understood as beyond substance, above all finitude, and incommensurable with the categories of human discursive reasoning. God in the original plenitude of His being is therefore no thing and, in a sense, nothing."[78] Now clearly, this passage resembles Heschel more than Isaac Luria. The notion that God remains incommensurable with human discourse, the

expression of awe before the mystery of existence—these are themes
taken from Heschel, whose own thinking about the ineffable was infused
by mystical categories. But Heschel never described God in terms of *ayin*
(nothing). He never called God a shattered plenum needing primal self-
restorations.

As Daniel Matt observes, the description of God in terms of *ayin* has
deep roots in Jewish mysticism.[79] But, in reality, Rubenstein's thought
has only the vaguest affinities with kabbalistic thought. Although intu-
itive and even insightful, his grasp of Kabbalah was neither well re-
searched nor far reaching. Unlike Arthur Green, for example, Rubenstein
never acquired the textual skills that would have allowed him to integrate
mysticism *effectively* into his own thought. He relies entirely on Scholem—
not on close study of primary sources. Nor does Rubenstein apply kabbalistic motifs to his own theory of ritual or Jewish peoplehood. To be
sure, Rubenstein has little use for kabbalistic and hasidic theurgy. His use
of Scholem was (for the time) daring and suggestive but ultimately
proves cursory.

Rubenstein's treatment of ritual and use of Leviticus are more far
reaching. In the chapter of *After Auschwitz* entitled "Atonement and
Sacrifice in Contemporary Jewish Liturgy," Rubenstein seeks to dispel
the historical embarrassment surrounding cult in liberal Jewish life and
thought. Against the grain of Jewish modernity, he privileges Leviticus
and its language of blood sacrifice over against Deuteronomy, prophets,
prayer, and ethics. The religion of Leviticus is no longer said to represent
a "primitive" and superseded stage in Jewish religious history. Rubenstein
suggests: "We are caught between the realization of the gratuity of the
magic and the concomitant realization of the inability of mankind to rise
above magic. Ultimately, the choice may be only between the compelling
magic symbols of death, such as the swastika, and the compelling magic
symbols of life, such as were represented in religious tradition."[80] Rubenstein therefore lauds the priests of ancient Israel. In his highly imaginary
view, they never allowed Yahweh to vanquish entirely the fecund powers
of pagan religion. They nullified the murderous, pagan quality in the
ceremony of the first-born son while retaining its essential insight into
inter-generational hostility. Canaanite agrarian festivals were transformed
into celebrations of sacred history, their inner connection with the cycles
of nature maintained, however.[81] Sacrifice and ritual, far more than prayer
and exhortation, appeal to the unconscious, evoke visceral emotions, and
intensify communal bonds and moral controls by containing otherwise
obdurate forces of violence and aggression. They help people manage the
tragic realities of human limit and failure.[82]

The "death of God" actually augments the value of traditional rituals
and institutions. In a world without the comfort of providence, they pro-

vide a modicum of meaning and security. The synagogue becomes the institution through which to dramatize the decisive moments of human existence: life, death, puberty, marriage, the rearing of children, the marking of time.[83] According to Rubenstein, Judaism represents, "the flickering candle we have lighted in the dark to enlighten and to warm us. Somehow it will continue for a very long time because there will always be some men who will accept and affirm what they were born to be."[84] Rubenstein agrees with Freud that religious ritual taps into the deepest level of the human unconscious. He also agrees that religious myths about an omnipotent (one might say phallocentric) father figure represent a hopeless illusion. But against Freud's critique, Rubenstein tries to unshackle religion and ritual from myths of covenant, command, and election. He upholds the social and psychological benefits that they can still secure. According to Rubenstein, religion and ritual help us "affirm" the life into which we have been absurdly thrown.

Rubenstein's discussion of archaic biblical ritual's life-affirming function recalls Nietzsche's positive appraisal of the early Israelite Yahweh cult. In *The Antichrist*, Nietzsche had described an original period in biblical religion when "Yahweh" expressed a consciousness of power, joy in and hope for oneself. The festival cult represented a people's self-affirmation—a people "grateful for the great destinies which raised them to the top . . . [and] grateful in relation to the annual cycle of the seasons and to all good fortune in stock farming and agriculture." In this light, archaic Israelite religion has less to do with good and evil or reward and punishment than with fecund joy and a nation's affirmation of its destiny.[85] Regardless of its obvious historical inaccuracy, Nietzsche's rendition of the ancient Yahweh cult provides a model with which Rubenstein could imagine religious life unshackled from the psychological burdens left by classical canons of sin and punishment.

In chapter 1 I distinguished between text, traditions, and traditional-readings-of-tradition. We now see that Rubenstein has not turned against text and tradition as much as against modern-readings-of-tradition. Rubenstein joins theories and motifs drawn from Leviticus, Freud, and Nietzsche in order to overturn the religious canon of *modern* Jewish liberalism. Originating in nineteenth-century Germany, Jewish religious liberalism represented a theological discourse ostensibly rooted in the ethical teachings of the prophets. The prophets' critique of priests and animal sacrifice thrilled Abraham Geiger. To Leo Baeck, the prophets were Judaism's greatest religious virtuosi. According to Hermann Cohen, the prophet Ezekiel represented the Bible's most advanced expression of his own "religion of reason." In Buber's writings, the prophets articulated in protean form his own I-Thou philosophy. Heschel upheld the prophets as heroes who intuitively experienced God's own anguished pathos. Needless to say, the priestly drama of ritual sacrifice neither preoccupied nor thrilled modern Jewish thinkers.

In contrast, Rubenstein casts the prophets in an entirely different light. Prophetic ethical demand came at the price of holding Israel guilty before a just and punishing God. As we saw in Chapter 3, Buber had tried to unhitch the prophets from Deuteronomy's discourse of reward and punishment. Rubenstein rightly insists that prophetic ethics are firmly rooted in Deuteronomist traditions of retribution. Prophetic rebuke relies on Deuteronomy's cacophony of threat, chastisement, promise, and reward—traditions that Rubenstein rejects entirely. In his view, those who consistently follow the prophet and Deuteronomist must conclude that the victims of the Holocaust suffered on account of their own sins. For Rubenstein, the prophetic literary tradition that was so beloved by modern Jewish liberals has suffered an irretrievable collapse. Leviticus offered a more persuasive way to describe theologically the suffering of innocent people. As even Jacob Milgrom admits, "The Lord appears as 'esh 'okelet 'a devouring fire' . . . that incinerates indiscriminately everyone in its path."[86] To Rubenstein, the divine exercise of impersonal, almost arbitrary force relieves innocent victims of the psychological burden of self-blame and guilt.

Rubenstein's reappraisal of prophets and Leviticus means rejecting the strand of Jewish tradition that had textually justified they way modern Jews abandoned strict ritual observance. In the nineteenth century, reformers like Geiger and Samuel Holdheim identified the "the essence of Judaism" with ethical monotheism. They used this idea to justify abandoning "outmoded" ritual and social forms. In contrast, twentieth-century thinkers like Rosenzweig, Buber, and Heschel appreciated the importance of language, ritual, peoplehood, and land. Yet they never quite emancipated themselves from the intellectual canons of nineteenth-century liberal Judaism. God, prophets, revelation, and ethics exercised their thought far more than did priests, ritual, and cult. In contrast, Rubenstein upholds the fragile and changing "forms" of Jewish life. By doing so, he has radicalized Rosenzweig, Buber, and Heschel's critique of nineteenth-century religious liberalism. Kashrut, the Land of Israel, the priestly drama of Yom Kippur, sexual mores, and bar mitzvahs are central to Rubenstein's vision of post-Holocaust Judaism.

Our picture of Rubenstein proves more complicated than the one of Rubenstein simply rejecting tradition. We can now see that Rubenstein has turned against a body of theological texts while selectively affirming others. This hermeneutic involves an intricate interplay between the texts, traditions, and traditional-readings-of-tradition that constitute Jewish "tradition."

First, Rubenstein reads theodic texts in radical isolation. He highlights

the presence of the theodic text or figure, whether it be the Deuteronomist, R. Ammi, or the capricious God in the Korah legends. He then
minimizes the importance of counter-texts and counter-utterances by literary figures like Job or R. Ammi's colleagues. At first, isolated theodic
texts are the only ones that matter.

Second, Rubenstein forms these representative, uniform theodic texts
into a "Judeo-Christian" tradition. This tradition includes the prophets,
the rabbis, Justin Martyr, and Heinrich Gruber. Isolated texts and figures
are said to typify classical religious thought in its entirety. Rubenstein
then rejects the "tradition" that he has so onesidedly reconstructed.

Third, Rubenstein inverts modern-readings-of-tradition by isolating
and then privileging figures and texts like Luria and Leviticus. In doing
so, Rubenstein seeks to reinvent the very same tradition that he himself
rejects. This type of counter-reading represents a first but uneven attempt
to construct a post-Holocaust Judaism predicated upon the radical rejection of theodicy and its texts.

The attempt to reinvent tradition, represents the point at which Rubenstein's contribution to post-Holocaust Jewish thought ultimately falls
short. Writing in the late 1960s and early 1970s, he missed the contemporary vogue in reader-response text reception. Rubenstein never seems
to have appreciated the interactive relation between traditional texts and
contemporary insight, how they form into what Hans-Georg Gadamer
calls a "fusion of horizons." He finds no in-between where traditional
texts and post-Holocaust readers might meet and change each other. For
Rubenstein, tradition stands over against his own sensibilities like an im-
placable other, not a dialectical partner. He struggles but ultimately fails
to translate his own theological insight into traditional trope and image.
Most notably, Rubenstein's hermeneutical assumptions prevent him from
identifying the antitheodic strands in biblical and rabbinic sources. He
cannot plait them into a strong post-Holocaust counter-tradition. In the
end he lacks the theoretical tools with which to contest from within
those strands of tradition—biblical, rabbinic, and especially modern—
that he rejects after Auschwitz.

Conclusions

The shortcomings that mark Rubenstein's theological and literary revisions should not blind us to his tremendous contributions to contemporary Jewish thought and text reception. Working in a virtual vacuum, his
own theological and hermeneutical revisions contradict the Judaism
taught by nearly all of the rabbis, scholars, and theologians of the time.
The task demanded rough and shocking language—precisely what nu-

merous critics have found so obnoxious. Rubenstein, I have suggested, chose a pagan argot, not because he himself was a pagan or thought that God had actually died. "Greek wisdom" constituted a blunt thematic instrument that Rubenstein used to disorient modern Judaism. Rubenstein introduced a voice of rage, revolt, and opposition into Jewish religious thought. For better or worse, he was the first Jewish theologian to reject providence, to complain that history remains a terrible mess that no God, reason, or meaning could ever hope to redeem. He integrated Ivan Karamazov's principled rebellion into the very heart of religious discourse—not as a marginal aside or rhetorical device, but as a permanent protest. One wonders whether he could have initiated this process without unfamiliar, foreign terms.

In addition to the introduction of new theological vocabulary, post-Holocaust theological revision necessitated a radical, even systematic, distortion of Jewish texts and traditions. Misreading was not an incidental blemish. It constituted the very motor of Rubenstein's project. At this point I can only speculate. Dislodging theodicy from the center of Jewish thought first required that one identify the problematic nature of its position there. Caricature (the isolation of prominent features, in this case prominent texts and motifs) enabled Rubenstein to show this in the boldest possible relief. One thinks of the paintings of George Grosz, the plays of Bertoldt Brecht, and other forms of social agitprop. The effect of caricature is neither fair nor subtle, but difficult to ignore. Rubenstein had made his point against theodicy (and with it his mark on contemporary Jewish thought).

Critics might still argue against Rubenstein that theologians should not aspire to be cartoonists. To be sure, willful acts of misreading do not make for scholarly virtue. However, this critique need not preclude the attempt to understand (critically and charitably) such acts. It makes little sense to condemn such misreadings out of hand without considering the function they play in stimulating religious reflection. As Harold Bloom has urged his readers to see, poetic revision demands precisely this type of torturous misreading. Bloom's characterization of Romantic poetry speaks to theological revision in general and Rubenstein's in particular. He writes: "Poetic Influence—when it involves two strong, authentic poets—always proceeds by a misreading of the prior poet, an act of creative correction that is actually and necessarily a misinterpretation. The history of fruitful poetic influence . . . is a history of anxiety and self-saving caricature, of distortion, of perverse, willful revisionism, without which modern poetry as such could not exist."[87] Bloom would have considered a virtue what Rubenstein's exasperated critics condemned out of hand. Rubenstein was what Bloom calls an ephebe—a young poet who misreads his predecessors in an attempt to create room for his own belated insight. Like the young Romantic poet, Rubenstein reread his precursors with seemingly willful distortion and perverse caricature. Following Bloom, we suggest that *nobody* could have considered the radical theological implications of Auschwitz without *grossly* reorganizing the theodic and antitheodic contents of biblical, rabbinic, and modern strands of Jewish tradition.

Traditions require an uneven process of transmission by which new conditions and insights continuously reconfigure a stored body of ideas, texts, and tropes. Indeed, a sharp discontinuity between modern and post-Holocaust Jewish thought rends the chain of tradition in the twentieth century. Rubenstein's writings indicate how the transmission of intellectual and spiritual traditions require discord. The resentment that he provoked testifies to the power of his misreading and to its genuine place within the broken chain of modern Judaism. According to Bloom, "Poems stay alive when they engender live poems, even through resistance, resentment, misinterpretation. . . . Out of the strong comes forth strength, even if not sweetness, and when strength has imposed itself long enough, then we learn to call it tradition, whether we like it or not."[88] Rubenstein's resistance to tradition and modern-readings-of-tradition constituted his surest contribution to the post-Holocaust-readings-of-tradition that have followed him. He rejected theodicy and expressed an overriding solidarity with suffering people. Kabbalistic, "feminine," and erotic religious metaphor filled his thought. Ironically, these very ideas, motifs, and sentiments have since become central features of contemporary Jewish thought.

Rubenstein, however, became something of a tragic figure himself—isolated by the community he had tried to defend and unable to complete his own theological project. He never possessed the requisite textual familiarity and hermeneutical tools with which to become a truly strong misreader of Jewish tradition. As Bloom describes the paradoxical relationship between strong ephebes and their precursors, "The mighty dead return, but they return in our colors, and speaking in our voices." Here even Rubenstein's most sympathetic reader must acknowledge that the dead never managed to speak in Rubenstein's own voice. We could never have had what Bloom describes as "that startled moment" in which it appeared that his biblical and rabbinic precursors were actually mimicking Rubenstein.[89] Unable to marshal the dead in his own voice, Rubenstein was ultimately unable to offer a truly powerful post-Holocaust misreading of Jewish thought and tradition. That task would fall to later post-Holocaust theologians who were to deny Rubenstein's imposing influence.

FIVE

DO I BELONG TO THE RACE OF WORDS?

ANTI/THEODIC FAITH AND TEXTUAL REVISION IN THE THOUGHT OF ELIEZER BERKOVITS

> I get up with the page that is turned. I lie down with the
> page put down. To be able to reply: "I belong to the race of
> words, which homes are built with"—when I know full well
> that this answer is still another question, that this home is
> constantly threatened.
> (Edmond Jabes, *The Book of Questions*)

IN THE SECOND CHAPTER of this study, we saw how classical Jewish thought swings between theodic and antitheodic response to the phenomena of suffering and evil. For its part, post-Holocaust Jewish thought is caught between the ruminations of Richard Rubenstein and those of Hasidic and other ultra-Orthodox Jews who describe the Holocaust in terms of the punishment of sin, the testing of the righteous, and the redemption of Israel.[1] However, the arguments sparked by Rubenstein's critique of tradition and theodicy were not confined to liberal Jews. Rejecting the "death of God" and ultra-orthodox renditions of Deuteronomy, Eliezer Berkovits was the first modern-Orthodox thinker to publish two full-length volumes about the impact of the Holocaust on Jewish thought. His first book, *Faith after the Holocaust* (1973), offered a dense description of Jewish faith after Auschwitz and the State of Israel's military victory in 1967. It is best known for the way Berkovits coupled the biblical notion of *hester panim* (God's Hiding Face) with the idea of human freedom. Berkovits entitled his second book on Judaism and the Holocaust *With God in Hell* (1979). In this deceptively simple collection of stories, Berkovits recounted the remarkable efforts by which pious Jews sustained traditional Jewish life in the ghettoes and camps. He described how Jews studied, prayed, fasted, marked holidays, and adhered to dietary regulations under the most extreme circumstances. In both books Berkovits sought to demonstrate how "authentic Judaism" retained its original vitality even after the Holocaust—an assumption that we will question by showing how Berkovits rewrote tradition in the process of championing its virtues.

In this chapter I argue that the traditionalism permeating Berkovits's understanding of "faith" was marked by the same types of rhetorical strategy and posturing as Rubenstein's radicalism. The question of faith had exercised Berkovits throughout his entire career. It occupied the title of *Faith after the Holocaust*. Central chapters in *With God in Hell* and *Major Themes in Modern Philosophies of Judaism* (1974) were devoted to it. We begin, however, with Berkovits's study of biblical theology that appeared four years prior to the publication of his first post-Holocaust deliberations. In *Man and God* (1969), faith (*emmunah*) did not mean mere belief in the existence of an infinite, omnipotent God. Rather, faith and faithfulness were said to signify trust, reliability, and endurance. Berkovits wrote, "The memory of God's works on behalf of Israel inspires reliance on God and trust in him."[2] Berkovits confidently proclaimed that "Without God's *emmunah*, the orderliness of the universe itself might come to an end at any moment and may return into some aboriginal chaos."[3] However, in his later writings, the world of faith no longer appeared so orderly. It now included a new element of anger and mistrust. According to Berkovits, "covenant . . . not only allows but, at times, requires the Jew to contend with the divine 'Thou.'"[4] This notion that covenant commands contention represented a distinctly post-Holocaust understanding of Jewish faith. Indeed, by the end of this chapter, it will be clear that Berkovits's attempt to throw the mantle of tradition over it required considerable guile. The examples of Job and rabbinic protest notwithstanding, this antitheodic formulation of faith and covenant shared more with Rubenstein's negations than with traditional Jewish pieties.

At first glance, Berkovits and Rubenstein could not have been more unlike. Born in Transylvania in 1908, Berkovits received a traditional yeshiva education. He was ordained at the Hildesheimer Rabbinical Seminary and received a doctorate in philosophy at the University of Berlin in 1933. He taught Jewish philosophy at the Hebrew Theological College in Skokie, Illinois, after serving as a congregational rabbi in Europe, Australia, and the United States. In 1975 he immigrated to Israel, where he died in 1992. Unlike Rubenstein, Berkovits was immersed in the world of Jewish thought and its classical sources. He wrote about biblical faith, prayer, modern Jewish philosophy, and Halakha. However, Charles Raffel has noted that Berkovits was himself a radical within the orthodox world. In his halakhic writings, Berkovits highlighted the role of "common sense," the "wisdom of the feasible," and the "priority of the ethical" in halakhic decision making. He proposed innovative solutions to a host of vexing contemporary legal questions by reasserting minority views from the Talmud in light of changing social, economic, or political circumstances. Raffel reminds us that Berkovits represented a new generation of

liberal modern Orthodox thinkers who favored more change and openness just when the Orthodox world as a whole was moving toward
greater conservatism. Like Rubenstein, Berkovits was damned with faint
praise, misunderstood, challenged with pointed hostility, and ignored
within his own community.[5]

In the pages to follow, I take issue with previous scholarship for failing
to question the conservative appearances of Berkovits's post-Holocaust
writings.[6] Critics like Steven Katz, Dan Cohn-Sherbok, and Eliezer
Schweid have typically emphasized two arguments found in *Faith after
the Holocaust*. First, they note how Berkovits contested claims made by
theologians like Rubenstein and Emil Fackenheim who argue that the
Holocaust was a unique evil that fundamentally ruptures traditional Jewish thought. According to Berkovits, Auschwitz constituted just another,
albeit extreme, example of the problem of evil. He wrote, "The shock of
those who perished or lived through the destruction of the Jewish com-
monwealth of antiquity or the Crusades or the Chmelnicki period was
not much different from the experience of our generation."[7] But Berkovits's position proved more complicated. Although he argued that the
Holocaust creates no *theologically* unique problems, he considered it to
have been *historically* unique. In fact, Berkovits virtually echoed Rubenstein when he wrote in *Crisis and Faith* (1976), "The phase of the Exile in
our times has to be recognized as total crisis because of the radically new
event—the total threat—that entered Jewish history. . . . In our exiles we
have experienced numerous holocausts. . . . This catastrophe, however, was
different from all of them, not just in degree, but in kind, in its essential
quality. . . . For the first time in our history, the Exile itself was destroyed."
[8] Berkovits believed that a period of total crisis, a new era, follows in the
wake of the Holocaust—a crisis qualitatively unique in Jewish history.

I also show how scholars have misassessed the theodic motifs that appeared in *Faith after the Holocaust*. Katz contends that one "could pick
at the edges of Berkovits's position at length but the center of his argument turns on his advocacy of a traditional 'free will' theodicy." Katz
then turns directly to Alvin Plantinga's presentation of this defence and
analyzes its shortcomings—both on independent philosophical grounds
and within the context of Jewish traditions that posit an interventionist
God who constantly interferes with history and its freedoms.[9] In the end,
however, Berkovits's position on theodicy proves far more nuanced and
complicated than Plantinga's. True, Berkovits argued that in order to
create free human agents, God must "hide His face" from them. God
cannot interfere with human freedom, even when it is abused. But Katz
never considered the possibility that Berkovits's free-will argument did
not constitute a defense of God.

I instead advance two fundamental counter-assertions about Berkovits.

The first is theological. Theodicy never occupied the sole center of Berkovits's response to the Holocaust. Theodicy and antitheodicy, trust and protest, formed the poles of a deep structure between which Berkovits's post-Holocaust writings alternated. Berkovits was caught between "answers" and "the failure to answer," between "trust" and "protest," between "acceptance" and "refusal." His post-Holocaust faith never really rested upon any one stable theodicy and certainly not upon a free-will defense of God. My second argument concerns Berkovits's manipulation of traditional texts. While suggesting that tradition remained intact, Berkovits himself was a subtle revisionist who rewrote and reread Jewish tradition in light of a uniquely modern disaster. To make these points, I pay close attention to the implicit theodic and antitheodic language that undergirds his writings. In texts about God and the Holocaust, deep religious valence underlies the use of simple words or expressions like "accept," "refuse," "not an explanation," "doesn't answer," "in spite of," "resolved," "exonerate," and "make sense." These verbal clues indicate an ongoing struggle with theodic and antitheodic response to the problem of God and catastrophe. Berkovits's post-Holocaust faith was neither as theodic nor as "traditional" as either he or his critics have heretofore suggested. Like Richard Rubenstein, he radically revised Jewish theological and literary traditions by reconfiguring their theodic and antitheodic components.

Faith: Between Theodicy and Antitheodicy

Faith after the Holocaust

The title of Berkovits's best-known text *Faith after the Holocaust* seems to evoke traditional affirmations in which God constitutes the proper object of faith and trust—even after Auschwitz. However, the significance of the word *faith* proves far from clear. Is it an intellectual assertion or an existential commitment? Is faith settled or unstable, calm or angry? Does Berkovits mean belief in God's existence, divine goodness, or trust in providence? Or (most importantly) does he mean faith in someone or something else besides God? At second glance, we suddenly realize that we do not know what Berkovits means by the very title of the text.

The suspicion that faith may involve someone or something other than God is immediately warranted in the book's foreword. Berkovits recounts how he had worked out the main thesis of *Faith after the Holocaust* during the weeks leading up to the 1967 Six Day War between Israel, Egypt, Syria, and Jordan. Referring back to what many at the time feared to be a new Holocaust, he writes:

In spite of the fears and notwithstanding the tension, carried along by one's faith in the immortality of Judaism and the Jewish people, it was possible to write. . . . Not once did I have to ask myself whether this faith in the eternity of Jewish survival was perhaps only a latter-day version of the "lying words," so radically rejected by the prophet Jeremiah. . . . It was this faith that I was affirming with every word I wrote in those critical weeks before the war and during the six days of the war.[10]

This passage, I think, is more curious than first appears. Note the context of fear in the wake of Arab threats to destroy the Jewish State. History signifies mortal danger, marked by war and threat. We then find an assertion of faith. However, this faith does not revolve around God! Berkovits does not remember trusting God to save the State of Israel. Indeed, God remains glaringly absent in the entire foreword. "The immortality of Judaism and [that of] the Jewish people" represent the first objects of faith that carried Berkovits through the 1967 crisis.

In the introduction to *Faith after the Holocaust*, Berkovits presents the theodic and antitheodic parameters between which his thought swings by outlining two conflicting responses to the Holocaust. Pious Jews submit to God in the belief that Auschwitz reflected divine will. As we recognize from previous chapters, this stance reflects the theodicies in which religious thinkers justify, understand, or accept the relation between God and suffering. The second approach described by Berkovits involves an "attitude of questioning and doubt, a position that may ultimately lead to outright rebellion against the very idea of a beneficent providence."[11] Proponents of this latter approach reject both "suffering and its rewards." They rebel against the idea that gross suffering represents God's loving providence or constitutes a mysterious good before which we must piously submit.

At this point one might have expected Berkovits to conclude that Orthodox Jews take the first path of submission and "radical theologians" like Rubenstein take the second path of rebellion. Berkovits, however, argues that one cannot discuss religious submission and rebellion in the abstract. A person must have earned, or rather suffered, the right to make any such assertion. Alluding to Rubenstein, Berkovits acknowledges that a "radical" response to Auschwitz may

lie in the phrases that God is dead, and life, absurd. In truth, however, the decisive question is rather: Who is the one who truly relates to this awesome issue? is it not the person who actually experienced it himself, in his own body and soul? who actually entered the hell of the ghettos, the concentration camps, the crematoria, with his wife and children, his family and friends, with innumerable fellow Jews from all over Europe, who loved, suffered, and endured, or who perished there? Or is it someone who read about it, heard about it, may have, perhaps, even experienced it in his identifying imagination. The response of these two cannot—dare not—be the same.[12]

One immediately suspects a case of special religious pleading that denies radical theologians like Rubenstein the right to draw "rebellious" conclusions. However, Berkovits warns that most believers have as little right to counsel pious submission as radical theologians have to rebel. *All* nonsurvivors lack the requisite experience with which to assert or reject faith after the Holocaust. "Needless to say," Berkovits writes, "what applies to the rebellion of the radical theologian applies with equal validity to the pious submission and the acceptance of the holocaust as an act of faith, by those who were not there either."[13]

Berkovits has found himself caught between two genuine religious approaches, neither of which he can genuinely adopt as his own. He sympathizes with those who lost their faith in divine providence during the Holocaust because of what they themselves had suffered. He justifies their defiance and even calls it holy. But, Berkovits adds, he himself cannot adopt their rebellion. To do so would mean that he must ignore those Jews whose faith survived intact. How dare he reject faith in providence when they did not?! And yet again how can he dare to believe in the face of those who refused?! Caught truly in the middle, he has to affirm with those who believed and protest with those who rebelled. This intermediate position defines the theological reflections that appear throughout the remainder of *Faith after the Holocaust.* Solidarity with the believers and the "heretics" precludes theological coherence. Berkovits's own thought will alternate between their faith and their rebellion. "This is not a comfortable situation," he admits, "but it is our condition in this era after the holocaust. In it alone do we stand at the threshold to an adequate response to the Shoah—if there be one. It is from this threshold alone that the break in and the breakthrough must come. . . . And if there be no breakthrough, the honest thing is to remain at the threshold. If there is no answer, it is better to live without it than to find peace either in the sham of an insensitive faith or in the humbug of disbelief."[14]

This unstable threshold-faith in God is not, however, without its own foundation. In my view, the love of Israel equals, may even outweigh, the importance of God in Berkovits's writings. True, Berkovits searches for what he calls a breakthrough, some "resolution" to the oscillation between theodicy and antitheodicy by which he might finally vindicate God and providence. For the moment, however, he defers any decision and remains in the middle. Believers and rebels equally belong to the community of Israel. Berkovits must therefore integrate both perspectives into his own thinking.

This nonpartisan solidarity with Jewish people clearly parallels the communal sympathies expressed in Berkovits's halakhic writings. In one particularly painful passage, Berkovits confesses how in 1938 he had refused a woman permission to divorce her husband so that she and her five-year-old child could flee Berlin. The husband had been confined to a mental institution after having contracted syphilis. But by law the woman remained an *agunah*, an "anchored" woman. Although his decision was confirmed by the leading halakhic authorities of the time, Berkovits regrets not annulling the marriage retroactively. His ruling had endangered the life of an innocent woman and her child by hampering her attempt to flee Nazi Germany. As Berkovits begins to reflect on the Holocaust, sympathy with that woman and her child outweighs fidelity to traditional halakhic interpretation.[15] Since then, Berkovits has taken extremely liberal positions around the legal status of women, non-Orthodox conversions, and religious coercion in the State of Israel.[16] In each case, the principles of *klal Yisrael* (Jewish unity) and *ahavat Yisrael* (the love of Israel) override strict halakhic interpretation.[17] We see more of his halakhic flexibility later in this chapter. But for now we suggest that the same compassion characterizes his theological thought. On the basis of Jewish unity and collective solidarity, Berkovits must seriously integrate into his own thought the theodic faith of those who believed and the antitheodic doubts of those who rebelled—even when these must run against the grain of tradition and logical coherence.

This solidarity with the Jewish people fuels the sense of outrage expressed in the first two chapters of *Faith after the Holocaust*. Responsibility for the Holocaust, Berkovits argues, belongs first and foremost to human agents. Chapters 1 and 2 contain angry indictments of Western civilization and Christian theology. Berkovits holds both responsible for setting the stage for the Nazi slaughter of the Jews. But, in chapter 3, Berkovits directs his anger against God. He retells Elie Wiesel's tale about a child hung in public by the Nazis at Auschwitz. The protagonist of Wiesel's novel hears someone behind him mutter "Where is God? Where is He?" Berkovits comments: "'Where is God now?' is the right question to be asked. Not to ask it would have been blasphemy. Faith cannot pass by such horror in silence. Faith because it is trust in God demands justice of God."[18] We remember from chapter 3 above that modern thinkers like Buber, Heschel, Soloveitchik, and Kaplan never seriously asked "Where was God?" They blamed evil on human viscousness and callous indifference and took refuge in a forward-looking hope to the future. Buber, Heschel, and Soloveitchik believed that human violence had obscured God's face but hoped that an absent God would soon return. For his part, Berkovits argues, God must be involved in "everything under the sun." Human depravity does not absolve God. Berkovits writes: "It is not our intention to justify God's ways with Israel. Our concern is with the question of whether the affirmations of faith may be made notwithstanding God's terrible silence during the holocaust."[19]

These antitheodic reflections, the refusal to vindicate God, constitute a bold challenge to the idea of providence. But what is their ultimate status? Indeed, we saw how Heschel, Soloveitchik, and Kaplan ostensibly challenged God only to answer in God's defense. Perhaps Berkovits has done the same. For now we leave open the possibility that chapter 3 of *Faith after the Holocaust* does not represent an integral antitheodicy, but rather an extended rhetorical device. Indeed, we do not discount the possibility that Berkovits may have strategically placed antitheodic doubts in chapter 3 in order to highlight a theodic conclusion in chapter 4.

Chapter 4 seems to warrant this suspicion (along with Katz' reading of *Faith after the Holocaust*). Here Berkovits denies that the Holocaust was theologically unique and argues that God's hiding ("God's terrible silence") guarantees human freedom. Berkovits notes that, in the Book of Isaiah, "God's self-hiding is an attribute of divine nature. Such is God. He is a God who hides himself."[20] For Berkovits, freedom constitutes the very essence of human existence. When God formed human beings, "He" created creatures who are constitutionally free. Even though it yields abuse, God must respect this freedom as the sine qua non that makes people human. Berkovits now radicalizes his point: "The question therefore is not: Why is there undeserved suffering? But why is there man? He who asks the question about injustice in history really asks: Why a world? Why creation? . . . We conclude then: he who demands justice of God must give up man; he who asks for God's love and mercy beyond justice must *accept* suffering."[21] For Berkovits, God's true power consists in self-restraint. "Such is the mightiness of God," he writes: "God is mighty, for he shackles his omnipotence and becomes 'powerless' so that history may be possible."[22] Since freedom constitutes human existence, God could eliminate evil only by eliminating humanity. Having thus raised the stakes, Berkovits concludes that it is "not very profitable to argue with God." Human existence entails sin and suffering—tragic conditions that we and God must tolerate in order that humanity might exist.

Katz, Cohn-Sherbok, and Schweid have all countered that this depiction of God's hiding does not square with biblical and rabbinic notions of a God who saves by acting in history.[23] However, Berkovits's own thought proves to be more dialectical than his critics suspect. He knows very well that, according to tradition, the God of Israel must save as well as guarantee freedom. Berkovits therefore allows the following tension to inform his thought. On the one hand, God withdraws from world history so as not to overwhelm human freedom. On the other hand, God must enter history and save humanity from its own undoing. Indeed, the historical survival of the Jewish people, especially after the Nazi onslaught, points to what Fackenheim might have called "God's saving presence." According to Berkovits, "the rabbis of the Talmud could speak of the silence of God . . . and yet remain true to His word, because notwithstanding the hurban Israel survived, remained historically viable, full of future expectation."[24] Berkovits's theology so far resembles a kind of *Heilesgeschicte* that reflects less on grandiose visions of "salvation" and more on mere survival. For Berkovits, the survival of the Jewish people is "miraculous" in proportion to its powerlessness. There is no wonder in the historical survival of large powerful aggregates like Christendom or Islam. Their survival can be explained according to purely empirical factors: the ebb and flow of power politics. The survival of Israel, however, is said to beg any such explanation. Although God hides from world history, His presence continues to manifest itself through the "miraculous" survival of "powerless" Israel.

To say the least, this theological interpretation of Jewish history proves deeply problematic. According to David Biale, Jewish powerlessness in the Diaspora, the Holocaust notwithstanding, has been less real than perceived. Biale writes (in what could have been a criticism of Berkovits) "Without an appreciation of the political acumen of the Jews in earlier times, their long history can only appear to be a miraculous accomplishment."[25] But for our purposes, it is sufficient to note the following: Berkovits has met the criticism of Katz, Cohn-Sherbok, and Schweid by "vindicating" God's way with the world and with Israel. It seems (but only seems) that he has justified God's absence while detecting trace signs of saving presence at the same time.

We would find, one might think, no more antitheodic utterance. However, the oscillation between theodicy and antitheodicy does not rest with these assertions. We first note the almost complete absence of theodic language in chapter 4 (the putative theodic center of *Faith after the Holocaust*). Words like *justify, absolve,* or *explain* barely appear. Berkovits has only described God's absence and elusive presence. While he seems to absolve God, he has not defended providence. In fact, he continues to argue with God—a stance that he himself has just called "unprofitable." At the conclusion of chapter 4, Berkovits suggests that "*even if no answers* could be found we would still be left with the only alternative with which Job was left, i.e., *contending* with God while trusting him, of *questioning* while believing, inquiring with our minds yet knowing with our hearts!"[26] One might have thought that the doctrine of God's hiding face, the importance of human freedom, the necessary toleration of sinners, and the survival of Israel were "answer" enough. Now we discover that there may be no answer. This curious conclusion possesses a double-edged quality. Berkovits, we see, has staked two contradictory positions in one breath. Trust and contention occupy the very same sentence. He has not achieved the breakthrough mentioned in the introduction of *Faith after the Holocaust*. The gap between an "inquiring mind" and a "knowing heart" suggests that he has not found a completely satisfactory theodicy by the end of chapter 4.

Antitheodic motifs reappear throughout chapter 5. Berkovits consistently rejects the doctrine of retribution no less than Rubenstein. In his eyes Israel is the Suffering Servant. Introduced in the fifty-third chapter of Isaiah, the Suffering Servant represents the suffering of the innocent tormented by the wicked for serving God. Long held by Christians to prefigure the guiltless Christ, the figure of the servant occupied a predominant place in modern Jewish theology. The doctrine of vicarious suffering allowed liberal Jewish thinkers like Hermann Cohen, Kaufmann Kohler, Abba Hillel Silver, and Buber to understand the grandeur, mystery, and dignity of Jewish suffering. Berkovits also describes the Suffering Servant in glowing terms. The Servant is said to have courageously accepted suffering in the service of God. However, as soon as Berkovits mentions the Holocaust, he casts the Servant under a different light. He exclaims; "The sacrificial way of the innocent through history is *not to be vindicated or justified!* It remains *unforgivable* . . . Within time and history God *remains indebted* to his people."[27] This counter-reading of the Suffering Servant motif represents a bold reversal of both classical and modern Jewish theology. No longer a symbol of compliance, the Servant becomes a figure of recrimination. In traditional Jewish thought, the divine love and grace (*ḥesed*) manifested in creation, revelation, and redemption, obligate the servant. In the Deuteronomy Song of Moses (discussed in Chapter 2 of this study), the children of Israel owe God an unpayable debt for redeeming them from Egypt. Berkovits, however, inverts this unequal debt. After the Holocaust, God is indebted to a recalcitrant Servant.

The State of Israel, we are now about to find, represents the payment of that debt. As such, chapter 6 finally contains the theodic "breakthrough" that Berkovits had sought in the introduction to *Faith after the Holocaust*. For Berkovits, Judaism has a "messianic essence"—a trust in the ultimate triumph of divine purpose in history. With the establishment of the State in 1948 and its "miraculous" military victory in 1967, Berkovits detects a glimmer of that messianic unfolding. Now and only now can he unequivocally conclude that "Jewish history *[makes] sense*: it is part of the cosmic drama of redemption. In it the massive martyrdom of Israel finds its *significance: nothing of the sorrow and the suffering was in vain*, for all the time the path was being paved for the Messiah. *Not a single tear was wasted*, for all of it will be *vindicated* in his coming. Only messianic *redemption* can *lend meaning* and bring *justification* to Israel's

martyrdom."[28] Up until this point, Berkovits has coupled theodic assertions with their antitheodic counter-assertion in tense, complicated
wholes. But in this brief statement we find the thick and unequivocal
concentration of theodic terminology that had been found missing in
chapter 4. No further antitheodic utterances follow—no more words signifying contention or protest. For the first time in the entire text, Berkovits describes suffering in terms of "sense," "meaning," "significance,"
"justification," and "vindication." According to Berkovits, the establishment of the State and the Six Day War vindicate God and providence.
He exclaims, "Now we have seen a smile on the face of God."[29]

Many critics find themselves repelled by the image of a God who reappears smiling so soon after the systematic destruction European Jewry.
Alan Berger calls this a case of "messianism's abuse." Berger prefers silence to Berkovits's attempt to locate the Holocaust within a meaningful
pattern of national redemption. In a similar vein, Amos Funkenstein admits that the State of Israel may partly owe its birth to the Holocaust.
But this signifies "a horrible burden, not a sign of election or divine
grace."[30] Funkenstein cites a famous passage from *Survival in Auschwitz*
where Primo Levi deprecates a religious Jew for thanking God after surviving a selection. By quoting Levi ("If I was God, I would spit at Kuhn's
prayer"), Funkenstein rejects the way in which Berkovits has used the
State to justify religious belief and faith. From our point of view, the
concluding appeal to messianic confidence in *Faith after the Holocaust*
suggests that Berkovits's earlier use of antitheodicy in chapters 3 and 5
constituted a short-term tactic. Its only purpose was to highlight in
bolder relief the faithful struggle in which Berkovits comes to reaffirm
God, providence, and tradition after the Holocaust.

There is, however, reason to qualify these criticisms. Messianism does
not constitute Berkovits's last word on the subject of suffering. In fact,
Berkovits's later writings contain no important discussions of messianism
(much less *hester panim*). We might also remember that Berkovits began
writing *Faith after the Holocaust* in the flush of excitement following the
Six Day War of 1967. Rubenstein's own reflections (discussed in the previous chapter) show that wild expressions of enthusiasm for the State
were not uncommon among American Jews at this time. In *Crisis and
Faith* (1976), Berkovits describes the State of Israel in the more sober
terms that began to inflect Israeli culture and American Zionism after the
1973 Yom Kippur War. While he still trusts that "what God has started
with us He will complete," Berkovits admits that "too much awaits its
justification; too much waits for its redemption."[31] The language of antitheodicy has reappeared in this later text. Indeed, we are now about to
see the oscillation between theodicy and antitheodicy resume in *With*

God in Hell (1979). The stabilizing breakthrough achieved in *Faith after the Holocaust* proves to have been only temporary.

With God in Hell

Berkovits's stated purpose in writing *With God in Hell* is to describe "the essence of faith within the system of Judaism." Berkovits explains that he will understand this faith by "establishing empathetic contact with the authentic [Jews] of the ghettos and camps."[3s] It is they who will embody for Berkovits the deepest expression of Jewish faith. After *Faith after the Holocaust*, one might expect these "authentic Jews" to trust God's messianic direction of history. Indeed, stories of pious, even confident, Jews fill the pages of *With God in Hell*. Berkovits retells the story of a young Hasid who insists that "a Jew [accepts] even suffering with love! Even to Gehenom [hell] one has to walk in joy."[33] Clearly awed by such trust, Berkovits lovingly imagines thousands of martyrs sanctifying God and life as they sing the traditional *Ani Ma 'amin* (I believe/trust) on their way to the gas chambers. In Berkovits's mind, they "lived as Jews with an intensity and meaningfulness never before experienced."[34]

Nevertheless, Berkovits cannot adopt this confidence as his own. Instead, his own presentation of "authentic Jewish faith" rests on the counter-example of Yossel Rakover—a Hasidic Jew whose wartime testimony was said to have been discovered in the ruins of the Warsaw Ghetto. Rakover is an intriguing and mysterious figure—just how mysterious we will see at the conclusion of this chapter. But for now, I merely note his importance for Berkovits. First, Berkovits quotes him for a full three and a half pages at the very end of the last major chapter in *With God in Hell*. Second, no new or qualifying utterances follow this citation. Literally and figuratively, Rakover represents Berkovits's last word on God, the Holocaust, theodicy, and, once again, antitheodicy.

Rakover's testimony possesses the double-tongued quality found in the early chapters of Berkovits's *Faith after the Holocaust*. On the one hand, Rakover speaks the argot of traditional Jewish faith. Rakover loves the Torah and its statutes and entrusts his soul to God. Like the fabled R. Akiba, he proclaims the *Shema* even unto death. On the other hand, the Holocaust has transformed Rakover's faith. Comparing himself to Job, Rakover realizes: "Formerly, in good times, my relationship to [God] was like to one who was continually pouring out His loving kindness on me and I remained forever indebted to Him for that. Now my relationship to Him is like to one who owes me something." Rakover's faith has been forever altered. His example informs us that, for Berkovits, authentic post-Holocaust Jewish faith stands between trust and tragedy.[35] This faith proves more Job-like than we would have thought had *Faith after the Holocaust* constituted Berkovits's last word on theodicy and antitheodicy.

To be sure, Rakover admits, even insists, that the Holocaust forms part of an "overriding divine reckoning, compared to which human tragedies are of lesser importance." Here we detect a glimmer of the messianism that Berkovits had expressed in *Faith after the Holocaust*. For Rakover, the importance of messianic history supersedes the individuals who suffer it. At the same time, he asserts that "this does not mean that a pious Jew ought to 'justify the judgment' and say: 'God is just and His judgment is just,' and that we have deserved the blows that we are receiving." For Rakover, the messianic process does not justify the catastrophe that has overtaken him. Nor does it mean that he deserves to suffer. It does not mean that Jewish history makes sense. It does not save every tear from going to waste (as Berkovits had concluded in chapter 6 of *Faith after the Holocaust*). Messianism no longer occurs within a strictly theodic context. Rather, Rakover recouples messianism with antitheodic language and expression.

Rakover's example exhibits the corporeal and performative quality of Jewish faith. For Rakover, faith does not constitute propositional belief or any other mental leap. It involves no intellectual assertions concerning the goodness of God or the justice of providence. Faith is instead an act of existential commitment to the life of halakhic covenant, performed by one's body. Neither God nor providence, but rather God's statutes become the object of his unequivocal trust. Rakover states that he "[has] trust in His statutes, although I cannot justify His deeds. . . . I bow my head before His greatness, but his staff with which he castigated me I shall not kiss." Rakover's faith is a partial physical movement, a bow of the head, but not a kissing with the lips. During the Holocaust, observant Jews like Rakover wrapped tefillin around their heads and arms. Their mouths uttered prayer. But perhaps the Halakha left Jewish minds free to assert and doubt. Rakover cannot always trust God's judgments, but he will always love the commandments inscribed within God's Torah. Rakover follows the prescriptions of statute and custom. Yet corporeal motions are not coupled with a mental assertion or statement that would justify the holy personage before whom he moves.

The performative, halakhic quality of Jewish faith is the center around which Berkovits's understanding of "authenticity" pivots. Drawing on Martin Heidegger, Berkovits argues that external conditions—the established social order in the midst of which human beings find themselves—do not determine authentic existence. In Heidegger's terms, authentic existence carries a quality of "mineness" (*jemeinigkeit*). To Berkovits, this means that Jews reject the values, cultures, and civilizations into which they have been historically thrown. Even in the camps, "authentic Jews" tried to uphold their own peculiar way of life. Religious Jews, Berkovits argues, defied (however so slightly) the SS-imposed logic of destruction by forcing upon it a humanizing template.[36] He writes, "In the midst of the filth of the SS kingdom, they established their own realm of Jewish continuity, giving structure to the wilderness into which they were cast."[37] Berkovits believes that observant Jews created a meaningful pattern of life that was uniquely their own even in the most abject environment. Their experience of time was determined by the Jewish calendar, not by the SS-imposed structureless sameness described by Primo Levi and Terrence Des Pres. Berkovits argues that halakhic practice accorded observant Jews a uniquely precious modicum of autonomy and dignity even in the ghettoes and camps. However precariously, they oriented themselves around a semblance of halakhic space and time: "study houses," Sabbaths, and holidays.

Berkovits's antitheodic faith in the Jewish people and their Halakha does not preclude, but certainly complicates, the love for God. Despite everything, Rakover clearly loves God's greatness, a holy greatness before which pale all things human. At the same time, Rakover demands that God "stop countenancing the torment of the unfortunate." He concludes his testimony by telling God that he dies, "peacefully, but not satisfied, beaten, but not despairing, trusting but not pleading, in love with God, but not a blind amen sayer of His." He loves God even though he says that God has "afflicted [him] to death." Although he envisions future redress, disappointment and anger infect his relationship with God. Rakover embodies for Berkovits a threshold faith between trust and love on the one hand and bitter protest on the other. His faith demonstrates an abiding love for Torah and its statutes, the life of halakhic Judaism. Following Levinas, we see that Rakover and Berkovits "love Torah more than God." But, we are about to see, it is a revisionary reading of classical Jewish texts and figures that drives Berkovits's own antitheodic faith.

Tradition

An impressive textual mastery has thrown an aura of "authenticity" and "tradition" over these theological reflections. First, Berkovits wields a large body of classical Jewish texts with remarkable ability, then finds the person of Yossel Rakover to lend this faith contemporary resonance. However, these appeals to authenticity and tradition prove far more complicated than appearances suggest. In my view they demonstrate a combination of exegesis and eisegesis, which reflects the space between "tradition" and invention. The author provides a persuasive array of traditional texts, but they appear within a radically transformed context. He adopts antitheodic sources whose semantics confirm his own intention. Yet he heightens the significance of these individual texts by placing them within a radically new *Sitz im Leben*. Berkovits never differentiates between individual texts, tradition, variant traditions, and traditional-readings-of-tradition. He affirms the protest of Job by ignoring authorities who reject it. He disregards Rab's comment that "dust should be put in the mouth of Job."[38] He offers no hint that Maimonides and Soloveitchik discredit the intellectual saliency of Job's complaint or that Saadiah Gaon tries to soften its radical edge. The anti/theodic tradition championed by Berkovits never existed prior to his own manipulation of its sources. The true identity of Yossel Rakover—representing Berkovits's standard of "authenticity"—will only confirm that rewriting and rereading lie at the very heart of what proves to be a profoundly revisionary approach to Jewish texts and thought.

Rewriting Tradition

Berkovits is most known for basing post-Holocaust thought on the motif of God's Hiding Face. However, the Book of Job proves much more central to his understanding of faith. Berkovits builds his own theology on the interplay between expressions of trust and protest found in this biblical text. However, he cannot pretend to understand Job's agony or assume his trust/protest. In the introduction to *Faith after the Holocaust*, he has described himself as a nonsurvivor who must sympathize with those whose faith survived and with those whose faith did not. He consequently invents a new character. Berkovits becomes Job's brother, the sympathetic bystander who can neither accept nor reject the suffering of others as the just will of God.[39] The entire antitheodic structure of Berkovits's post-Holocaust faith depends on Job's brother. By writing him into the biblical text, Berkovits can now express his own "believing rebellion and rebellious belief"[40] while remaining loyal to the suffering Job. By adding this new character to the parable, he supplements the biblical text and expands its range of expression to include his own oscillating post-Holocaust faith.

Berkovits further expands the Bible's thematic range by creating two Jobs. In the original text, Job seems to retract his complaint when God appears in the whirlwind. No less than Rubenstein, Berkovits understands that this image of a reconciled Job does not convey the anguished quality of faith after the Holocaust. In the twentieth century, God does not appear out of the whirlwind to address the complaints presented by suffering human figures. Berkovits therefore suggests that "there were really two Jobs at Auschwitz, the one who belatedly accepted the advice of Job's wife and turned his back on God, and the other who kept his faith to the end. . . . Those who rejected did so in authentic rebellion; those who affirmed . . . did so in authentic faith."[41] Having already added a new character to the text, Berkovits inserts into the Bible two Jobs who adopt radically disparate views. These diametrically opposed personae do not, however, cancel each other out in the rewritten text. The Bible is said to contain them both. Or rather, Berkovits deftly allows them to sit together in a single character and in a single text—again, in order to authenticate his own shifting post-Holocaust faith.

Berkovits's bald manipulation of the Book of Job is rooted in a peculiar philosophy of Halakha found in the liberal wing of modern Orthodoxy. The names Joseph Soloveitchik, Irving Greenberg, Blu Greenberg, and David Hartman come immediately to mind. According to this liberal wing, the application of Halakha to novel situations demands ingenuity and innovation; above all, the standpoints of human dignity and sympathy complement obedience to the law. We have already seen Berkovits's concern for the plight of the *agunah*—an "anchored" woman who cannot remarry because she has been unable to obtain a legal bill of divorce from a husband either recalcitrant or missing. He has proved profoundly sympathetic to the suffering of women faced with unequal legal rights in initiating divorce. To redress these situations, Berkovits has proposed that contemporary authorities rewrite the traditional marriage contract (the *ketubah*). He would have them introduce a clause or conditions into the marriage contract that would empower women to annul a marriage retroactively.[42] It is not my intention to delve into the details that underpin these halakhic innovations. Yet one cannot but remark upon the following. Berkovits would cut into the letter of a halakhic text in order to insert his own contemporary sensitivities.

Note too the similarity between the rewriting of nonlegal and legal texts. In both cases Berkovits confronts the need to rewrite contracts and covenants. He reimagines the covenantal relationship between God and the Jewish people. He would rewrite legal contracts. In both cases Berkovits has demonstrated profound sensitivity to the pain suffered by aggrieved partners. He rebukes God for tolerating Jewish agony during the Holocaust. He upbraids the Halakha for causing women needless suffering. In both of these cases Berkovits refuses to blame the victim. He remains a loyal brother to a protesting Job and to his aggrieved Jewish sisters. At the same time Berkovits affirms faith both in God and Halakha. Despite the injustices they have countenanced, Berkovits is confident that they remain open to redress. Both God and Halakha are said to have a conscience and ultimately sympathize with those in pain. Berkovits therefore trusts them, convinced that they fundamentally support the protests and revisions necessary to relieve suffering persons.

An additional component to Berkovits's hermeneutical methodology involves erasure—a skill that proves central to his halakhic theory. Berkovits points to precedents where the rabbis in the Talmud temporarily or permanently suspended biblical law. He refers to instances where they refused to apply biblical law or where they frustrated its real life application. Examples include laws concerning bastard children, the rebellious son, the idolatrous city, and the death penalty. The Bible takes a harsh stand, but Berkovits relies on rabbinic precedent and states, "The law may say what it pleases; it has no application in human experience."[43] More radical still, Berkovits shows how the rabbis actually "uprooted" biblical law in order to protect and preserve community and Torah in times of crisis. The paradigmatic case used by the rabbis in the Talmud is the prophet Elijah's building an altar to God and offering sacrifices on Mt. Carmel—in direct violation of the Torah's laws concerning the centralization of the sacrificial cult in Jerusalem. Berkovits points to the establishment of "fences" and temporary emergency decrees recorded in the Talmud. In each case he invokes rabbinic authority to annul tradition in light of temporal necessity, ethical considerations, and common sense. Sometimes, he writes, the only "feasible thing is to break a law of the Torah in order to preserve the Torah."[44]

Berkovits has also erased figures and passages from nonlegal texts. For instance, the Job who seemingly recants in Job 42:7 virtually disappears from view. In Berkovits's early study of biblical theology *Man and God*, Job accepts that "in the plan of a universal creator there are other considerations, too, apart from justice alone, whose validity may only be understood from the viewpoint of the Creator alone."[45] No such Job appears in *Faith after the Holocaust*. Still another telling example of revisionary erasure involves the prophets Jeremiah and Habakkuk. In *With God in Hell*, Berkovits cites those passages in which they question God and providence. He even associates them with an unrepentant Job by forgetting how the bulk of these prophetic books constitutes a rebuke of Israel. In short, he allows Jeremiah and Habakkuk to articulate his own antitheodic thought by obscuring the dominant theodic strain that informs the original texts.

Rereading Tradition

Berkovits rewrites tradition in order to advance his own post-Holocaust insight concerning God and suffering persons. But what about traditional texts that can't be rewritten? What about texts that require fixed, regular, and public recitation? As an orthodox Jew, Berkovits has no authority to supplement or erase mandatory prayers no matter what they say about the suffering of innocent people.[46] This problem becomes clear when we compare Berkovits with Rubenstein. Unable to recite prayers whose meanings he rejects after Auschwitz, Rubenstein stands mute in synagogue. After the death of his son, he refused to pray Yom Kippur's *un- etaneh tokef.* Berkovits does not have this luxury. He cannot ignore, much less omit, the verbal forms of traditional liturgy.

However, even without rewriting specific prayers, Berkovits can transform their meaning by rereading them. Jewish law obligates Berkovits to proclaim three times daily "the Eternal is good to all and His tender mercies are over all His works." He must bless God, "the Redeemer of Israel." But how, Berkovits asks, could he or the rabbis utter such assertions remembering the complaints of Jeremiah, Habakkuk, and Job, or the destruction of the Temple? Has God preserved the faithful and redeemed Israel? Has God resurrected the dead? To resolve this problem, Berkovits reimagines the rabbis at prayer. He describes them as follows:

> One can almost see the sad smile on the faces of the rabbis who left us with this comment. "God preserves the faithful?" God the Redeemer, the Resurrector? Indeed? Yes, indeed. Nevertheless and in spite of it all it is so. We adorn God with a great many attributes which mean to describe his actions in history even though they are contradicted by the facts of history. Fully aware of the facts, with open eyes, we contradict our experience with our affirmations. Yes all these attributes of God in history are true; for if they are not true now, they will yet be true.[47]

The process of rereading has subtly changed the meaning of the prayers. Instead of constituting unequivocal exclamations, they turn into questions and tentative assertions. Berkovits has thereby introduced an oscillation between doubt and assertion within an utterance that appears at face value to be a simple assertive declaration. Rereading these texts, he inserts a protest into exclamations that ostensibly praise God. Berkovits thus transforms a liturgical expression with questions and demands while still evidencing trust in the future.

Perhaps Berkovits's most surprising re-reading involves the figure of Elisha ben Abuyeh (a.k.a. Aḥer). The Talmud describes Elisha as a leading scholar who, upon witnessing the suffering of the innocent, concludes that "there is neither judgment nor judge." Elisha becomes the archetypical rabbinic apostate who abandons Jewish belief and practice in the face of suffering. The Talmud names him Aḥer, Hebrew for "other." In *Faith after the Holocaust,* Berkovits takes up his tale by retelling the dispute between Aḥer and R. Meir. R. Meir interprets R. Akiba's notion that "God hath also made the one [thing] over against the other," by referring to mountains and hills, oceans and rivers. Berkovits understands this to mean that the dialectics of creation do not represent pure opposites. The contrast between a mountain and a hill is relative, not absolute.

The highest mountain is only a high hill. Aḥer interjects by giving R. Akiba's teaching a radical meta-ethical import. According to Aḥer's interpretation, God creates the righteous and the wicked, the Garden of Eden and Gehenna. If the opposites of creation prove absolute, then so does the contrast between good and evil. God remains responsible for creating both and therefore stands beyond good and evil.[48]

Berkovits demonstrates more sympathy with the position taken by Aḥer than with the opinion of R. Meir. "Rabbi Meir," Berkovits writes, "spoke in general terms; he did not expatiate on the dialectics of good and evil, of the righteous and the wicked." In contrast, Aḥer is said to have understood the ethical implications of R. Akiba's statement. Once again, Berkovits reads an ironic smile into the traditional text. Imagining Aḥer's rebuke of R. Meir, Berkovits writes: "One imagines the impishly appreciative smile in [Aḥer's] face as he was saying, "Not like this did your master explain it. . . . " Indeed, not like this; yet exactly like this." On one hand, Berkovits agrees with R. Meir. Good and evil define each other. Without the freedom to choose, one can be neither righteous nor wicked. God had to allow for the possibility of both. On the other hand, Berkovits agrees with Aḥer when he writes, "In a sense, God can be neither good nor bad." If God is incapable of evil, then God can do no good either. God, being incapable of the unethical, is therefore not an ethical being. Justice, love, peace, mercy, and their pursuit belong to human beings.[49]

Berkovits has attributed positive significance to Aḥer's contribution to a central theological debate. He rejects R. Meir's attempt to establish a continuum between good and evil. Good and evil stand mutually opposed. Berkovits therefore supports the arch apostate of rabbinic literature who would hold God responsible for both. Indeed, the rabbis at prayer and Aḥer are made to share similar ironic smiles as they weave a proposition and its contradiction into single, untidy statements. Berkovits thus binds Aḥer and the rabbis together by having them articulate nearly similar anti/theodic statements and sentiments.

We argued in Chapter 1 of this study that traditions are created by "clumping" individual texts and figures into a common discursive framework. These frameworks inevitably contain a center along with margins. Historically marginal texts or figures gain new meaning and significance when they enter into the center of tradition. They now subsist within the privileged center of a broad textual network. In Berkovits's writings, Aḥer's theological quandary and radical conclusions are not as "other" as they were for the rabbis. In fact, Berkovits associates Aḥer with the figures of Jeremiah, Habakkuk, and Job in order to claim that the rebellious sage "looms large in the pages of the Talmud and forces upon the conscience of Judaism the awareness of the seriousness of this issue."[50] Berkovits has overstated his point. Obviously, Aḥer haunts the rabbinic imagination. But this does not mean that he "looms large in the pages of the Talmud." To begin with, most pages of the Talmud are occupied with halakhic reasoning. And in contrast to such aggadic heroes as Moses or R. Akiba, Aḥer occupies but a small part of the Talmud. Only rarely do the rabbis wrestle with the figure of Aḥer and the problems he presents. Marginal in the Talmud, Elisha appears large only in Berkovits's post-Holocaust-reading-of-tradition.

The recreation of tradition very often depends on exactly this kind of overinterpretation. Traditions, we now know, are neither stable nor unified entities. They contain heterogenous sources that often contradict each other. But traditions do acquire a semblance of stability at any given historical juncture. Relatively unified structures, with roughly defined centers and margins, are provisionally established by historically powerful individuals and institutions. Certainly Aḥer never "forced" rabbinic Judaism to grapple with the problem of innocent suffering. The problem of suffering instead turned Elisha into "Aḥer," an other. The Talmud tells how he debauched and murdered after his apostasy. One rabbi comments that Aḥer would not have sinned had he been aware that the righteous receive their reward in the world-to-come. In the twentieth century, Soloveitchik understood Elisha/Aḥer to symbolize secular Israelis, distinguishing between Elisha, the pious Jewish soul in the heart of every Jew, and Aḥer, the apostate who openly derides Jewish piety. While Elisha can still repent, Aḥer remains forever alien to Jewish tradition.[51] Soloveitchik's position reflects by far the majority view, a fact that does not discredit Berkovits's appreciation of Aḥer, but simply points to the radical hermeneutic with which Berkovits has just reread Jewish tradition. He has brought an isolated voice from the margins of the Talmud into the very center of his own post-Holocaust theology.

Conclusions

Harold Bloom's discussion of poetic revision clarifies, if only by way of contrast, Berkovits's position within the chain of Jewish tradition. In the previous chapter we saw how Rubenstein's writings fit Bloom's description of the "revisionary ratio." According to Bloom, a young romantic poet's Promethean denial of literary influence is part and parcel of the reinscription of that very influence into his own work. We argued that Rubenstein's own misreading of tradition helped create a post-Holocaust variant of it. We concluded with Bloom that "meaning cleaves more closely to origins the more intensely it strives to distance itself from origins."[52] Berkovits, however, represents a reversal of this revisionary ratio.

Rather than deny influence, Berkovits highlights the traditional Jewish sources represented in his thought. Yet the more insistently he claims the influence of tradition, the more evident it becomes that he has radically revised it. To reverse Bloom's observation, Berkovits reinvents origins the more intensely he strives to approximate them.

The revisionary quality of Berkovits's post-Holocaust Jewish thought illuminates the identity between theology and reading in scripture-based religious traditions. One never happens without the other. Berkovits's rejection of theodicy makes textual revision *necessary*. To unequivocally justify or accept the relation between God and the Holocaust in the spirit of Deuteronomy and R. Akiba would contradict the holy disbelief that he has sworn to respect. But Berkovits must justify tradition. Theodicy threatens its post-Holocaust relevance. Berkovits therefore re-enters the store of tradition and finds antitheodic expressions once uttered, recorded, and then "forgotten" by succeeding generations of readers. Scrambling through classical texts, Berkovits has reassembled the verbal cues from which to construct his own distinctively post-Holocaust rendition of tradition. At the same time, textual revision has in turn made theological revision *possible*. Berkovits can make antitheodic claims because he has found their trace in traditional texts. Otherwise, his post-Holocaust theology would have lacked traditional warrants. Berkovits can communicate his own unique point of view only insofar as he has found/invented a prior traditional vocabulary. This exegetical skill provides him an interpretive grid with which to understand the Holocaust and the freedom and authority to advance bold theological revisions.

Tradition and its texts bind and empower Berkovits at one and the same time. On one hand, they limit his theological options. He does not have Rubenstein's freedom to explore unchartered theological territory with new religious language. The audacity of Rubenstein's early attempts to ground Jewish theology in existentialist philosophy and pagan rhetoric is foreign to Berkovits.[53] He lacks the recklessness. On the other hand, Berkovits has advanced a faith that is both historically textured and radically innovative. His command of tradition provides a depth that critical readers often find lacking in Rubenstein. Berkovits's theological writings are complicated intertexts, a meeting point for God and Torah, Aggadah and Halakha, tradition and modernity, heroes and antiheroes, victims and survivors, martyrs and rebels, trust and contention. Berkovits's stands in radical solidarity with them all as he weaves an untidy post-Holocaust complex of convention and revision, theodicy and antitheodicy.

We argued in Chapter 4 that Rubenstein's attempt to rewrite tradition lacks what Bloom calls strength. For Bloom, a strong misreading of tradition is one in which a young poet succeeds in forcing his precursors to speak in his own voice. "The mighty dead return," Bloom writes, "but they return in our colors, and speaking in our voices."[54] I am now pre-pared to conclude, but with one major caveat, that Berkovits offers ex-actly the kind of strong misreading described by Bloom. Berkovits recre-ates tradition in his own image by recasting its theodic and antitheodic tropes and figures. Berkovits succeeds in forcing Aher into the center of the Talmud by interpolating his own post-Holocaust insight into the tra-ditional text. Perhaps indeed, he has brought the mighty dead back to life, but in his own color and voice.

With this said, I would only close these reflections with a final remark about the irony that undergirds the process of theological revision and the rhetoric of tradition. Berkovits has staked too much authority on the question of authenticity and this proves to be his major weakness. In his book on modern Jewish philosophy, he censures Buber, Heschel, and Kaplan for missing the "essential nature" of Jewish theology found in its classical sources. In his legal writings, he seeks to restore what he con-siders to have been the "original" flexibility and moral conscience found in traditional halakhic writings. In *With God in Hell*, Yossel Rakover rep-resents the "authentic Jew of ghetto and camp" who embodies the es-sence of Jewish faith. But Berkovits (like many other writers in the 1970s) quotes Rakover without apparently recognizing that Rakover is a fictitious character. His testimony, said to have been found in a small bottle in the ruins of the Warsaw Ghetto, was actually told by an Israeli writer named Zvi Kolitz. First published after the war in a Yiddish news-paper in Buenos Aires, the story then made its way to Israel, the United States, and Paris where it was presumed to be an authentic testimony. The tale appears in Albert Friedlander's edited collection of short stories *Out of The Whirlwind* (1968) under the title "Yossel Rakover's Appeal to God." In the foreword to the story, the editors explain that Kolitz had come to know the story of the Rakovers and reconstructed Yossel's last thoughts in the spirit of Levi Yitzhak of Berditchev. Even this, it appears wasn't true. No such person named Yossel Rakover ever existed.[55] As such, the almost pseudepigraphic quality of Berkovits's use of Kolitz's character undercuts the rhetoric of tradition and appeal to authenticity that inform his writings. The authentic Jew of the Holocaust proves to be a post-Holocaust literary figure, a revisionist's invention.

SIX

WHY IS THE WORLD TODAY NOT WATER?

REVELATION, FRAGMENTATION, AND SOLIDARITY IN
THE THOUGHT OF EMIL FACKENHEIM

> When all the psychic moorings had been pulled loose, the
> last remaining poet raised a great and unfamiliar cry. The
> people, he now discovered, had to be recreated before a
> memorial could be built in its memory. "I have imagined
> you!" he exclaimed from his last and temporary refuge. "I
> have invented a Jewish people!" All past divisions would
> ultimately cease to have meaning, for *all* of the people were
> now holy . . . Liberated from their physical reality, from the
> vast contradictions of their life and their death, the Jews of
> eastern Europe entered the realm of myth.
> (David Roskies, *Against the Apocalypse*)

EMIL FACKENHEIM stands at the midpoint of post-Holocaust
Jewish theology having combined Richard Rubenstein's rhetoric
of radicalism with Eliezer Berkovits'a rhetoric of tradition. Like
Rubenstein, Fackenheim has described the Holocaust as a fissure in Jewish history that scuttles traditional categories and recasts classical literary
figures in a harsh new light. Like Berkovits, Fackenheim never quits belief in a supernatural God or abandons traditional Jewish sources. However, in marked contrast to both Rubenstein and Berkovits, Fackenheim's
writings contain only a handful of cryptic, theological comments. In fact,
Fackenheim has said little about God or God's presence in catastrophic
history. Instead, as I show in this chapter, Fackenheim's philosophical
career demonstrates an ongoing preoccupation, not with God, but with
revelation, rupture, and the fragmentation of value. We will find that
Fackenheim retains an uneasy set of often-contradictory philosophical,
theological, and literary affirmations within an anxious worldview. I conclude this chapter by observing that the blind solidarity with the Jewish
people and the State of Israel that governs this worldview constitutes a
weak (even dangerous) link in an otherwise sophisticated discussion of
Jewish existence after Auschwitz.

Born in Germany in 1916, Fackenheim was briefly interned by the

Nazis at the Sachsenhausen concentration camp in 1938. Soon thereaf-
ter, he fled Europe for Canada, where for years he occupied the pulpit of
a Reform synagogue and taught at the University of Toronto's Depart-
ment of Philosophy. A committed Zionist, he moved to Israel and now
resides in Jerusalem. Although he was trained as a liberal rabbi at the
Hochshule für die Wissenschaft des Judentums, philosophy has always been
his true vocation. Fackenheim inaugurated his post-Holocaust writings in
a 1967 symposium entitled "Jewish Values in the Post-Holocaust Future."[1] In it he outlined a contemporary crisis in which Jewish existence
functions as the first act of Jewish faith. Fackenheim became notorious
for formulating what he called the "614th commandment," which he
said now supplemented the traditional 613 commandments of Jewish
law. By this, he meant to say that "the authentic Jew of today is forbidden to hand Hitler yet another, posthumous victory."[2] The 614th commandment ordered Jews to survive, to remember the Holocaust. It for-
bade religious Jews from despairing of God and prohibited secular Jews
from despairing of the world. It demanded a stubborn steadfastness by
which secular and religious Jews alike might infuse life with meaning and
hope.

In this chapter I take issue with Fackenheim's critics and argue that the
614th commandment was but an awkward first attempt to adapt early
ideas about revelation to post-Holocaust Jewish life. Among Fackenheim's most astute critics, Michael Wyschogrod objected vigorously to
the central role of the Holocaust in Fackenheim's thought. How, Wyschogrod wanted to know, can one generate any positive commitment to
Jewish existence from so radical an evil? Can mass death and attention to
it yield life? For Wyschogrod, the Holocaust radically undermined the
Jewish commitments that Fackenheim wanted to advance. Auschwitz revealed no 614th commandment; it manifested nothing but a demonic
presence that only God's redemptive promise could ultimately smother.[3]

In the following pages I seek to blunt Wyschogrod's critique by providing a broader overview of Fackenheim's philosophical thought. I argue that the ultimate success or failure of Fackenheim's work has almost
nothing to do with the poorly formulated 614th commandment per se.
It was just a trope (in and of itself barely adequate) that stood for the far
more critical motif of supernatural revelation. Fackenheim had begun his
philosophical career trying to justify Jewish obligations in the modern
philosophical worlds bequeathed by Kant and Hegel. However, a sustained intellectual encounter with the Holocaust fragments his earlier,
fideistic faith in God, world, and human destiny. Having sought system
and serenity, Fackenheim now finds rupture and disquiet. A pronounced
theological minimalism and unequivocal love for Israel begin to govern
uniquely ambivalent readings of the Hebrew Bible and its God. In the

end Fackenheim's post-Holocaust thought represents a self-consciously anxious attempt to find a small shard of good upon which to reconfigure modern (Jewish) life after Auschwitz. In retrospect the 614th commandment—like the iconography inflecting his discussion of the State of Israel—proved to have been a matter of overheated rhetoric. This has brought Fackenheim considerable criticism, much of which we will share. And yet we ourselves must but admit that overstatement is unavoidably imbedded within the intensified symbolism that all icons provide. I say more about icons further along in this chapter. But for now, an equal measure of charity and suspicion might help readers critically appraise Fackenheim's hyperbole (both the hyperbole itself and its effects).

The Early Fideism

The conflict between reason and revelation, history and transcendence preoccupied Fackenheim's early philosophical thinking. In a short text entitled *Metaphysics and Historicity* (1961), he wrote, "Never have men had so much cause to seek a transcending wisdom in terms of which to understand and influence the course of events, and yet to fear that such a wisdom is beyond their reach."[4] According to Fackenheim, Hegel provided the key to this dilemma. In his view Hegel had understood that human consciousness was both historical and trans-historical, finite and infinite. Fackenheim sympathized with Hegel's description of the divided self: "I raise myself in thought to the Absolute . . . yet at the same time I am finite consciousness. . . . Both aspects seek each other and flee from each other. . . . I am the struggle between them." But Fackenheim ultimately criticized Hegel for trying to teleologically sublate finite consciousness into the infinite.[5] Instead, he pursued what he called a post-Hegelian Hegelianism—a philosophical craving for transcending comprehensiveness that can only expect partial satisfaction in a fragmented "post-Christian," "postmodern" world.[6]

Fackenheim, we begin to see, had placed great hope in the search for a transcending perspective that might situate finite, historical human existence within a broader nexus of supernatural value and moral direction. In 1968 Fackenheim published *Quest for Past and Future*, a collection of his early theological and philosophical essays, most of which were written in the 1950s. Excluding the introductory first chapter, they do not reflect a "post-Holocaust" sensibility but rather, a philosophical style that Fackenheim was, by 1968, in the process of abandoning. For our purposes, however, *Quest for Past and Future* proves to be an important document that illuminates his later thought by way of contrast.

The Fackenheim reflected in the early essays was a radical foundationalist who wanted to provide religious life in general, and Judaism in particular, with stable philosophical warrants. He sought to combat a corrosive philosophical critique and a dangerous subjective relativism that he saw threatening modern Jewish and religious life. Above all, he sought to protect Judaism by finding an indisputably objective basis for Jewish particularism. In an essay defending "the revealed morality of Judaism" against Kantian ethics (1965), Fackenheim asked with anxious passion: "How can thinking be at once truly philosophical and essentially Jewish? . . . How then can it at once have the objectivity and universality which is required of it as philosophy, and yet be essentially committed to a content which has Jewish particularity?"[7] Like medieval Islamic and Jewish rationalists, Fackenheim hoped to reconcile reason and revelation, philosophical and religious thought. Modernity, however, had rendered belief in revelation more precarious than ever before. Fackenheim saw Judaism particularly embattled before Kant's threatening presence. The philosophy of Kant (with its universal concepts, categories, and judgments) was the authoritative bar before which Fackenheim tried to justify Jewish thought.

According to Fackenheim, only an absolute, supernatural revelation yielded the objectivity required by philosophy to ground Jewish particularism. At best, reason can yield only a plethora of historically contingent and contradictory claims concerning revealed truth. This absence of a firm revelation threatened Jewish identity and religious commitments. But Fackenheim also knew that revelation no longer constitutes a bona fide source of knowledge in the modern period. In an essay entitled "Can There be Judaism Without Revelation?" (1951), Fackenheim apprehensively argued, "In the absence of a binding commandment supernaturally revealed to a particular people, it makes as little sense to have a Mosaic religion for the Jewish people today, as say, a Platonic religion for the modern Greek nation."[8] According to his own logic, he could justify Jewish religious life *only* if it "made sense." Following Enlightenment philosophical norms, this meant that Judaism had to be "universal" and "necessary." In an essay entitled "In Praise of Abraham, Our Father" (1948), Fackenheim sought a normative Jewish identity independent of any single individual's relative judgment. Again he asked why Jews should remain Jews instead of capriciously following Unitarianism, Bahai, or Ethical Culture. Fackenheim looked to classical Judaism to solve this quandary. Revelation was said to have served the ancients as an "absolute instruction," rendering Jewish obligations clear and "theologically demonstrable."[9]

In addition to providing Jewish life a stable philosophical foundation, supernatural revelation formed the basis of Fackenheim's broader philosophical anthropology. Throughout the entirety of *Quest for Past and Future*, Fackenheim described the human person as a "broken vessel" that only God could mend. The tensions tearing human life were said to include those between biological necessity and spiritual freedom, self-confidence and humility, authority and autonomy, joy and suffering, the finite "is" and the infinite "ought." Now following Hegel (not Kant), the task of philosophy was to integrate these human potentialities into a meaningful and even harmonious whole.[10] At the same time, Fackenheim realized that human insight yielded no such integration. Finite and contradictory, it only produced more contradiction. Fackenheim therefore sought a supernatural dimension of revealed truth that transcended the conflicted human self and the ideals and standards relative to it.[11]

The early Fackenheim wanted supernatural revelation to secure both Jewish commitment and human self-fulfillment. Yet ironically Fackenheim did not find it sufficient in and of itself. In the modern world objective revelation required a "fideistic" support that is subjective in nature. Fideism refers to that stubborn act of faith by which religious believers persist in their belief notwithstanding powerful, empirical counterevidence. In a controversial essay entitled "On the Eclipse of God" (1964), Fackenheim argued that "there is no experience . . . that can possibly destroy religious faith. Good fortune reveals the hand of God; bad fortune, if it is not a matter of just punishment, teaches that God's ways are unintelligible, not that there are no ways of God. . . . Religious faith can be, and is, empirically verifiable; but nothing empirical can possibly refute it."[12] These comments testify to the radical nature of Fackenheim's early fideism. He knowingly, perhaps perversely, flouted the falsifiability principle upheld by analytic philosophers of the time. For Fackenheim, philosophers can only support religious faith—in this case by appealing to good fortune. However, they could never refute belief by pointing to misfortune. Fackenheim thereby rendered faith immune to any possible criticism, catapulting it beyond the confines of rational discourse.

This fideism was particularly vulnerable on logical grounds. Fackenheim piled important philosophical and ethical affirmations onto the objective and absolute revelation of a supernatural God who is said to transcend finite human existence. Jewish particularism and an integrated human self were made to rely on nothing less. Yet the basis on which he loaded so much was itself unstable. Ultimately, belief in supernatural revelation hung upon the very subjectivism that Fackenheim had hoped to transcend by means of it. He relied on a putatively objective revelation, but only on the basis of a stubborn, personal act of faith that willfully blinds itself to disconfirming counterevidence. The willfully subjective nature of Fackenheim's fideism undermined his own radical foundationalism. Even the revelation of a supernatural God alone could not secure the basis for clear-cut Jewish obligations or human fulfillment.

The tension between an absolute revelation and its subjective reception through the finite media of human consciousness, language, and mythic symbols had long been a staple of German-Jewish philosophy. Martin Buber and Franz Rosenzweig had also sought to ground human subjectivity upon absolute truth and moral direction—even while recognizing the subjective reception-component underlying religious experience. But what had proved to be a subtle tension in the thought of Buber and Rosenzweig turned into a bald contradiction in Fackenheim's early writings. Rosenzweig (and this was true of Buber also) encouraged a nonfanatic form of religious thought and culture, one that was *open* to modern secular culture and modern intellectual canons. In contrast, the fideism of Fackenheim's appeal to revelation was extreme to the degree to which it *closed* itself off from critical philosophical inquiry.

The problem of human suffering undermined Fackenheim's fideism further still. The combination of fideism and theodicy appear in stark form at the end of an essay entitled "Self-Realization and the Search for God" (1952). Fackenheim rejected the notions that the human self was perfectible and that evil constituted a controllable aberration. He argued that the self was marked by destructive and irreducible tensions. However, Fackenheim held out the hope that "man finds his self only when he surrenders himself to God because thus only does he come to accept the contradictions of his state. . . . He can live thus, and do so serenely, because of his confidence that ultimately all contradictions rest in the mercy and justice of God. Man continues to live in pain and anguish . . . but after his humble and serene acceptance of his human lot as a whole, this question is no longer paralyzing, this conflict no longer catastrophic, And even his pain and anguish are now a praise of God."[13] A high degree of abstraction characterized Fackenheim's early confrontation with the problem of suffering. Rather than address concrete examples of human pain, he talked about serenely accepting "contradiction," "the human condition," "anguish." Nowhere did he indicate any concrete terror that these philosophical buzzwords might have signified. Unlike Dostoyevsky's fictitious Ivan Karamazov, the early Fackenheim ignored real-life stories recounting the fate of particular children. He did not take into account the image of burning babies as told by Elie Wiesel. It is hard to imagine how he could otherwise have spoken of turning anguish into a praise of God or how conflict "ceases to be catastrophic."

Fackenheim had already abandoned theodicy and fideism by the time he wrote the later essays found in *Quest for Past and Future*. In its introductory first chapter, he critically reappraised his thought from the preceding twenty years. Fackenheim now acknowledged that "there is both despair within faith and serene confidence without it."[14] He granted that catastrophe constitutes historical counter-evidence that threatens Jewish thought. He admitted that God's presence before Job reveals no satisfactory answer. He realized that Auschwitz resists theological meaning. He began citing the writings of Elie Wiesel. Never again would Fackenheim "commit [himself] to a God of History through whom the tragic is redeemed, all contradictions reconciled, and nothing lost."[15] Never again would he assert that "after all, God is omnipotent and history is safe in His hands despite the evil done by men."[16] By the time Fackenheim published *Quest for Past and Future* in 1968, he had concluded that even revelation cannot resolve all existential contradictions, that everything can be lost, that nothing remains safe. His thought had already become "post-Holocaust."

Fragments

God's Presence in History (1970) ratifies the shift from the confident theological fideism of Fackenheim's early philosophical writings to the brooding reflections that characterize his post-Holocaust writings. Indeed, the book's very dedication to Elie Wiesel indicates a profound break. According to Fackenheim, Wiesel "[forced] Jewish theological thought in our time into a new dimension."[17] As Michael Berenbaum has noted: "Where previous Jewish theologians found some security in God and His revelation, in man and his creaturely status, and in Israel and its divine mission, Wiesel now finds an abyss of chaos . . . and radical insecurity. Wiesel's fundamental experience is one of absence in a world that was once pregnant with Presence."[18] Berenbaum's description of Wiesel captures the spirit of Fackenheim's post-Holocaust writings. God, creation, revelation, and mission no longer secure Fackenheim's post-Holocaust faith. At the same time, we should not overstate the difference bifurcating Fackenheim's philosophical career. Even in his post-Holocaust writings, Fackenheim understands Judaism in supernatural terms. For him, revelation still expresses "the strange, extraordinary, and even paradoxical affirmation that an infinite God acts in History and was unmistakably present at least once."[19]

Fackenheim now calls revelation a "root experience"—a past event with the normative power to legislate to the present. A root experience must be a normative, public, national event that future generations reenact within liturgical frameworks. With these (semi-objective) sociological criteria, appeals to personal epiphanies are precluded from the ambit of revelation. Fackenheim turns instead to the two major mythic events that have historically shaped Jewish religious life: God's saving presence at the

Red Sea and God's commanding presence at Sinai. Quoting Buber, Fackenheim characterizes such root experiences as explosive events marked by "astonishment," "wonder," and "surprise." Such terms are not the casual remarks of an impassioned enthusiast. Rather, they coalesce into what Susan Shapiro has called a "phenomenology of astonishment."[20] The occasion of these semitechnical terms signals a discussion of revelation in Fackenheim's thought. The wonder of a root experience is either immediately experienced or reenacted in the memories of a people, inscribed as stammering traces within sacred texts and liturgical cycles. Future generations access past root experiences by liturgically reenacting the event and making its abiding astonishment their own.[21]

History, however, complicates the process of reenactment. Historical crises (Fackenheim calls them "epoch-making events") contest supernatural revelation by disrupting the reenactment of root experiences. People who experience epoch-making events (like the Maccabean Revolt, the Temple's destruction, or the Spanish Exile) struggle to relive moments of abiding wonder experienced in the past. The Holocaust was also an epoch-making event. Jews who reenact God's saving presence at the Red Sea must now remember the Holocaust—a time when God failed to save.[22] Those who would sing with Israel at the Red Sea stand crestfallen before the visage of Auschwitz and its victims. In this respect the Holocaust is not unique. Epoch-making events constitute integral moments in the dialectical tug between history and tradition. They have forced Jews in every generation to renew Judaism while undermining any reenactment of the revelations upon which Jewish religious life feeds.

The continued reflection upon root experiences in the wake of epoch-making events shapes what Fackenheim has called the "midrashic framework." Midrash, of course, refers to the literary genre in which the rabbis following the destruction of the Second Temple formulated an inconsistent set of doctrines, beliefs, and opinions in the form of story, parable, and exegesis. In Fackenheim's view, the midrashic framework allowed the rabbis to reflect on classical root experiences and reenact the abiding astonishment that they have traditionally evoked. Just as importantly, the midrashic framework also allowed the rabbis to remain cognizant of the way in which contemporary epoch-making events disrupt the possibility of reenacting that experience. According to Fackenheim, modern Jewish faith must exhibit genuine openness to the counterclaims posed by philosophy and historical tragedy. Fackenheim provides the example of the traditional Passover Seder in which Jews reenact the wonder experienced by the Israelites at the Red Sea. The contemporary Jew participates in the Seder, open to the possibility of reenacting a root experience, but aware of the critical tensions that render the reenactment of any divine presence implausible.[23]

Steven Katz has complained that Fackenheim never clarifies how the Holocaust fits into the midrashic framework.[24] On one hand, it is an epoch-making event that disrupts the reenactment of any root experience. On the other hand, Fackenheim has to claim that the Holocaust was not just another epoch-making event. Otherwise, it is not unique. In response to Katz, I would argue that Fackenheim meant to call the Holocaust an epoch making event *and* a root experience. Paradoxically, Auschwitz undermines belief in God and providence while at the same time revealing the presence of a commanding supernatural voice—i.e., the 614th commandment. According to Fackenheim, the "Commanding Voice of Auschwitz" was a "voice as truly other than man-made ideals— an imperative as truly given as was the Voice of Sinai."[25]

In terms of content, the discussion of the 614th commandment in *God's Presence in History* remains identical to the one formulated in the 1967 symposium. However, Fackenheim expands upon his theme by fragmenting what had previously appeared to be an unequivocal command into four conflicting pieces. The first fragment orders Jews to remember. The second fragment dictates Jewish survival. The third prohibits Jews from abandoning the world to the forces of Auschwitz and forbids despair. The fourth prohibits religious Jews from abandoning God and also forbids despair. Appearing more or less determinate in content, these fragments recall how the early Fackenheim had hankered for classical Judaism's supernatural revelation and ostensibly clear-cut obligations. However, in this post-Holocaust text, revealed Jewish duties involve considerable confusion. In particular, the duty to remember Auschwitz conflicts with the ones that forbid despair. For religious Jews, following the fourth commandment means contending with a God whose presence in history has proved uneven. For their part, secular Jews can neither forget the past for the sake of life nor destroy life by relentless mourning. They must retain belief in human goodness without forgetting Auschwitz. Religious and secular Jews alike "exist, survive, endure, [and] witness to God and man even if abandoned by God and man."[26]

Fackenheim's own theological claims are more modest than the bombastic rhetoric suggested by expressions like "The Commanding Voice of Auschwitz." In fact, the commanding voice does not signify a clear and overwhelming presence. Fackenheim only maintains that secular Jews cannot regard Jewish survival as the sole product of self-sufficient reason. To remain a Jew after Auschwitz appears stubbornly counter-intuitive when prudent reason would compel Jews to secure safety for themselves and their descendants through rapid assimilation. Secular Jewish identity, the commitment to maintain Jewish life without belief in God, evokes the same sense of mystery and wonder that Fackenheim accords to religious revelation. For their part, religious Jews remain virtually God-forsaken—just like their secular counterparts. Religious Jews after Auschwitz can "hardly hear anything more than the mitzvah" of survival. They detect an overriding command without apprehending the God who commands it. After the Holocaust the only bond possible between Israel and God is "hardly more than the mitzvah itself."[27]

God, world, and Israel subsist in total conflict after the Holocaust. Contrary to first appearances, the 614th commandment leaves Fackenheim with very few clear-cut obligations! How can one remember the dead and not despair? How can one pray to God or trust one's neighbor? By the end of *God's Presence in History*, all that remains to Fackenheim are antitheodic fragments and the dumb will to endure. Like the voice that comes to Job out of the whirlwind, the commanding voice of Auschwitz has explained nothing. Fackenheim's avowal of ignorance differs fundamentally from those made by theologians who faithfully accept a mysterious providence whose workings they cannot fathom. Fackenheim had already announced in the opening essay of *Quest for Past and Future* that the Holocaust will never bear religious meaning and called the attempt to find one "blasphemous."[28] In *God's Presence in History*, Fackenheim continues to argue that the Holocaust yields no theological significance, purpose, or value. Paraphrasing the rabbis, he writes: "Even moments of supreme darkness in history are [not] simply inexplicable while, at the same time, not even moments of supreme light are moments in which all is explained. . . . [There] are times of salvation which yield no explanation."[29] Fackenheim sadly suggests that even the rabbis doubted whether the messianic future would explain the death of a single child.[30]

The 614th commandment constitutes God's presence in twentieth-century Jewish history. But what does Fackenheim mean by "presence"? Readers of the postmodern literature know that the term has a long history in Western thought (readers of modern Jewish thought will detect echoes of Buber and Rosenzweig). In the Western tradition "presence" has acted as a code for *logos*, certainty, communicability, identity, the encounter with God, the end to alienation, redemption. In its place postmodern critics (including self-styled a/theologians like Mark Taylor) advance the counter-themes of absence, fragment, deferral, dispersal, and difference. As such Fackenheim's rhetoric of presence would seem to contradict the postmodern mood. However, "presence" has taken on a radically different sense in Fackenheim's post-Holocaust writings. He admits, "Because His presence is *in* history and does not (or not yet) transfigure history, it can only be a particularized presence, and for this if for no other reason, it is a *fragmentary* presence."[31] God registers but a partial, fleeting presence. A trace presence, virtually absent, a still small voice, it is not quite here. Divine presence no longer constitutes the transcendent plenum that we find in the history of Western theology (or in

Fackenheim's early writings). Deeply entangled in history, it fragments to such an extent that it can no longer transfigure finite life in an unambiguous fashion. Its claims are minimal and even confused, its appearance more elusive and less certain. This piecemeal presence leaves history unredeemed and Fackenheim unsettled. Even after the establishment of the State of Israel and the 1967 war, his vision remains comfortless. Nothing has removed the Holocaust's sting. Fackenheim therefore concludes *God's Presence in History* with bitter feelings of longing, defiance, endurance, and fear.

Arthur Cohen once complained that Fackenheim has offered too bleak a vision of the world. He argued that Fackenheim "is left with the slender thread of hope and a sextant aligned to a God who has his center everywhere and his circumference nowhere."[32] Indeed, Fackenheim does not confine the negativity that worried critics like Cohen and Wyschogrod to the 614th commandment. Radical negations permeate the entire rhetorical structure of *God's Presence in History*. We see them in Fackenheim's refusal to explain or attribute meaning to the Holocaust. They appear in motifs like protest, resistance, longing, defiance, and endurance. The entire midrashic framework—the ability to reflect upon and reenact a root experience despite the contradictions that it entails—teeters on the verge of collapse. Fackenheim explains: "The pious Jew during the Passover Seder has always reenacted the salvation at the Red Sea. The event remained real for him because He who once had saved was saving still. And this latter affirmation could continue to be made, even in times of catastrophe, because the divine salvation remained present in the form of hope."[33] In contrast, Fackenheim offers little hope on which to base defiance or reconstruct the broken midrashic framework. The 614th commandment offers no reason, rationale, or even heart behind Jewish existence. By the book's conclusion, critical readers were right to wonder about the "Jewish affirmations" that Fackenheim had promised in its preface. He seems to have crippled the religious imagination with a commanding voice of staggering negativity.

Tikkun

Perhaps by way of counterpoint, Fackenheim promises healing in *To Mend the World* (1982). In the title of his most intensive post-Holocaust rumination, Fackenheim explicitly draws upon Isaac Luria's kabbalistic theory of divine catastrophe. The world's creation entails a powerful surge of destructive force shattering the mystical structure that forms the Godhead. With the breaking of the vessels, God and world are torn into pieces. In response, human acts of *tikkun* (mending, repair) help restore this broken Godhead to a state of primordial wholeness. The kabbalist conducts this *tikkun* by performing mitzvot with mystical intentions. Like the kabbalist, Fackenheim must also reconstruct that which catastrophe has rent. But unlike the kabbalist, his *tikkun* is philosophical. He grapples with nothing less than the "foundations of future Jewish thought." Over and over, Fackenheim wonders how Jewish philosophical thought is possible since the Holocaust has paralyzed the very possibility of "thought itself."[34]

What could this have possibly meant?

First and foremost, "philosophy" and "thought" mean Hegelian system. Hegel has exercised an ongoing fascination upon Fackenheim. He calls Hegel "the great unmatched mediator of all things, and especially of all modern and religious and secular things."[35] Fackenheim credits Hegel for trying to integrate all historical phenomena into an all-inclusive philosophical vision. Following Hegel, he understands "thought" to be this attempt to grasp the absolute in conceptual form. The foundations of future Jewish thought involve nothing less than synthesizing the conflicting truths of revelation and reason, religion and secularism. This explains the attention devoted to Spinoza and Rosenzweig in *To Mend the World*. Rather than treat them in their own right, Fackenheim turns them into Hegelian signifiers. "Spinoza" stands for modern secularism and universal humanism, the "free modern man." In dialectical contrast, "Rosenzweig" signifies a nonfanatic openness to revelation and Jewish particularism, the modern image of the committed religious Jew. For Fackenheim, future Jewish "thought" means sublating Rosenzweig and Spinoza, Judaism and Jewish secularism, in the historical light of genocide and statehood.

When Fackenheim claims that the Holocaust ruptures "thought," he therefore means that it has ruined Hegelian system. Fackenheim argues that "confidence" in faith and secularism, already strained in Hegel's own time, becomes impossible after the Holocaust.[36] This is an argument already found in Fackenheim's *The Religious Dimensions in Hegel's Thought*. According to Fackenheim, Hegelian dialectic involved [1] a modern religious confidence in an infinite God who enters the finite world and redeems it, [2] a secular self-confidence in modern culture, and [3] a confidence in philosophy's ability to comprehend reality. But Fackenheim contends that post-Holocaust thought has lost confidence in the very terms that Hegel had desired to mediate.[37] There are neither certainties nor securities in a post-Christian, postmodern world. God speaks "obscurely and intermittently" at best. Secular self-consciousness is also rendered insecure. Modern self-confidence and the spiritual hegemony of Western humanism are broken as science and terror mix after Auschwitz and Hiroshima. Fackenheim concludes, "that from so fragmented a world, the Hegelian philosophy would be forced to flee. . . . "³⁸ In *To Mend the World*, Fackenheim explains that philosophical systems require completion whereas history remains open-ended. Spirit cannot comprehend the All since life continues to generate social and cultural nova. In this view, there can be no system until human beings finally exhaust the history that stimulates philosophical thought. Until then, one only holds fragments of a philosophical system.³⁹

Second, "thought" is the opposite of turbulent affect. When Fackenheim talks about thought, he consistently characterizes it as calm, serenity, and composure. In this extremely contentious schema, secular philosophers allow nothing to astonish them or otherwise distract them from the contemplative life. Take for instance Spinoza's image of the "free modern man." Fackenheim describes him as one who "seeks to understand and thus to master the emotions. This he does by weakening those that negate or diminish life, and by enhancing those that affirm and expand life. . . . While accepting the fact of 'wonder,' he does not 'come to a stand' with it, for it is a mere 'distraction.' "⁴⁰ For Fackenheim, *thought* means the detached serenity that Spinoza upheld as the highest philosophical virtue. In particular, philosophical composure checks the "wonder" fired by revelation. Martin Heidegger, who in his later writings came to characterize thought as an aesthetic submission before Being, presents still another example. Fackenheim explains, "Thought achieves the freedom it requires by adopting . . . a stance of 'composure' that 'lets things be.' "⁴¹

Few critics have noted that the gross sentimentality that has exasperated so many of Fackenheim's readers is philosophically significant. When Fackenheim claims that the Holocaust ruptures "thought," he means that it has shattered tranquil thought (along with Hegelian system). Fackenheim describes how a sentimental tide of outrage floods any attempt to maintain philosophical composure. Upon apprehending the Holocaust, "the philosophizing person, like other flesh-and-blood persons, can think no thoughts and ask no questions but can only be appalled by the criminals and filled with grief for the victims."⁴² Affect interferes with cool deductive reason and measured inquiry. At this most immediate and prereflective level, the act of remembering opens us to deep, distracting feelings of outrage and anguish. The only effective way to evade these is to ignore the Holocaust or smother it in generalizations. Condemning Heidegger's silence, Fackenheim writes, "Only because in his generalized *Seinsverlassenheit* the screams of the children and the silence of the Musselmänner are not heard is there any possibility of adopting toward the age, as the ultimate philosophical stance, a 'composure' that 'lets things be.' "⁴³ In contrast, an overwhelming abyss disrupts any post-Holocaust thought that bothers itself with the Musselmänner (the living dead described by Primo Levi) and the murdered children. The Holocaust floods any self-composed reflection, much less calm attempts to let things be or mediate reason and revelation. That is why Fackenheim asks, "If Auschwitz permits no composure . . . how can thought be at all?"[44]

The Holocaust, however, has not completely undermined Jewish philosophical "thought." In fact, the Hegelian synthesis of revelation and secularism survives in a new form. Rather than build abstract systems, thought now reflects upon narratives that recount the resistance of "*amcha*." By *amcha*, Fackenheim means "the Jewish people," ordinary women and men, religious and secular alike. Their resistance to the Holocaust provides philosophers sufficient basis for post-Holocaust thought. Fackenheim describes ordinary Jewish women and men resisting the Holocaust, women who braved pregnancy in the camps, ghetto fighters, and Hasidim. By resisting genocide both physically and spiritually, *amcha* surpassed Hegel. In Fackenheim's mind, the Molotov cocktails of secular resistance fighters fuse with the tefillin of their religious counterparts. Uniting secular and religious forms of resistance, *amcha* began to manifest the heretofore denied Hegelian synthesis of religion and secularism. "Here at last," Fackenheim claims, "we have reached the Ultimate that holds together and unites all these forms of resisting, all these ways of being." On the basis of their resistance, Fackenheim can now envision the future of Jewish "thought." Molotov cocktails and tefillin sublate Spinoza and Rosenzweig into what Fackenheim calls a new "ontological category," a way of being both secular and religious.[45]

This renewed ability to envision a synthesis of religion and secularism proves to be a revelation. Remembering how "wonder" and "surprise" function as code words that signal revelation, we are alert to the significance of *amcha*'s resistance leaving Fackenheim "astonished." In ordinary language one might easily comment that any attempt to resist the Nazis was "amazing." Fackenheim, however, turns this otherwise-colloquial expression into a religious signifier. Following the collapse of philosophical reason, he applies the terms *amazement* and *wonder* to Jewish resistance. Fackenheim endows that resistance with mystery. He "cannot explain" why pregnant Jewish women did not abort their pregnancies or why more people did not suffer the complete collapse described in Primo Levi's discussion of the Musselmann. Of course, Fackenheim knows that all of these accounts are subject to any number of physiological, psychological, and sociological explanations. But these natural explanations only heighten the sense of wonder that signifies the trace-presence of a supernatural revelation. Fackenheim exclaims repeatedly, "Once again the categories 'willpower' and 'natural desire' seem inadequate. Once again we have touched an Ultimate."[46]

With the tacit introduction of such revelation rhetoric and the witness of one Pelagia Lewinska in *To Mend the World*, we can better understand what Fackenheim came to mean by the commanding voice of Auschwitz and its 614th commandment. Lewinska's testimony proves critical. Lewinska (a Pole, not a Jew!) tells how she one day decided that she would either survive or die with dignity. Lewinska represents one of Fackenheim's most important witnesses. In his mind, she heard and resolved to obey the commanding voice of a supernatural God. Fackenheim is so taken with her testimony that he cites it twice verbatim. We quote in brief:

> At the outset the living places, the ditches, the mud, the piles of excrement behind the blocks, had appalled me with their horrible filth. . . . And then I saw the light! I saw that it was not a question of disorder or lack of organization but that, on the contrary, a very thoroughly considered conscious idea was in the back of the camp's existence. They had condemned us to die in our own filth, to drown in mud, in our own excrement. They wished to abase us, to destroy our human dignity, to efface every vestige of humanity . . . to fill us with horror and contempt toward ourselves and our fellows.

> From the instant when I grasped the motivating principle . . . it was as if I had awakened from a dream. . . . *I felt under orders to live.* . . . And if I did die in Auschwitz, it would be as a human being, I would hold on to my dignity.[47]

Of course, Fackenheim realizes that this does not constitute much of a revelation. He does not suggest that Lewinska "proved" anything about God. He does not use her testimony to deduce any positive set of ritual commandments. Indeed, Lewinska herself never identified a divine source to the order commanding her to live. She only described a brief incursion of good into an anti-world of death. At best, such moments represent unclear, fragmentary signs. But for Fackenheim, Lewinska's testimony, expressed in the passive voice, points beyond itself. Fackenheim quotes Buber's citation of Nietzsche's cryptic comment, "One takes and does not ask who gives."

In my view Lewinska's testimony represents the commanding voice of Auschwitz condensed to its most minimal and pristine core. It resembles what Robert Alter, citing Gershom Scholem, has called a "zero point of revelation." Virtually contentless, Alter described such revelations as "religion pushed to the brink of nihilism."[48] Fackenheim's discussion of the 614th command in *God's Presence in History* had demanded some determinate, albeit unclear, content. It told Jews to resist Hitler, to survive, struggle, and hope. But, in *To Mend the World*, Fackenheim has reduced the voice to its barest possible essence. It says only, "Live." A simple affirmation (capable of meaning almost anything), it constitutes the commanding voice of Auschwitz's purest content. We therefore agree with Katz that the 614th commandment does not constitute a divine imperative, but only a human response.[49] The compulsion to live in a world defined by death was the sole divine presence whose echo Fackenheim detects in the stories of those who resisted the Nazis. Everything else— the 614th commandment's four conflicting fragments and especially awkward expressions like "the duty not to hand Hitler posthumous victories"—comprises Fackenheim's own imperfect interpretation of a vaguely sensed supernatural trace.

Katz's critique suggests the following comparison. In our view, the 614th commandment and Lewinska's revelation recapitulate the distinction between *Gesetz* (law) and *Gebot* (commandment) found in Rosenzweig's thought. Rosenzweig had recognized (along with Buber) that the 613 laws said to have been revealed by God to Moses represent human forms. They are the product of human interpretation. But over against the human form of *Gesetz*, Rosenzweig juxtaposed the single supernatural commandment (*Gebot*) "Love Me!" acting as the revealed content of *Gesetz*. In Rosenzweig's words, the imperative form of the command "Love me!" represented a "wholly perfect expression, wholly pure [*ganz reine*] language of love."[50] This purified expression constituted a distilled, minimum core of revelation open to the modern person. Barely a content, the commandment contained two words. Following Katz's lead, we now see the relationship between Rosenzweig and Fackenheim. The 614th commandment, its four conflicting fragments, and awkward expressions like "the duty not to hand Hitler posthumous victories" formed *Gesetz*. These fragments reflect the work of human interpretation. More to the point, they represent Fackenheim's own imperfect response to the supernatural *Gebot* whose purified expression he finds in Lewinska's testimony.

Lewinska's testimony represents one *tikkun*—a mending of the world. The stories of Kurt Huber, Bernhard Lichtenberg, Jewish partisans, and the establishment of the State of Israel constitute further examples. Huber was a professor of philosophy executed by the Nazis for his leading role in the White Rose student movement. He invoked Kant and Fichte on behalf of his resistance. For that reason, he provides a counterweight to those Germans, including Adolph Eichmann, who appealed to Kant in performing their "duty" to the Reich. Kantian ethics and the Idea of Man [*sic*] do not entirely collapse after the Holocaust because of Huber's resistance. For his part, Lichtenberg was a Protestant pastor whom the Nazis arrested for publicly praying for the Jews. Lichtenberg provides a counterweight to the tragic legacy of Christian anti-Semitism. Christianity does not entirely collapse after the Holocaust, because Lichtenberg resisted the Nazis in Christ's name. We will see in the next section of this chapter how the State of Israel mends Jewish life ruptured by the Holocaust. It too represents a figure of resistance. Fackenheim treats them all like supernatural revelations, foreign incursions of moral good into (or in the wake of) an anti-world of mass death. Like any root experience, they were public and historical. Their examples command normative force and fill Fackenheim with "surprise" and "wonder."

One must nevertheless ask, respectfully, what their resistance was really worth. How many lives could Huber, Lichtenberg, and Lewinska save? How many Nazis did the ghetto fighters kill? The stories presented by Fackenheim are deeply stirring, but one cannot help but suspect. Why do these stories stir feelings of "surprise" and "wonder" and not depression and despair? Much depends on the telling. True, the stories testify to the dignity of the human spirit. Perhaps they even point to some transcendent trace. However, they also remind us that human good and divine sparks remain powerless before the face of evil. Indeed, Fackenheim makes too little, a bare minimum of revelation, mean too much. These small isolated figures of resistance (pregnant women, a lonely philosophy professor, an isolated clergyman, desperate ghetto fighters) prove disproportionate to the gross fissure that Fackenheim hopes to heal by their example. The future of Jewish life, the future of the world, are made to rest on an edifying but meager stock of moral good. This may, in fact, represent a profound religious truth. Abraham sought to save Sodom and Gomorrah on the basis of ten righteous people. But the Bible tells its tale tersely. In contrast, Fackenheim's profoundly impassioned hyperbole threatens to lose all sense of proportion and balance.

In Fackenheim's defense, I would argue that the sentimental, even gross hyperbole with which he overinterprets these stories obscures his own levelheadedness. Fackenheim's heavy-handed style has led Susan Shapiro to argue that his celebration of resistance overshadows the memory of the Holocaust and its victims.[51] In my view, however, Fackenheim never exaggerates the historical or spiritual significance of resistance. The *tikkun* rendered by it remains an incomplete, though highly charged, token. Fackenheim himself insists that "the *tikkun* . . . was not a good requiring and thus retroactively justifying the evil that it was to mend."[52] He writes: "We cannot mystically either fly above history or leap forward to its eschatological End. The screams of the children and the silence of the Musselmänner are in our world. We dare not forget them; we cannot surpass or overcome them and they are unredeemed. . . . Hence in our search for a post-Holocaust *tikkun* we must accept from the start that at most only a fragmentary *tikkun* is possible."[53] This rhetoric of fragmentation pioneers a unique theological stance. Fackenheim acknowledges that any post-Holocaust *tikkun* remains incomplete at best. No redemption subsumes painful memories into a larger pattern of meaning and good. His theological and philosophical vision remains insistently antitheodic, disquiet to the very end. At best, history has left Jewish thought but a fragmentary trace of good on which to reconstruct post-Holocaust life.

We return to Shapiro's argument below in our discussion of Psalm 118, but for now we suggest the following. The problem with the thesis advanced in *To Mend the World* is not (as Shapiro contends) that images of resistance overwhelm the memory of Auschwitz and its victims. The problem is that overinterpreting figures of resistance allows fideism to slip surreptitiously back into his thought. Fackenheim's strength as a theologian rests on his ability to tolerate the ambivalence of fragments and fissures. But Fackenheim tries too hard to mend a religious landscape constructed totally of unquiet fragments. Something other than God must remain "whole," the thought of which will leave him "serene" after the Holocaust. *Amcha* and the State of Israel assume that function. The authentic Jew described by Fackenheim is no disjointed, decentered postmodern subject. In a post-Holocaust world of broken transcendence, Fackenheim champions unapologetic, uncritical Jewishness. Without a fully present God, he needs at least this one surety.

Fideism Redux

Four years prior to the publication of *To Mend the World* (1982), Fackenheim had penned even balder appeals to unapologetic Jewishness in *The Jewish Return into History* (1978). These collected essays serve as a prolegomena to the more sophisticated philosophical analysis in *To Mend the World*, while helping us to perceive the weakest link in Fackenheim's mature thought. Inured to any possible criticism, Fackenheim defends a political-historical entity (the State of Israel) with the same fideism he once employed in defense of supernatural revelation. Many critics have found this particularly irksome. Indeed, we will agree that his image of the State resembles an empirical datum only in the crudest form. We too will exercise suspicion and fault him for that. Nevertheless, Fackenheim's critics have overlooked the iconography inflecting his use of theological, philosophical, and political motifs. Now surely, no one today would condemn the makers of icons for failing to represent devotional objects in strictly realistic terms. I suggest we make the same allowance for Fackenheim and exercise a measure of charity. "Israel" is an icon in Fackenheim's thought. It reflects a concentrated image of good over against the backdrop of unspeakable suffering. The luster of its image centers devotion and inspires "wonder." It constitutes a catalyst for communal solidarity and political action, including Fackenheim's own *aliyah* to Jerusalem. We further note (also in Fackenheim's defense) that this iconography has a quality peculiar to post-Holocaust thought. The light thrown by it remains shadowed by the memory of suffering. In our view, Fackenheim's uncritical solidarity with the Jewish people (marked by the grief of memory) pivots a uniquely turbulent approach to the traditional sancta of God and Torah.[54]

"Israel" does not constitute an incidental or merely sentimental motif in Fackenheim's thought. It represents a powerful trope with precise theological and philosophical resonance. First and foremost, we note the reverential tone. Self-consciously evoking the medieval philosophers Nachmanides and Judah Halevi, he paints this idyllic picture: "Today one travels throughout the replanted valleys of Galilee and is lost in wonder. And one walks through the Jewish Quarter of the Old City, ravaged by the Jordanians a generation ago, and is filled with a strange serenity."[55] These are not the casual remarks of a Canadian Jewish tourist enchanted by Eretz Yisrael. The very words *wonder* and *serenity* automatically ascribe a superordinate theological and philosophical significance to the State. For Fackenheim, Israel holds Hegelian and hence universal significance as a site where the antimonies between religion and secularism actually achieve successful synthesis.

This philosophical interpretation of Israel explains an otherwise banal fascination with images that conjoin the profane and the sacred in the form of military materiel and Jewish ritual objects. Fackenheim reflects upon a photograph of soldiers praying during the 1973 Yom Kippur War. Molotov cocktails turn into Jewish tanks; religious Jews become soldiers.[56] Fackenheim maintains that the State manifests a commingling of secular self-reliance and religious hope. The image of a religious Jew praying by the side of a tank has reduced the dissonance between piety and power. They no longer constitute antinomies. In an essay on Hegel, Fackenheim makes this audacious claim: "The reborn Jerusalem is overcoming the religious-secular split . . . with world-historical consequences as yet unknown." Fackenheim concludes the essay by imagining how Hegel himself might have "wondered" at this *aufhebung*.[57] For Fackenheim, the State of Israel represents more than geography, demographics, economics, institutions, or policy. It constitutes a politically embodied Hegelian signifier.

Israel plays the role that faith in a supernatural God once played in Fackenheim's earliest theological writings. It inspires wonder. It manifests supposedly contradictory human impulses such as self-reliance and religious hope. Fackenheim strikes a strongly fideistic attitude toward the State. We remember that in his essay "The Eclipse of God" Fackenheim held that no empirical counter-evidence could refute faith in God and supernatural revelation. His faith left him free of despair in the face of "human contradiction." We then saw how Fackenheim later abandoned this view, arguing in his post-Holocaust writings that Jewish theologians must seriously consider empirical, historical counter-evidence and admit that faith can be refuted. In the wake of this admission, Fackenheim's religious worldview seemed to be composed solely of disjointed fragments. Now, however, we see that fideism reappears around the figure of Israel. His faith in the people and State remains invulnerable to any historical reality that would disturb his astonishment. Neither war nor military occupation can upset his enthusiasm. Gross internal conflicts, especially between religious and secular Israeli Jews, never unsettle his reflections upon a "New Jerusalem."

For Fackenheim, Israel evokes "Jewish heroism," not contemporary political fissure. Images and figures constantly ground these reflections, creating a heady kitsch. Fackenheim draws philosophical implications from the popular slogan and folksong "*Am Yisrael Chai*" (the people Israel lives). He wonders at the photograph of soldiers at war and prayer. He reflects upon the statue of Warsaw Ghetto hero Mordecai Anielewicz before blooming fields. A book of philosophical essays (*Encounters between Judaism and Modern Philosophy*) is dedicated to "the Israelis," *The Jewish Return into History* to Yonathan Netanyahu, the slain commander of the 1976 Entebbe operation. In both books we note the fleeting figure of Bar Kochba, whose "heroism" was a factor in Rome's destruction of Judea in the year 135.[58] Fackenheim's pervasive fascination with Israeli power is common enough among Diaspora-born Jews. However, his almost incidental reference to Bar Kochba strikes a particularly odd tone, regardless of one's historical appraisal of the Bar Kochban revolt. It strongly suggests that Fackenheim's Zionist reflections prove less open to the ambiguities of Jewish history than to stylistically crafted historical images.

In the context of the 1990s even the rhetorical effect of Fackenheim's Zionism appears myopic. True, a consensus regarding the future of Palestine may emerge between Israel's secular left and right wing. However, it is too early to know if religious and secular Israeli Jews will converge to create new cultural forms or whether they will exhaust each other in a hopeless *Kulturkampf*. But even more importantly, Fackenheim has misjudged the relation between religion and violence. In his writings they represent strict antinomies. But if Judaism and violence were intimately coupled from the very start, would they require Hegelian mediation? According to René Girard, religion and violence are inextricably entangled. Following Freud, Girard argues that the sacred originates in primal

scenes of sacrificial violence. According to Girard, social structures are
threatened by the violence spawned by mimetic desire. The ritual slaughter of an innocent victim protects the community from the devastating
effects of reciprocal mayhem. Girard writes, "Religion shelters us from
violence just as violence seeks shelter in religion."[59] This theory may exaggerate human propensities for violence and the violent origins of religion, but it also illuminates biblical events like the prophet Samuel hack-
ing Agag to death. It jibes with the acts of terror committed by members
of the Israeli religious nationalist "Underground" in the 1980s and includes the assassination of Yitzhak Rabin. Indeed, if "violence is the heart
and secret soul of the sacred,"[60] Fackenheim should have been less astonished at the commingling of power and piety in the modern State of Israel.

It would be a mistake, however, to entirely dismiss Fackenheim's Zionism. Like so many symbolically coded images, the State of Israel constitutes a powerful modern-day iconographic figure. Fackenheim's love for
this intentionally stylized and mythical image of the State reflects the
power of desire. The bleak vision in *God's Presence in History*, had seemed
to offer no good in a post-Holocaust world. Fackenheim himself notes in
The Jewish Return to History that suffering challenges the value of this-
worldly existence. In an essay entitled "The Human Condition after Auschwitz: A Jewish Testimony One Generation After," he writes, "Without
doubt to say yea or nay to existence is the ultimate question in all religion and all philosophy."[61] The Holocaust represents an existential nay. It
appears to finally wash away the moral foundation upon which the world
wobbles. In this dim light, "The State of Israel" functions as a precarious,
symbolic bulwark. Fackenheim's love for it is decidedly unempirical. It
constitutes a stubborn, a priori affirmation. For Fackenheim, the State
means that "life and love, not death and hate, shall prevail."[62] Rejecting
pessimism, he upholds an image of the survivor who "affirms [life] by an
act of faith which defies comprehension."[63]

God and Torah

The ability to love the Jewish people and the State of Israel with all his
heart, soul, and might allows Fackenheim to render critical readings of
God and Torah without abandoning the midrashic framework. As we see
it, this very blindspot has produced unique readings of the Hebrew Bible
and its God that are powerful in proportion to the ambivalence they
express. In *To Mend the World*, Fackenheim had appealed to Hans-Georg
Gadamer's hermeneutical theory. He wondered how post-Holocaust
readers could, in Gadamer's terms, "fuse" their intellectual and spiritual
horizons with those of traditional texts. Like Gadamer, Fackenheim ar-

gued that a reader's own historically situated pre-understandings radically determine his or her readings of texts transmitted from earlier times. But Fackenheim parted with Gadamer by arguing that an unbroken line of continuity—one that Gadamer saw binding readers and texts—had snapped for Jews after the Holocaust. Auschwitz threatens to sever post-Holocaust readers from the past and its texts. Unlike some postmodern theorists, however, Fackenheim did not reify the category of discontinuity. Without fully developing the idea, Fackenheim strongly suggested that any repair of Jewish life depends on retrieving traditional texts.[64]

Fackenheim finally offers a sustained exposition of a traditional text in his most recent book, *The Jewish Bible after the Holocaust* (1990). He promises in its foreword a "post-Holocaust biblical hermeneutic"—a method with which to reread the Bible in light of Auschwitz. The motifs of rupture, struggle, and solidarity that characterized his post-Holocaust thought continue to inform this new biblical hermeneutic. Sensitive to the changes wrought by historical upheaval, Fackenheim recognizes that readers of the Bible today are likely to be more vexed than those of previous generations.[65] Echoing Buber's famous essay "The Man of Today and the Jewish Bible," Fackenheim insists that "the Jewish Bible must be read by Jews today—read, listened to, struggled with, if necessary fought against—as though they had never read it before."[66]

In *God's Presence in History*, Fackenheim had suggested that the "citing of God against God may have to assume extremes that dwarf those of Abraham, Jeremiah, Job, [and] Rabbi Levi Yitzhak."[67] This magnified protest now assumes form in his own biblical hermeneutic. We have seen in this study's second chapter how the rabbis in the Talmud and midrash had defended Israel—even against God. But they rarely defended rebels like the stiff-necked generation wandering through the Sinai desert after the exodus from Egypt. The biblical text, its God, its chief prophet, and a long tradition of Jewish commentators have largely sided against them. In stark defiance, Fackenheim supports their repeated complaints for water. He asks, "What difference does [the salvation at the Sea] make three days later to the mothers, when their children are dying of thirst?" Likewise, Fackenheim finds himself torn between Joshua and Caleb on one hand and the Israelites on the other. He supports Joshua and Caleb's refusal to return to Egypt but understands the fears that their report provokes among the people. In Fackenheim's rendering, they fear for their children in an unknown land and (in an obscure allusion to the Palestinian people) resist the idea of devouring another nation. This support of fearful, rebellious, even morally delicate Israelites takes the extreme form of defending those who worshiped the golden calf. Even the most gross infidelity could never justify complete extermination. Al-

though Fackenheim claims to "hover" between God and Israel, he in fact
champions the community in practically every conflict. Even in the case
of Korah, Fackenheim refuses to censure Jews. On one hand, he refuses
to side with Korah's rebellion against Moses and Aaron. Fackenheim re-
proaches Korah's band for "arrogating unto themselves a holiness attrib-
utable only to God." However, in doing so, Fackenheim identifies them
as left-wing Hegelians. He thus preserves his solidarity with the Jewish
people by transforming these unsavory Israelites into gentiles!

Blind love for the people of Israel has led Fackenheim into new hermeneutical and theological territory where the visage of God has become
unclear. An overriding solidarity governs his rereading of the Bible and
appraisal of its protagonists—a love before which God inevitably pales. In
each case Fackenheim evokes the children when adjudicating disputes
between God and Israel. They symbolize for him the endangered community at its most innocent and vulnerable. Fackenheim explains that
post-Holocaust Jews "perceive how radically their religious situation has
changed: they have but no choice but to take sides with the mothers of
the children, against the narrator, against Moses, and, if necessary, against
God Himself."[68] In Fackenheim's unequivocally anthropocentric religious
worldview, God becomes an uncertain figure. One critic has consequently
faulted him for not articulating a clear theology, but this I think was
Fackenheim's point.[69] Indeed, Fackenheim says almost nothing about
God, as if on purpose. Attributes of goodness or power go virtually unmentioned in light of Auschwitz. As we saw in our discussion of *God's
Presence in History* and in *To Mend the World*, God represents at best a
minimal figure.

Fackenheim's own theological voice hides implicitly within the folds of
textual commentary. A reworking of Psalm 118—with its invocation of
God's "enduring mercies"—is a case in point. Significantly, this psalm
constitutes a central part of the liturgical *Hallel*, a thanksgiving prayer
traditional Jews recite on holidays such as Passover that celebrate divine
deliverance. The future of this liturgy worries Fackenheim. In the first
chapter of *The Jewish Bible after the Holocaust*, he repeats a question
posed by Buber in "The Dialogue between Heaven and Earth" concerning a modern-day Job and "God's enduring mercies." With renewed intensity he cites Buber verbatim: "Dare we recommend to the survivors of
Auschwitz, to the Job of the gas chambers, 'Thank ye the Lord, for He is
good, for His mercy endureth forever'"?[70] We remember from Chapter 3
that Buber answered this question in the negative. For his part, Fackenheim could not have chosen a better text. The thanks expressed by Psalm
118 appear in triplicate: in the biblical text itself, in the traditional *Hallel*,
and in Buber's negation. In the last chapter of *The Jewish Bible after the
Holocaust*, Fackenheim introduces an additional layer. Should Jews recite

Psalm 118/*Hallel* on *Yom Ha-ʿatzmaut* (Israeli Independence Day)? Or does the memory of the Holocaust undermine the thanks that the State's establishment would otherwise demand?

This discussion of Psalm 118 forms a cryptic meditation on God's manifest goodness. As such, it also speaks to Shapiro's argument that an image of the good overwhelms the memory of catastrophe in Fackenheim's thought. In my view Fackenheim retains a subtle balance. Caught between the memory of genocide and the event of statehood, Fackenheim does not praise God's goodness indiscriminately but recommends that thoughtful readers acclaim "God's enduring mercy" *sotto voce* (with lowered voice), simultaneously praising and withholding praise. Even while thanking God on *Yom Ha-ʿatzmaut*, Fackenheim must also remember the Holocaust. He asks: "What if dire times called for faith in self-fulfilling prophecies? For giving thanks to divine Goodness, hoping that this will awaken it? For praising divine Mercy, hoping that this will call it forth?"[71] With these suggestive questions, Fackenheim has transformed the significance of the psalm and the meaning of *Hallel*. No longer an utterance describing reality, it becomes a prescriptive utterance demanding goodness from God. In the process of rereading psalm 118, Fackenheim has tacitly advanced a fragmentary theological statement. God is not omnibenevolent. Characterized by absence, divine mercy does not permanently endure *in actu*. Indeed, almost mystically, the religious worshiper deploys Psalm 118 in order to conjure God's *latent* goodness.

A similar understanding characterizes Fackenheim's discussion of divine power. Divine power, like God's goodness, is not always manifest. It too requires prayer and other forms of human *tikkun* to call it forth. Once again, this leads Fackenheim to the problem of reciting Jewish liturgy. Once again, he culls theological observation from textual commentary. Toward the end of *To Mend the World*, he imagines the reflections that accompany Jewish prayer after the Holocaust. Resisting the Yom Kippur martyrology *Ele Ezkera*, he writes:

> For the children, the mothers, and the Musselmänner had not chosen to be martyrs, had not died as martyrs: and that God needs *that* death is unacceptable. Hence even the most devout Jew at prayer must today ask, on the holiest day of Judaism: why is the world today not water? . . . Why does anything—Man, World, God—still exist now—and not water? Why does he himself still exist—an accidental remnant? . . . Where the divine Judgment? As his prayer is informed by these questions it is transformed. It becomes a gift whereby is returned to God "His crown and His scepter."[72]

Fackenheim inverts the meaning of Yom Kippur in this liturgical revision. Instead of God cleansing human sin, Yom Kippur becomes an occasion in which Jewish prayer restores "crown and scepter" to God. This reference to crown and scepter comes from Elie Wiesel's novel *Gates of the Forest*. Wiesel, in turn, most likely took this image from tractate Yomah of the Babylonian Talmud. Representing divine power, the trope of God's crown and scepter occurs repeatedly throughout Fackenheim's post-Holocaust writings.[73] It suggests that human usurpation has rendered God impotent. Human action in the form of prescriptive speech-acts, must therefore call it forth. Prayer, again almost mystically, restores to God the broken attribute of divine power.

In sum, we have seen unequivocal solidarity with Israel transforming the traditional sancta of God and Torah into ambivalent figures. Ruptured by historical catastrophe, God's presence in history appears fragmentary at best. This God no longer resembles the "worshipful" entity described by Anglo-American philosophers of religion or the magisterial God of History pilloried by Rubenstein. God has become more "postmodern," no longer a self-sufficient entity, perfect in power and goodness. God's presence fragments, divested of these attributes that would have otherwise constituted divine perfection. Torah also breaks in Fackenheim's biblical hermeneutic. No longer the faithful repository of perfect wisdom, Fackenheim reads it with post-Holocaust eyes. He cannot defend God, Moses, and the biblical narrator against those who have murmured against them. He must therefore reread biblical texts. He lowers his voice. He turns liturgical exclamations into desperate invocations. In the process, the biblical text and liturgy have also become "postmodern," rendered open by the twists and distortions of a strong interpreter. The resemblance to postmodern theory should not, however, obviate this feature of Fackenheim's thought. A God whose historical presence proves alarmingly uneven remains the God of History. A fragmented textual tradition retains its privileged status as Torah.

Penultimate Conclusions

Fackenheim's primary accomplishment as a theologian lies in this ability to incorporate radical negativity into overarching religious commitments. The demand to represent good after Auschwitz may pose a more difficult challenge. How does one trace the movement from catastrophic suffering into joy and vigor? What does it mean to enjoy life when others still suffer? "To life, to life, *l'ḥayim*" becomes doubly grotesque after Auschwitz. And yet, the rabbis (e.g., in tractate Moed Katan of the Talmud) had the good sense to warn against excessive mourning. Perhaps one has no choice but to risk bad taste—both in celebrating life and remembering the dead. Hence perhaps the ironic penchant among some postmodernists to tolerate and even embrace "flamboyant" displays of kitsch;

hence perhaps the presence of hyperbole in Fackenheim's writings. There may be no other way to represent and celebrate the good before the memory of evil. This said in Fackenheim's defense, I would not want to abandon entirely our own hermeneutic of suspicion. Fackenheim's reflections could stand a little irony. We have seen the image of the State of Israel acting like a powerful icon blinding Fackenheim. Irony might have prevented him from stumbling in the process of leaping backward from radical evil toward an imperfect, empirical good.

To borrow a term from Derrida, Fackenheim's reflections on resistance and the State of Israel depend on how a good might "supplement" death. The supplement is a philosophical category in Derrida's writings. It represents that which remains unthought or unthinkable (banished, overlooked, "mysterious") by any single totalitizing system. For our purposes, we note the word's twofold meaning. Derrida explains that, on the one hand, a supplement constitutes a surplus, a plenitude superadded to another plenitude. It does not supersede. On the other hand, a supplement may operate as a substitute that "intervenes or insinuates itself in-the-place-of." One figure comes to displace another. In either case, Derrida identifies this common feature, "whether it adds or substitutes itself, the supplement is exterior, outside of the positivity to which it is superadded, alien to that which, in order to be replaced by it, must be other than it."[74] In Derrida's *On Grammatology*, writing supplements speech, deferral supplements presence, difference supplements identity, culture supplements nature, masturbation supplements coitus. Fackenheim's supplement is moral: good supplements evil. Jewish life in the State of Israel and in the Diaspora astonish Fackenheim after Auschwitz. No matter how fragmentary, they represent life-affirming supplements to an anti-world predicated on a teleological logic of destruction. Figures of life, they become mysteriously other when juxtaposed to the Holocaust. In a movement integral to his thought, Fackenheim *superadds* them to his reflections on Auschwitz. Like the figure of love in Rosenzweig's thought, they usher him back "into life."

Rosenzweig had built his reflections about death, love, and life upon the triad of God, man, and world intersecting through the media of creation, revelation, and redemption. In Rosenzweig's system, no single point subsumes the All. Rather, totality takes the shape (*Gestalt*) of this six-figured constellation; and at the center of the system, love redeems death. In contrast, totality shatters in Fackenheim's thought under the impact of catastrophe. No supplement "redeems" the negative in Fackenheim's post-Holocaust thought. No supplement "intervenes or insinuates itself in-place-of" Auschwitz. On a nationally televised broadcast in what was then West Germany, Fackenheim commented: "Once Hegel, the greatest German philosopher, observed that the wounds of the spirit heal without leaving scars. This he could no longer say today. Scars do remain, and 'healing' is not the right word. But to alleviate the pain is possible, and this is why we are here today."[75] The supplement represented by the State does not solve the problem of evil. A modicum of hope, the *tikkun* it offers signifies a fragmentary trace and nothing more. Nevertheless, after the Holocaust, even the slightest trace-presence of good signifies something rather than nothing. The fragmentary trace provides the guarded basis for Fackenheim's hesitant affirmations while he accounts for the Holocaust's radical testimony against God, Torah, and human character. Like Derrida's description of the supplement, a trace good represents "less than nothing and yet, to judge by its effects, much more than nothing. The supplement is neither a presence nor an absence. No ontology can think its operation."[76]

Derrida indicates to us just how difficult it is to think clearly about a supplement. This proves especially the case when trying to think about ambiguous but life-affirming supplements in the aftermath of catastrophe. In my view Fackenheim's thought does not ultimately stumble over the problem of evil but over the problem of love. How should one love a morally imperfect person or entity? Can love blind one to the suffering of others? Is love worth the pain that frequently accompanies it? What are its limits? The beloved "New Jerusalem" never obscures the visage of Auschwitz. It redeems nothing. In Derrida's words, the State represents less than nothing. It cannot heal the scars left by Nazi Germany's assault upon the Jewish people. At the same time, again according to Derrida, it comes to represent much more than nothing. It ushers Fackenheim back "into life."

In the end, however, Fackenheim ultimately fails to consider the consequences that attend any attempt to sanctify an imperfect, empirical entity with superordinate status. His own discussion of history consistently ignores the moral ambiguity of violence. Despite a rhetoric of historical realism, Fackenheim effectively turns the State into a trope, a set of dramatically stylized images. His reflections upon a rebuilt Jerusalem remain supra-empirical, marked by the power and limits that characterize religious discourse. This blind love belies an observation made by the art historian Moshe Barasch, who writes, "Even the most enthusiastic champion of pictures acknowledges, by the very fact that he or she has to defend the image's validity, that the object of veneration is problematic."[77] Fackenheim has failed to describe the State of Israel and Jewish identity with the same measured ambiguity, the same rhetoric of rupture and fragmentation, with which he meets God and Torah. Supplements, even life-affirming ones, are never innocent. The State of Israel need not ever have been morally pure to have constituted a good after Auschwitz.

CONCLUSION

DISCOURSE, SIGN, DIPTYCH

REMARKS ON JEWISH THOUGHT AFTER AUSCHWITZ

Unity is about different people with different opinions talking
about the same things.
(Michel Foucault, *The Archeology of Knowledge*)

I.

IN *THE ARCHAEOLOGY OF KNOWLEDGE*, Michel Foucault
faulted attempts by intellectual historians to establish continuities
between rapidly shifting historical periods. Foucault proposed instead an "archaeological" method to explore ruptures, discontinuities,
and interruptions. Following this plan, historians probe the thresholds
that "suspend the continuous accumulation of knowledge, interrupt its
slow development, and force it to enter a new time."[1] Foucault sought
new lines of continuity *within* historical periods, not between them. He
wanted to show how diverse but contemporaneous statements coalesce
into "discursive formations." By discourse, Foucault meant a limited
number of statements governed by a definable group of rules, regularities, and conditions.[2] In a discursive framework, rules and regularities
give rise to new concepts, regroupings of objects, social exclusions, and
types of enunciation.[3] This does not mean that Foucault accepted the
Hegelian notion that national or temporal spirits of progressively greater
self-consciousness unite the diverse expressions of a people or age. Indeed, the regularities that govern discourse formation work anonymously
across fields of difference. These regularities do not necessarily come to
self-consciousness nor do they point to a definite telos. Intellectual work-
ers (e.g., historians, botanists, psychiatrists) who participate in the same
discursive framework typically fail to recognize the links that bind one
another. They form a variegated web whose breadth they comprehend
very inadequately.[4]

Foucault's notion of the archive enables us to conceptualize the broad
range of post-Holocaust theological and hermeneutical revision. Despite
fundamental disagreements, Rubenstein, Berkovits, and Fackenheim
helped fashion a common discursive framework—one with its own
unique rules, thematic objects, subjects, and class of experts. We have

noted the radical rupture separating their own contemporary reflections from classical and modern Jewish traditions. Buber, Heschel, Soloveitchik, and Kaplan barely spoke about the Holocaust. Their reference to it remained largely allusive and impressionistic. In contrast, post-Holocaust theologians spoke of practically nothing else. They formed part of an inter-discursive grouping of antagonistic writers, artists, and politicians as different from one another as Hannah Arendt, Bruno Bettelheim, Raul Hilberg, Lucy Dawidowicz, Terrence Des Pres, Elie Wiesel, Primo Levi, Jean Amery, Cynthia Ozick, Philip Roth, Irena Klepfisz, Abba Kovner, Dan Pagis, Aaron Appelfeld, Leon Uris, Menachem Begin, Dov Shilansky, Meir Kahane, Avi Weiss, Arthur Cohen, Irving Greenberg, Steven Katz, Claude Lanzmann, and (most recently) Steven Spielberg.[5] The types of sacred scripture, contemporary literature, political utterance, and historical knowledge were no longer of the same variety that had exercised modern Jewish theology prior to the Eichmann trial in 1963. Viewed from within this larger nexus, Rubenstein, Berkovits, and Fackenheim represented pivotal figures forming a new theological discourse in which the memory of Auschwitz and the State of Israel virtually displace God and Torah.

By this I do not mean to suggest that post-Holocaust religious thought is defined by thematic objects (e.g., Auschwitz, Israel) that pre-exist the discourse. Indeed, Foucault insisted that discourse and discourse formation do not "form" around pre-given thematic objects. Discursive objects do not generate discourse! Rather discourse creates discursive objects. Historically peculiar criteria—institutional in nature—generate the emergence or disappearance of any given concept, object, figure, idea, and statements about them. For example, the emergence of psychiatric concepts and subjects in the nineteenth century was predicated upon a set of relations governing hospitalization, internment, procedures of social exclusion, rules of jurisprudence, and the norms of industrial labor and bourgeois morality.[6] "The homosexual" was one such subject. In the first volume of his *History of Sexuality*, Foucault explained how psychiatry (along with medical and pedagogical discourses) actually saw to the proliferation of heretofore peripheral human sexualities. Under ancient and canonical civil codes, sodomy had constituted a category of forbidden acts. In the nineteenth century, "the homosexual" became a full-blooded personage, "a case history, and a childhood . . . a type of life, a life form, and a morphology, with an indiscreet anatomy and possibly a mysterious physiology." Foucault argued, prior to this period, "the sodomite had been a temporary aberration; the homosexual was now a species."[7]

As nineteenth-century psychiatric discourse saw to the proliferation of human sexualities, so too has discourse about the destruction of European Jewry generated new theological subjects. Soon after 1945 the murder of Europe's Jews took on the name Holocaust. Auschwitz assumed unique and mordant iconographic status. Against this backdrop Rubenstein embodied the picture of the young, rebellious theologian, boldly advancing the dignity of his people against tradition. Berkovits helped disseminate the bitterly conflicted Yossel Rakover. Fackenheim pushed stylized images of endangered children, desperate resistance fighters, and heroic Israeli soldiers to the forefront of religious thought. We have argued that Rubenstein, Berkovits, and Fackenheim reflected less on actual historical persons than on carefully crafted images. Like psychiatry creating the "homosexual subject," post-Holocaust religious discourse generated its own thematic subject: The Privileged Antitheodic Subject. We paraphrase Foucault to suggest that throughout the course of this study we have seen the following: once a more or less temporary aberration in Bible and midrash, this Privileged Antitheodic Subject has now come to represent a species.

The technique of forming new subjects out of traditional texts has always shaped Jewish thought. With no little hermeneutical ingenuity, Philo crafted a new type of religious authority by turning Moses into a philosopher. According to Maimonides, the excellence of Moses' prophecy lay in his unmediated apprehension of the Active Intellect. In this century Buber and Heschel transformed prophets and Hasids into existentialists (one is tempted to say expressionists). The tradition as they read it advanced the faith that suffering could generate spiritual value. For their part, Rubenstein, Berkovits, and Fackenheim abandoned theodicy and theodic texts. They ignored theodic figures who justify, explain, or accept the relation between God and catastrophic suffering. Against the grain of rabbinic Judaism and modern Jewish thought, post-Holocaust thinkers turned to the drama of priestly cult, a morally absent deity, the protesting Job, the heresy of Elisha b. Abuye, abandoned wives, a plaintive community. These once marginalized but now privileged antitheodic subjects acted as a warrant allowing post-Holocaust thinkers to voice their own doubts about God and suffering.

The question of textual warrant constitutes one further feature of discourse that bears on post-Holocaust thought. Foucault observed how discourse formations rely on interlinking groups of experts authorized to speak at particular moments in particular venues: to transmit knowledge, to offer prognosis, to pass sentence. The effect is to control discourse by restricting its exercise to an authorized class. In his writings Foucault paid particular attention to physicians, pedagogues, psychiatrists, and, criminologists. For its part, post-Holocaust discourse formation has relied upon groups of experts all its own. Religious leaders, university professors, community functionaries, artists and architects, museum directors—all contribute to the control of discourse about the Holocaust. Of course, in Foucault's writings, the pronouncements of experts enjoy legal sanction. In our case, Holocaust experts (except in Germany where it is illegal to deny the existence of the Holocaust) employ only extralegal, moral powers of censure and rebuke. Debate revolves around respect for the dead, common sense, moral decency, and even good taste.

The question of who controls the right and authority to speak has always been central to religious life and thought. The attempts by Rubenstein, Berkovits, and Fackenheim to restrict theodicy (by calling it "obscene," "blasphemy," "shipwrecked") reflect but a recent case in point. We have seen that the encounter with evil challenges religious discourse at many different levels. The Holocaust (and attention paid to it) threatens the narrative frame and ritual expression that constitute Jewish communal affiliation and spiritual identity. Can one dare reiterate Deuteronomy's rhetoric of retribution or recite the Yom Kippur *unetanah tokef* after Auschwitz? How can one continue to speak at the Passover Seder about God redeeming Israel? Is it possible to say that supernatural commandments undergird Jewish existence with meaning? Must we make these affirmations sotto voce? Or do rules governing acceptable post-Holocaust discourse preclude such assertions? Rubenstein, Berkovits, and Fackenheim arrived at radically different solutions to these kinds of questions. At the same time, each sought distinctly religious and moral sanctions to surmount any myopic obsession with God and theodicy.

Foucault would have recognized that the genuine difference between one religious thinker's traditionalism and another's radicalism need not preclude common participation in a discursive formation. The post-Holocaust theological discourse was (to paraphrase this chapter's epigraph from Foucault) one in which different people with different opinions talked about the same things. Rubenstein rejected belief in the God of History while Berkovits railed against Him. Like his radical counterpart, Berkovits refused to call God perfect. Both assumed a posture of stubborn solidarity with suffering people. Rubenstein bought his radicalism at the price of ignoring antitheodicy from the canon. Rejecting tradition, he paradoxically recast it. In contrast, Berkovits accepted Torah by rejecting theodicy. That is, he sought to conserve tradition but wound up reshaping it. I believe that Jewish religious thought will continue to demonstrate this tension between mixed intentions, innovation, and conservation well into the future. However, I suspect that it will fall within the antitheodic parameters set by post-Holocaust discourse. At least for a long time to come, none but the most stringently ultra-Orthodox are likely to justify God at Job's expense.

More recent theological writings evidence the pervasiveness of post-

Holocaust discourse, respecting this secret concord between Rubenstein and Berkovits. Arthur Green recognizes with Rubenstein the absurdity that fills existence. He writes: "We have seen the arbitrariness of fate, the depths of human cruelty, the indifference of both man and nature. We do not deny absurdity, but we reject it, defy it."[8] For his part, Jonathan Sacks (currently the chief rabbi of England) ridicules the "death of God" and "the moral revolution."[9] However, he admits, "neither creation nor history carry their meaning on their surface. . . . The primary encounter is not with something outside the text but with the text itself."[10] By acknowledging that one cannot immediately detect God's presence in history, Sacks stands in a fundamental, albeit unacknowledged, agreement with Richard Rubenstein. For their part, the strategies employed by critical feminist theologians such as Judith Plaskow closely resemble those devised by post-Holocaust theologians writing in the late 1960s and early 1970s. Neither Rubenstein, Berkovits, nor Fackenheim accepted texts that countenanced divine injustice. In a similar vein, Plaskow resists theological and textual traditions that support gendered injustice.[11] In short, doubt about the meaning of history, solidarity with the victims of injustice, fidelity to an expansive view of the community of Israel, and visions of repair have dictated fundamental theological and hermeneutical revisions across a wide ideological spectrum. Indeed, these disparate voices indicate the historical process by which discursive patterns anonymously generate binding criteria, powerful thematic foci, and hermeneutical innovation.

II.

Foucault's archaeological method did not in principle deny that lines of cultural continuity distend through historical time. He himself knew that not all elements in a discursive formation change at once. Historians do not find worlds composed of entirely new objects, concepts, etc. emerging in toto.[12] Unfortunately, Foucault did not explain how a variegated cultural system can subsist throughout many historical strata. His strength has been to articulate a profound sense of historical rupture, not to follow lines of continuing cultural mutation. For this we turn to Umberto Eco's semiotic theory.[13]

By definition, semiotics (or semiology) refers to the science of signs. For Eco, this entails a methodology for perceiving any cultural unit as a plastic system of interlocking parts. A "sign" may be a literary motif, a philosophical argument, a historical or mythological figure, a musical note. Patterns are created by arranging and rearranging the order of specific signs and bringing them to bear upon each other in complex and potentially infinite form. As one author has suggested, semiotics offers an encyclopedic way of looking at a world and its constituent parts as "a net, a rhizome—a tangled clump of bulbs and tubers—or a labyrinth, a vast aggregation of units of meaning among which an infinite variety of connections can be made."[14]

Eco has paid particular attention to what he called the "open work." An open work is an artistic piece composed of carefully devised signs whose ultimate composition remains undetermined by the artist. In one essay Eco looks at how avant-garde musical composers present the performer with the option to freely arrange and rearrange the units that compose their work. For instance, one composer leaves the performer a large, single sheet of music paper with a series of note groupings. The performer must select among these groupings and weld them into new aggregates. In another example, the first section of a musical piece is made up of ten different pieces on ten sheets of music paper. These can then be rearranged in different sequences, like a stack of filing cards.[15] The avant-garde composition as understood by Eco is intentionally designed to contain parts that can be detached and moved, thus opening the work to an almost indefinite number of possible configurations.

As tradition-based social forms, Judaism and Jewish thought do not allow the same measure of idiosyncratic determination as does avant-garde musical composition. Yet many scholars in the field of Jewish Studies (and I count myself among them) would insist that the practical operation of Judaism and Jewish thought is more like an open work than appearances might first suggest. Judaism and Jewish thought also remain subject to what Eco called the "unexpected freedoms" and "the unlimited discovery of contrasts and oppositions that keep multiplying with every look."[16] Judaism consists of signs (texts, beliefs, social institutions, literary figures, and ritual observances) that form into a semiotic web of interlinking pieces. By signs we also mean affective states of consciousness brought about by ecstatic experience and catastrophic event. Such states include the elation of election and expressions of hurt. To be sure, the relations between each and every sign coalesce into more or less historically determinate configurations. One won't find medieval thinkers entertaining the intellectual virtues of Job's protest or identifying prophecy with the political cause of social justice. These belong to a different age. But the cultural nexus that constitutes "Judaism" in any given period is itself built upon detachable parts. Its units can be moved between the center and margins of the community's attention to reveal new meanings at different historical moments.

The conditions that made for the emergence of Rubenstein, Berkovits, and Fackenheim's theological and textual revisions were semiotic. Each thinker manipulated a more or less fluid web, composed of "signs" taken from more or less determinate historical strata. Those strata that have directly concerned this study are biblical, rabbinic, and modern. Rubenstein, Berkovits, and Fackenheim moved what had since become marginal outbursts of anger along with priestly, mystical, and feminine figures into the center of their discourse. They hardened tradition's central concern for the community of Israel into stubborn solidarity. They deactivated central tropes like retribution, the world-to-come, afflictions of love, and prophetic rebuke by moving them out into the margins of their thought. In the process, post-Holocaust religious thought came to constitute a *unique*, antitheodic loop in the semiotic web of Jewish tradition.

Such a conclusion contradicts those who argue that the murder of European Jewry has produced no new theological expression not already present in the pages of Bible, midrash, or modernist poetry and literature. It contradicts those who suggest that Auschwitz was just another, albeit extreme site of Jewish suffering. In terms of strict *content*, the antitheodic tropes used by Rubenstein, Berkovits, and Fackenheim admittedly remain the same throughout time—but not their *formal* arrangement vis-à-vis previously hegemonic theodic patterns. As I posited in this study's introduction and argued throughout its pages, the Holocaust and its memory have radically recast the theodic and antitheodic contours of Jewish theology. Antitheodic expression shifts from the margins of classical Jewish literature, moving from the literary horizons afforded by Yiddish and Hebrew literary modernism into the very center of religious thought. This shift speaks to the changed face of catastrophe in the modern era. Antitheodicy (the refusal to justify, accept, and value suffering) proves especially compelling in an age of extermination camps and nuclear weaponry. After all, traditional Jewish eschatology had pinned its confidence on a surviving remnant. The threat of global annihilation (combined with the human propensities for methodical destruction and systemic apathy revealed during the Holocaust) erodes this confidence. Taken together, the memory of Auschwitz and the fear of a nuclear catastrophe paralyze the dialectical movement of catharsis and redemption central to both classical and modern theodicy.

I do not know if Rubenstein, Berkovits, or Fackenheim ever acknowledged the hermeneutical and semiotic presuppositions upon which they built their own antitheodic discourse. The young Richard Rubenstein knew that confronting the Holocaust required momentous change from Jewish theology. I wonder if he suspected that the radicalism of his thought had less to do with theological propositions per se than with his recoding the contents of an entire religious culture. Nor do I know if Rubenstein realized at the time just how plastic traditions might become; and that it was this very plasticity that allowed him to turn to the religiosity of priests, ritual, and community over against the more "prophetic" emphasis on God, morality, and prayer. Neither did Berkovits ever acknowledge the radical implications of rehabilitating the good names of Job and Elisha b. Abuye. We wonder if he ever realized the consequences of moving these marginal figures into the center of his own response to suffering. For his part, Fackenheim was better read in contemporary hermeneutical theory. He recognized the uneasy dialectic that governs the relation between tradition and change. But even in Fackenheim's work, the "midrashic framework" that he defended against Rubenstein seemed too unified a structure to explain his own manipulation of it. Fackenheim transforms the root experience of Sinai by reenacting it with a cast of confused, insecure, and angry people.

The fact that post-Holocaust Jewish theologians remained so unaware of their own method suits Foucault's description of the anonymous quality of discourse. Their examples only confirms poststructuralist doubts regarding the importance of authorial intent. At the time neither Rubenstein, Berkovits, nor Fackenheim entirely controlled the revisions they began to produce. Rubenstein's deliberate intent in *The Religious Imagination* was to eulogize tradition, not to generate a nontheistic reading of it. Conversely, Berkovits tried to salvage traditional Jewish thought, not to create a revisionary counter-tradition. Nor did Fackenheim seem to realize how close he approached Rubenstein when he affirmed belief in God's presence in history by depicting it as elusive and fragmented. Never fully in control of their own discourse, Rubenstein, Berkovits, and Fackenheim behaved like semiconscious sleep-walkers. They rifled the margins of tradition for signs that spoke to them in their own voice after Auschwitz. It is no surprise that results marked by such reckless courage were so uneven.

III.

Religious thought (even thought about the Holocaust) does not occur in an aesthetic vacuum. In part, claims about the relationship between religion and art state a cultural fact—one brilliantly explored by Mark Taylor in *Disfiguring: Art, Architecture, Religion* (1992). An opening chapter surveys theories about art, the absolute, and the sublime found in the philosophical writings of Kant, Schiller, Schelling, and Hegel. He shows how the theologian Friedrich Schleiermacher and the painter Caspar David Friedrich (each through their own media) sought to demonstrate the aesthetic power of religion and the religious nature of art. Taylor's discussion continues into the twentieth century. A chapter detailing the explicitly expressed spiritual tendencies of modernist painters (e.g., Kandinsky, Malevitch, Neuman, Rothko) segues into a chapter on, Karl

Barth. Against romanticism in theology and in the arts, Barth had withdrawn divinity from all things creaturely and human, including art and artistic creativity. It is with no small irony that Taylor draws this uncompromising theological stance into conversation with the architectural purism of Le Corbusier, Walter Gropius, and Ludwig Mies van der Rohe.

To frame the entanglement between religion and art, Taylor coins the unwieldy terms *theoesthetics* and *a/theoesthetics*. By the former, Taylor means a romantic and then (in this century) modernist religious aesthetic. Romantics and modernists sought to bind together an organic spiritual nexus that modernity had supposedly sundered. Modernism in particular was marked by heady and often militant forms of utopianism. The Jewish philosopher Franz Rosenzweig sought to reconfigure a shattered All into a new and supple constellation. Martin Heidegger strove to uncover the ontological root of human Dasein. Walter Benjamin speculated upon an originary, comprehensive Pure Language. Politically, socialists and communists ventured to reconstitute the social fabric through the medium of Revolution while fascists sought their own vicious brands of utopian renewal. Taylor identifies theoesthetics with the promise by religion and art (and here we add ideology) to heal wounds and mend the tears rending self, society, and world. In contrast to these totalizing visions, Taylor advocates a skeptical and anti-utopian a/theoesthetic. As understood by Taylor, postmodern a/theoesthetics demands "an ethic of resistance in which irreconcilable differences are repeatedly negotiated" without hope for resolution. God still plays a role in this resistance, but only "from the proximate distance of an Other I can never know." God is rendered through figures that are rent—not through the luminous categories of Being, identity, essence, subject, or presence.[17]

Building on Taylor's analysis shows that the relationship between religion and art shares formal as well as cultural characteristics. By aesthetics, neither Taylor nor I mean theories about the beautiful per se. Indeed, so much of modernist and postmodernist art has taken the grotesque as its theme. Rather, the term *aesthetics* refers to fields of perception, to the formal organization (or disappearance) of figure, line, plane, tone, and texture within compositional frameworks. In our view, the art of religious thought resembles the craft of painting compositions. Some religious compositions offer revelations composed of determinate content that orient the spiritual eye around clear-cut theophanies and moral norms. Some trace disembodied visions of fleeting sublimity. And still others paint pictures of redemption or enlightenment that promise lyric harmony and balance now or at the end of days. Names invoke figures, verbs generate movement, adjectives cast color and tone.

What, then, do post-Holocaust compositions look like? The first thing that must be said is that the Holocaust itself resists *any* attempt to capture it in terms of color, light, and probably even word. It constitutes a surd, a stubborn postmodern topos. What does it mean to exterminate a people? How do "ordinary men" become mass murderers? What was Auschwitz like? Where was God? Taylor quotes Edith Wyschogrod: "The holocaust is itself intrinsic to postmodern sensibility in that it forces thought to an impasse, into thinking a negation that cannot be thought and upon which thinking founders."[18] Readers of the post-Holocaust literature will recognize this and similar-sounding epistemological negations in the writings of Primo Levi, Elie Wiesel, Emil Fackenheim, Arthur Cohen, and countless others. Now clearly, I do not wish to enter into an entire philosophical debate about language, thought, and experience. For the purposes of this project, I have tried to respect the more limited claim that our "ordinary" language proves inadequate to convey the subjective impact of the Holocaust on its victims (what they experienced, perceived, and felt).

While the experience of the Holocaust itself resists representation, the same does not hold true for the post-Holocaust ruminations that have been the subject of this study. Rubenstein, Berkovits, and Fackenheim select antitheodic figures, order them within narrative frameworks, and apply casts of "coloring" or mood. They use as their backdrop the architecture of the death camp and the land of Israel.

To whom may we then compare them? In no sense do post-Holocaust compositions resemble the landscape depicted in Caspar David Friedreich's *Monk by the Sea* (1808–10). In this painting a sublime sky fills nearly the entire canvas. Its cloudscape is a formless mass virtually eclipsing the figure of a lone monk standing before the sea. The scene simultaneously threatens and inspires, but in the end we know that the monk is safe and will leave this place a "deeper" man. Nor can early twentieth-century modernism help us here. Post-Holocaust landscapes share nothing with the complex but harmoniously balanced totalities of a Kandinsky composition. Kandinsky evoked the kinetic luminosity created by the coming together of disembodied color, geometric shape, or biomorphic form. The contrast between nineteenth- and early-twentieth-century compositions and post-Holocaust thought could not be greater. Sublimity (in nature or in abstract form) withdraws before enlarged visions of Auschwitz. The eye stops dead; no theophany here. Post-Holocaust compositions work along the fissured surface of now-abandoned killing centers. The broken "lines" of the Musselmann (described to us by Levi) never come together to form luminous totalities.[19]

Following Taylor, I propose that post-Holocaust religious thought reflects the cavernous interiors and ruptured landscapes depicted in the paintings of Anselm Kiefer (1945–). His paintings exploring Germany's mythical and recent historical past had led many German critics to accuse him of glorifying the Nazi era. Less hostile viewers will have noted that this body of work elicits satire, irony, mourning, and melancholy. Kiefer offers deserted reenactments of the Nibelung myths. A memorial hall to "Germany's spiritual heroes" is empty. Photographs of the artist raising Nazi salutes in ridiculous tableaus appear anything but reverential. Monuments to Nazi neoclassical architecture resemble ruined crypts. In the 1980s Kiefer looked to ancient Near Eastern, biblical, and kabbalistic myths. Longing for the coming of a new world, Kiefer depicts Osiris and Isis, astral serpents, the Exodus from Egypt, Aaron's staff, seraphim, divine emanations, pillars of clouds, ladders to heaven, the city of Jerusalem. Like an alchemist, Kiefer attempts what he himself knows to be impossible. He seeks to rework materials drawn from ruined German landscapes into new formations. Using lead, emulsion, and gold leaf as media underscores this alchemy. Although the blasted figures that inhabit these latter compositions never come to harmonious balance in the present, they allude to something better.[20]

Two of Kiefer's paintings (discussed by Taylor in *Disfiguring*) interest me in particular. Both typify the intersection of the Holocaust and biblical myth in his work. The first is a 1983 piece called *Shulamite* (see figure 1). The painting's title refers to the Bible's Song of Songs and the black-haired woman of Paul Celan's *Todesfuge*. In one of Kiefer's later "books" also called *Shulamite* (1990), she appears under the figure of torn-out hair. However, in this painting the subject is a massive, brick crypt. The charred ceiling of the vault suggests a conflagration. In the back, seven dimly burning lights evoke the memory of that fire. The colors throughout are ashen. The lights do not illuminate. As Taylor notes, the canvas has brought the viewer into a monstrous oven.[21] A second piece offers a different landscape. *Flight from Egypt* (1984–85) is a massive black and white photograph of a desert landscape superimposed with brush strokes (see figure 2). A mountain rises to the right along the foot of which runs a road with no foreseeable end. An amorphous blue-gray cloud hovers over the scene. A glob of paint distending from the cloud and a golden thread break the line separating heaven from earth that runs across the canvas. According to Taylor, the desert represents desertion, ash, and night. Quoting Maurice Blanchot, he points to "the menacing proximity of a vague and empty outside, a neuter existence, null, without limit, sordid absence, a suffocating condensation where being ceaselessly perpetuates itself as nothingness."[22]

In my opinion Taylor overstates the desertion depicted in *Flight from Egypt*. His citation from Blanchot better fits the tone and texture of *Shulamite*. True, the road in Kiefer's desert landscape is empty of people and points to no definite redemption. The molten cloud may or may not threaten. So at one level, this desert scene does not comfort. However,

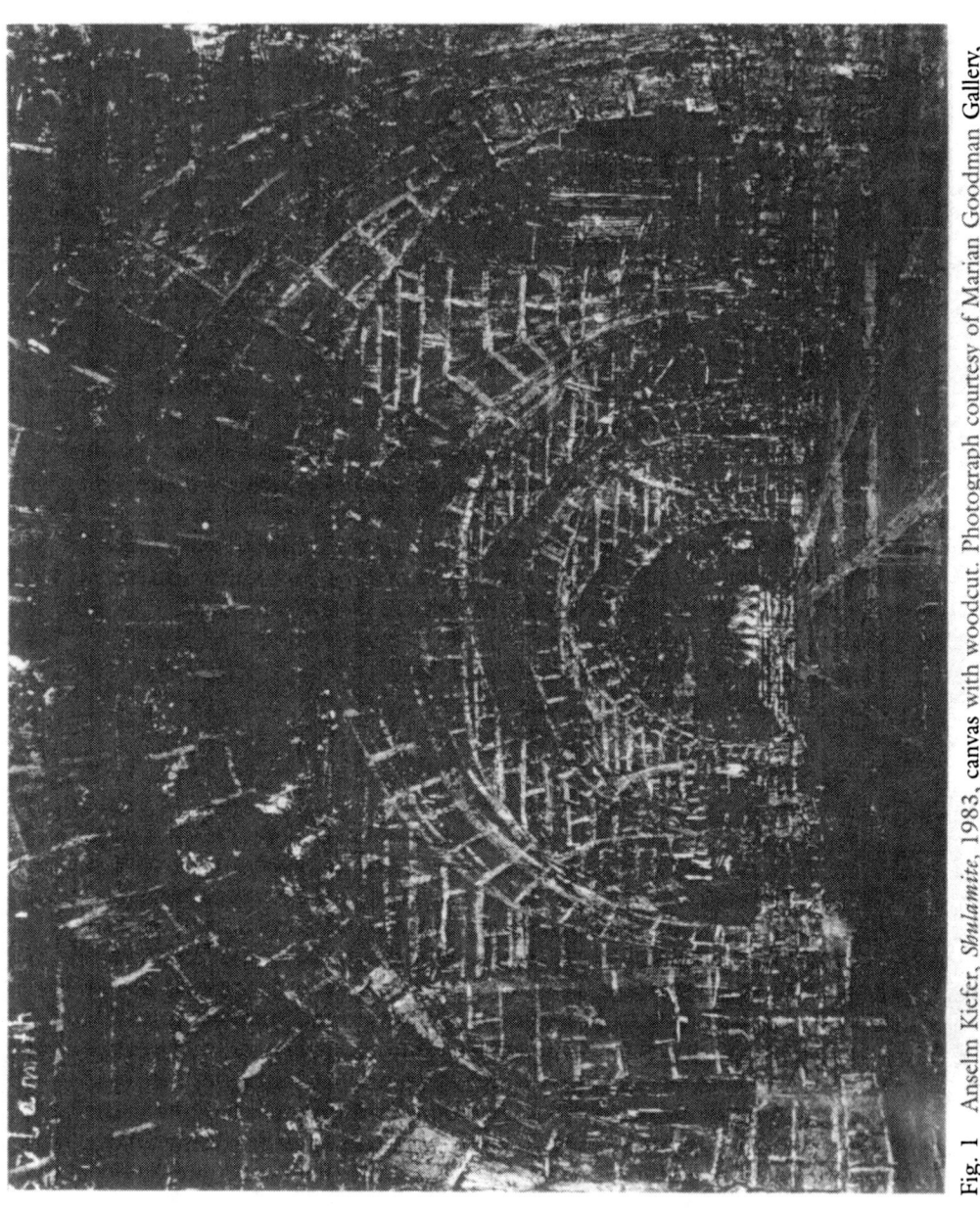

Fig. 1   Anselm Kiefer, *Shulamite*, 1983, canvas with woodcut. Photograph courtesy of Marian Goodman Gallery, New York.

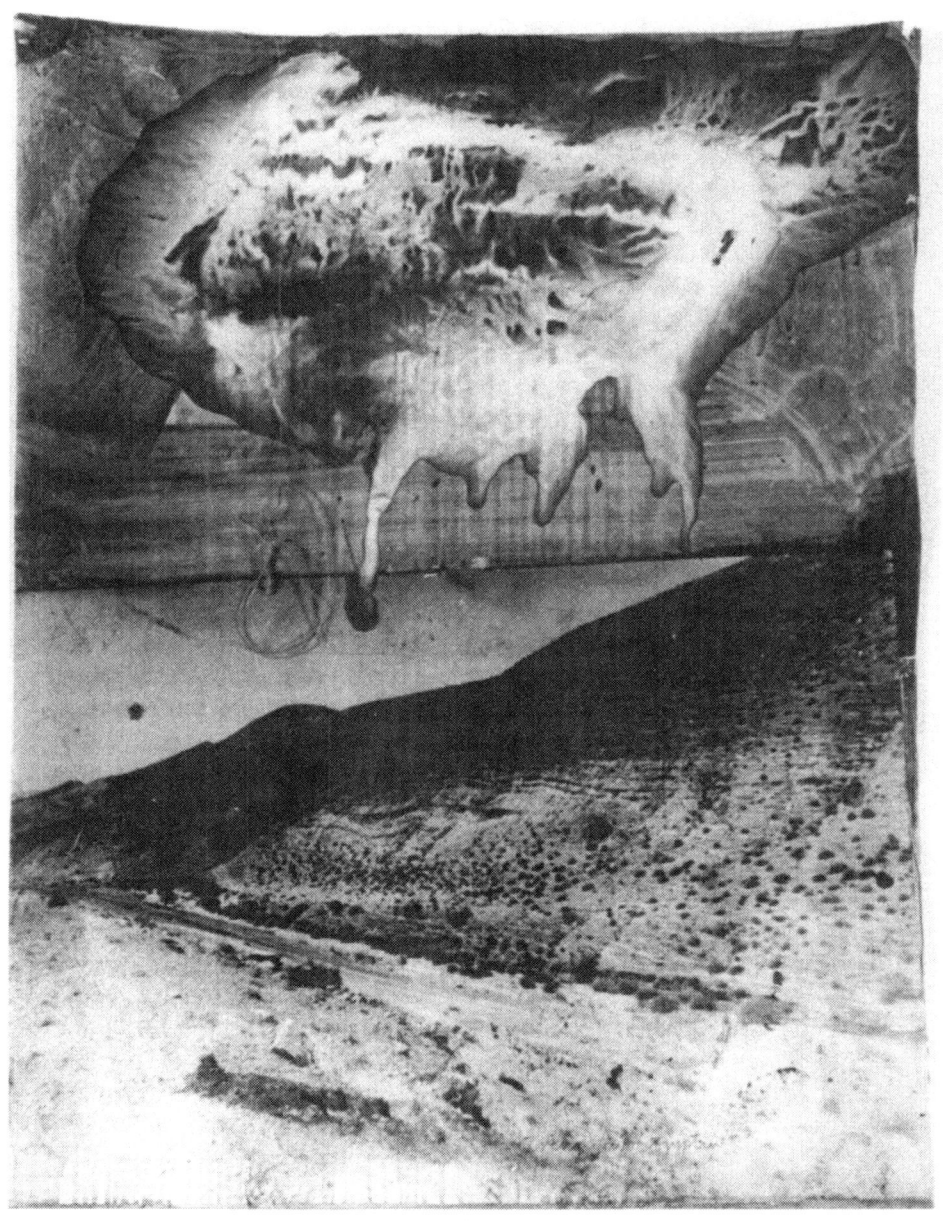

Fig. 2 Anselm Kiefer, 1984, *Flight from Egypt,* collage. The Denise and Andrew Saul Fund. Photograph © 1997. The Museum of Modern Art, New York.

looked at differently, *Flight from Egypt* presents an opening after the stark interiority presented in *Shulamite*.²³ After the grim certainty of the crematoria image, the uncertainty of this desert scene represents a small relief. The molten cloud, although amorphous and potentially dangerous, breaks the utter solitude in *Shulamite*. And while Taylor comments upon the gold thread (which may very well form into a noose), his analysis ignores the molten paint distending from the cloud's main body. Readers of the post-Holocaust literature might recognize in this figure a resemblance to Arthur Cohen's idea of the filament. According to Cohen, God exists neither in conjunction nor in disjunction with the historical: "I understand divine life to be rather a filament within the historical. . . . As filament, the divine element of the historical is a precarious conductor. . . . [Man]—not God—renders the filament of the divine incandescent or burns it out."²⁴ Following Cohen, we make neither too little nor too much of Kiefer's figure. A trace sign tentatively overflows into our desert scene. As it enters this world, the molten blue coloration has already blackened. Burnt out, the filament has lost its luster. It does not illuminate. Still, it points beyond itself. And even without this filament, the scene has opened. Unlike the claustrophobic site in *Shulamite*, here at least we find ourselves outside.²⁵

Combining these two paintings creates a diptych that forms the scene of post-Holocaust Jewish thought. At the most obvious level of meaning, the word *diptych* refers to a pair of pictures covering two separate panels, usually hinged. In our case, the first painting (*Shulamite*) memorializes the recent past; the second painting (*Flight from Egypt*) indicates an uncertain future. In the same way, Rubenstein, Berkovits, and Fackenheim hinged the memory of the Holocaust next to the figure of Jerusalem. True, the creation of the State of Israel in 1948 would seem to obviate metaphors of deserts and desertion. However, such metaphors continue to hold insofar as the inhabitants of any political entity remain vulnerable to the uncertainties of history. While the State is more secure in the 1990s, its survival seemed far more precarious throughout the 1960s and 1970s. Berkovits and Fackenheim (no less than Rubenstein) had no firm reason to trust that God would save the Jewish people from a second Holocaust. Such doubt at least reflected the panic prior to the Six Day War in 1967 and the nervous sense of disenchantment following the Yom Kippur War of 1973.

Two additional meanings to the term *diptych* draw out the scene of post-Holocaust Jewish thought still further. According to a second definition, the word *diptych* refers to a two-leaved wooden tablet. One side of the tablet lists the names of the living, the other names the dead for whom prayers and Mass are said. According to a third meaning, a diptych is a hinged two-leaved tablet used in ancient times for writing. Now undoubtedly, Jewish thinkers in the 1990s and into the next century are unlikely to center their thought around the Holocaust. One cannot expect it to exercise future generations with the same force that exercised Rubenstein, Berkovits, Fackenheim, and Kiefer. They belonged to the generation that first brought the Holocaust to the self-conscious forefront of the public memory. Nonetheless, I suspect that the theological diptychs they created will retain their use. Combining these last two meanings of the word diptych, post-Holocaust interiors and landscapes represent surfaces upon which Jewish thinkers into the next century might continue the process of writing after Auschwitz: orienting religious thought toward an uncertain future while remembering the dead, the technologies with which they were murdered, and the fragility of goodness. As Rubenstein warned in 1966, those who ignore the Holocaust but try to talk about the God, society, and self still run the risk of hopeless naïveté.

By and large, Jewish thinkers in the 1980s and 1990s have worked within the parameters of this diptych. We indicated above that contemporary thinkers like Arthur Green, Judith Plaskow, and Jonathan Sacks stand in an often-unacknowledged concord with Rubenstein, Berkovits, and Fackenheim. While space and time do not permit us to demonstrate this family resemblance, we conclude this study with a meditation on the work of Michael Wyschogrod. Green, Plaskow, Sacks, and others work within the shadow of the Holocaust, but not as radically as Wyschogrod. To my mind, Wyschogrod has crafted a theological composition that uniquely reflects and builds upon the post-Holocaust landscapes offered by Rubenstein, Berkovits, Fackenheim, and Kiefer. And he has done so while only rarely talking about the Holocaust itself.

In *The Body of Faith* (1983), Wyschogrod intentionally remythologizes the biblical doctrine of election. With the rabbis and Maimonides as his chief antagonists, Wyschogrod presents a profoundly "carnal" understanding of Jewish life. Carnality refers to the incarnation of God within a particular, flesh-and-blood, corporate body. It constitutes the imbedding of divinity within the physical and historical life of the Jewish people. Wyschogrod insists that Jewish thought attend to this carnality. First and foremost, this means rethinking God and God's relationship with this people. The God of Israel is an uncanny personage with whom covenant is fraught with uncertainty and danger. Carnality therefore means care for the people's body politic, its aesthetic creations, spiritual renewal, and ultimate redemption. Last, the "carnal" constitutes an epistemological category signifying that which eludes reason. The carnality of the Jewish people implies that so very much about it does not bear rational analysis: its God, its ritual life, its historical destiny. While Judaism does not abrogate the human right to ask questions, it nevertheless recognizes that reason's power to illuminate existence remains limited at best. According to Wyschogrod, "The reason of Israel is . . . a dark reason, a reason that remains entangled in the dark soil in which the roots of reason must remain implanted if it is not to drift off into the atmosphere."[26]

Wyschogrod's book is too rich a text to exhaust in the short time left to this study. We take this time only to juxtapose his thought with our imaginary diptych. The first point to note is that a definite aesthetic marks the discussion of carnality. "Shadow" and "darkness" represent the governing visual metphors that drive Wyschogrod's thought. Most notably, this "dark" aesthetic governs his depiction of the Temple cult. Echoing Rubenstein, Wyschogrod recounts the cathartic power pulsing through the biblical scene of animal sacrifice. The animal writhing in its own blood dramatically points to our own mortality. In Wyschogrod's rendering, the Bible has thrown up a bridge between slaughter and the holy by bringing horror into the house of God.[27] Wyschogrod completes this scene further along in the text. Commenting upon the binding of Isaac, he writes: "The love that Israel receives from God cries out for a return, for the giving by Israel to God of its substance, as God gives of his. And this giving is self-sacrifice, in some form."[28] Without a Temple cult, the people of Israel itself becomes the sacrificial victim for the sanctification of God's name (*kiddush ha-Shem*). The social and historical fact that Jewish existence inevitably invites aggression Wyschogrod calls a "dreadful truth." He writes, "If there is no need for sacrament in Judaism, it is because the people of Israel in whose flesh the presence of God makes itself felt in the world becomes the sacrament."[29] In other words, the near sacrifice of Isaac and the sacrificial blood within the Temple precincts prefigure slaughter throughout the Diaspora and into the twentieth century.

This picture of cultic (and political) exile brings us deep into the vaulted crypt in *Shulamite*. Kiefer's memorial can help us set the ultimate scene for Wyschogrod's discussion. The effect of combining [1] the *akeidah*, [2] the Temple cult, and [3] *kiddush ha-Shem* leads the religious imagination directly from the open sky of Moriah, through the perimeter of a ruined Temple, and into a radically dead space. In turn, Wyschogrod's reflections upon the past (and he clearly includes the recent past) provide discursive depth to Kiefer's visual creation. They suggest a further set of archetypal associations with which to trace the burnt-out crypt in Kiefer's painting. Horror magnifies horror. The *Shulamite* heightens the truly dreadful character of Wyschogrod's image. At the same time, associating a charred, empty crypt with divine carnality makes Kiefer's image all the more appalling.

Wyschogrod's text leads its reader from the memory of this terrible place to the tentative and uncertain opening of Kiefer's *Flight from Egypt*.

Like the desert road in Kiefer's painting, Wyschogrod's text is forward looking. Both point toward the future. But in both Wyschogrod and Kiefer's work, the path toward that future is obscured. While the temporal structure of Jewish myth tries to assure us that redemption awaits at its terminus, how many terrors lie in wait along the way? According to Wyschogrod, Jewish thought promotes a dark knowledge about a future that it does not know. The person who lives in dialogue with the God of Israel knows that he or she has no security other than in that dialogue.[30] By now we know from Wyschogrod's reading of the *akeidah* that this relationship involves love but precludes safety. Trying to explain why theology has not traditionally enjoyed the same centrality in Judaism as in Christianity, Wyschogrod points to the carnality of Israel's election. Theory can encompass teachings, not the life of a people. And since the destiny of this people remains incomplete, it remains insecure.[31]

So far, Wyschogrod's thought works within the post-Holocaust parameters set by Rubenstein, Berkovits, and Fackenheim. On one point, however, *The Body of Faith* stands in contrast with this discourse. In our view, Wyschogrod's book ends on a messianic hope that is a little too bright for the landscape that he himself describes. His messianism is maximalist, expecting that unexpected moment when a divine act will bring history to an apocalyptic climax. According to Wyschogrod, this act will redeem a broken cosmos by mending the spiritual and political ruptures that rend it.[32] However, by his own accounts Wyschogrod has no right to conclude so confidently. Wyschogrod himself has argued that the future envisioned by Judaism is not assured by the nature of things but rather hinges upon a divine promise.[33] Surely Wyschogrod must know how thin this promise appears in the twentieth century. Perhaps God has seen it proper to protect the Jewish people. But why should it be God who protects now when God did not protect then? And that God protects now does not ensure that God will continue to do so in the near or distant future. In my view, Rubenstein, Berkovits, and Fackenheim better expressed the restless uncertainty that Wyschogrod himself shares throughout most of *The Body of Faith*. For Rubenstein, death constituted the only escape from the vicissitudes of life. Berkovits ended *With God in Hell* with Yossel Rakover wrestling with God. Fackenheim's *God's Presence in History* concluded with notes of longing, anger, and defiance. At the very best, the confidence that Wyschogrod has placed at the end of his book in a divine promise seems unevenly earned. But we suspect that Wyschogrod knows this all too well.

One does not begrudge any attempt to find a good that might illuminate the second half of our post-Holocaust diptych. Rubenstein, Berkovits, and Fackenheim also recognized good after Auschwitz. However, the tentative goods they identified belong to this-world and its present, not to a still-uncertain future. The fragility of good represents a theme that runs throughout the post-Holocaust literature. Its authors pointed to the survival of the Jewish people, to its rebirth in the State of Israel, to Jewish life and ritual. These goods remain vulnerable, perpetually at risk, never taken for granted. They lack the power to transform the very order of our moral world. Wyschogrod might have made his messianic future-scape more subtle and less secure by adopting a similar circumspection. There is of course no ultimate way to adjudicate conflicting claims about this-worldly goods and apocalyptic good, except to say that verifying claims about the former involves a lot less waiting.

It should be obvious by now that the Holocaust has been left behind in the wake of its memory. *Flight from Egypt* already points to the future. *Shulamite* remains but an imperfect memorial to the past. These and the theological landscapes that I have described throughout this study are *post*-Holocaust. They surround a lived past that I myself cannot imagine. Those of us untouched directly by the event (whether by geography or birth) have nothing more than the memories and memoirs of survivors, the emerging historical record, and documentary images and dialogues. When the last survivor dies, these will be as close as we get to the lived experience of the event itself. To be sure, the children of survivors carry their own traumas. However, even the best-informed attempts to remember and draw conclusions from the testimonies of this event will miss the mark. This includes my own study of theodicy and antitheodicy. For that I am sorry. I have tried my best to address insoluble theological problems created by the catastrophic suffering of other people.

NOTES

INTRODUCTION
MODERNITY SURPASSED

The source of the epigraph is Marc Chagall's preface to Abraham Sutzkever, *Siberia*, 6–7.

1. Zygmunt Bauman, *Modernity and the Holocaust*, x.

2. Jean-François Lyotard, *The Differend*, 56–58; *Heidegger and "the jews"*; Bauman, *Modernity and The Holocaust*; Edith Wyschogrod, *Spirit in Ashes*; Anthony Giddens, *The Consequences of Modernity*, 7–10, 124–34, 151, 172–73.

3. The term *antitheodicy* was first suggested to me by the subtitle of Victor Turner's *The Ritual Process: Structure & Anti-Structure*. Many months later I ran across the term in John Hick's response to the "protest theodicy" of the Protestant theologian John Roth. Hick briefly suggested that it would be better to call such a response an antitheodicy. However, Hick's use of this term was incidental. He did not develop it further. (It is worth noting that Roth's own antitheodic reflections were powerfully influenced by the writings of Elie Wiesel and Richard Rubenstein).

4. There are ample studies of "Jewish modernism" on the part of literary critics and art historians who have examined the work of Bialik, Agnon, Scholem, Kafka, Benjamin, and Chagall. To date, however, no scholar has applied this term to modern Jewish theologians like Buber, Baeck, Rosenzweig, Heschel, and Soloveitchik. This belongs to a future study.

5. See Nathan Glazer, *American Judaism*, 172; Richard Rubenstein, *After Auschwitz*, 1st ed., x; Eliezer Berkovits, *Faith after the Holocaust*, 67. Cf. A. B. Yehoshua's citation of Saul Friedlander's formulation of the psychological thesis in *Between Right and Right*, 3. Readers should keep in mind that Rubenstein published two editions of *After Auschwitz*, one in 1966 and the second in 1992. The second edition judiciously selects from the 1966 version of *After Auschwitz* while adding substantially revised articles and essays published under separate cover. As a result, I have taken care throughout these notes to distinguish between the first and second editions.

6. To avoid gender-biased generalizing, one of my recourses throughout this book has been to put the generic term *man* within quotation marks.

7. David Roskies, *Against the Apocalypse*, 241.

8. Ibid., 221.

9. Ibid., 196.

10. Eliezer Berkovits, *Faith after the Holocaust*, 166.

CHAPTER ONE
THEODICY AND ITS OTHERS

1. Clifford Geertz, *The Interpretation of Culture*, 10.

2. Arnold Eisen, "Covenant," in Arthur Cohen and Paul Mendes-Flohr, eds., *Contemporary Jewish Religious Thought*, 107–8.

3. Anson Laytner, *Arguing with God*; David Stern, *Parables in Midrash*; David Kraemer, *Responses to Suffering in Classical Rabbinic Literature*.

4. Fyodor Dostoyevsky, *The Brothers Karamazov*, 226.

5. John Hick, *Evil and the God of Love*, 256.

6. David Ray Griffin, *God, Power, and Evil*, 12.

7. Ibid., 268–69, 273.

8. Philip Hefner, "Is Theodicy a Question of Power?" 89; see also Philip Hefner, "God and Chaos: The Demiurge versus the Urgrund"; Frederick Sontag, *The God of Evil*, 4–5, 111–12.

9. John Hick, *Evil and the God of Love*, 30.

10. Anthony Flew, "Divine Omnipotence and Human Freedom," 157.

11. H. J. McCloskey, *God and Evil*, 65.

12. Arthur Green, "The Role of Jewish Mysticism in a Contemporary Theology of Judaism," 10–14.

13. Eliezer Berkovits, *With God in Hell*, 128.

14. Pearl Benisch, *To Vanquish the Dragon*, 347.

15. Peter Berger, *The Sacred Canopy*, 54.

16. Clifford Geertz, *The Interpretation of Culture*.

17. Max Weber, *Sociology of Religion*, 58–59.

18. Peter Berger and Thomas Luckmann, *The Social Construction of Reality*, 101–2. Cf. 97–102.

19. Peter Berger, *The Sacred Canopy*, 29.

20. Ibid., 3–28.

21. Arnold Eisen, *The Chosen People in America*.

22. Irving Greenberg, "Voluntary Covenant," 35.

23. See David Roskies, *Against the Apocalypse*; Alan Mintz, *Hurban*; Terrence W. Tilley, *The Evils of Theodicy*, 1, 85–86; Kenneth Surin, *Theology and the Problem of Evil*, 8–19; Larry Bouchard, *Tragic Method and Tragic Theology*, 228.

24. David Tracy, *Plurality and Ambiguity*, 11.

25. Judith Plaskow, *Standing Again at Sinai*, 25.

26. Mary Daly, "After the Death of God the Father," 57.

27. Blu Greenberg, *On Women and Judaism*, 105–23.

28. Genesis Rabbah 22:9.

29. Numbers Rabbah 14:6.

30. Exodus Rabbah 5:22.

31. Jacques Derrida, *The Gift of Death*, 60–61.

32. Eliezer Berkovits, *With God in Hell*, 124.

33. Ibid., 124–25.

34. Ibid., 117–18, 128–31.

35. Daniel Boyarin, *Intertextuality and the Reading of Midrash*, 12.

36. Ibid., 39.

CHAPTER TWO
ANTI/THEODICY

1. Richard Rubenstein, *After Auschwitz*, 2d ed., 157.

2. Eliezer Berkovits, *With God in Hell*, 118.

3. Rubenstein, *After Auschwitz*, 1st ed., 127.

4. Ephraim Urbach, *The Sages*, 515–16.

5. Mieke Bal, *Death and Dissymmetry*, 16–17.

6. Ibid., 5. Cf. 20–21.

7. Recent scholars have seen the presence of antitheodic thought in classical Jewish texts without naming it. See David Kraemer, *Responses to Suffering in Classical Rabbinic Literature*; David Roskies, *Against the Apocalypse*; David Stern, *Parables in Midrash*, 130–145, cf. 145–51; Anson Laytner, *Arguing with God*. However, none of these scholars have systematized their thoughts around a formal philosophical signifier.

8. Laytner, *Arguing with God* pays particular attention to the lawsuit motif in his exposition of antitheodic thought in traditional Jewish texts.

9. Deuteronomy 11:13–21.

10. See Moshe Weinfeld, *Deuteronomy and the Deuteronomic School*, 307.

11. Gerhard von Rad, *Deuteronomy*, 198.

12. G. Ernest Wright, *The Interpreters Bible. Book of Deuteronomy*, 516.

13. Sifre 307 (emphasis added). Please note that in this instance I am respecting Hammer's transliteration of the Hebrew letter "tzadi" as Ṣ. My own transliterations that appear throughout the text will render the Hebrew as *tz* (as in *tzadik*).

14. Avot 2:6.

15. Shabbat 55a. See Solomon Schechter's discussion of R. Ammi in "The Doctrine of Divine Retribution," 362–79.

16. Avot de Rabbi Nathan, #38.

17. Ibid., #2.

18. Ephraim E. Urbach, *The Sages*, 514.

19. Avot 4:16.

20. Adolph Buchler, *Studies in Sin and Atonement in the Rabbinic Literature of the First Century*, 170–74, 319–74. Michael Fishbane, *The Kiss of God*, 91.

21. Tanḥuma, Lech Lecha, #10.

22. See Michael Fishbane, *The Kiss of God*.

23. Adolph Buchler, *Studies in Sin and Atonement*, 171–72.

24. Genesis Rabbah 32:3; cf. Genesis Rabbah 34:2, 40:3, 55:2; and Song of Songs Rabbah II:16:2.

25. Sanhedrin 101a.

26. Berakoth 5a.

27. Ibid.

28. Avot 1:3.

29. Avot 6:1.

30. Avot 4:2.

31. Deuteronomy 6:5.

32. Berakoth 61b.

33. Sifre 43.

34. Alan Mintz, *Hurban*, 77.

35. G. Ernest Wright, "The Lawsuit of God: A Form-Critical Study of Deuteronomy 32," 47.

36. Norman Habel, *The Book of Job*, 187–88. Bruce Zuckerman, *Job the Silent*, chap. 10.

37. Cited in Zuckerman, *Job the Silent*, 104.
38. Ibid., 116.
39. Edwin M. Good, *In Turns of Tempest*, 375.
40. Habel, *The Book of Job*, 576, 582–83.
41. Good, *In Turns of Tempest*, 375–78, cf. 170.
42. James 5:11.
43. Baba Bathra 16a–b.
44. Alan Mintz, *Hurban*, 52–53. Cf. 35–36.
45. Lamentations Rabbah, proem 24.
46. Mintz, *Hurban*, 61–62.
47. Lamentations Rabbah, proem 24.
48. Max Kadushin, *The Rabbinic Mind*, 215–17.
49. Roskies, *Against the Apocalypse*, 34.
50. Deuteronomy 32:20.
51. Deuteronomy 32:19–20, (JPS 1985).
52. Psalms 44:24–25.
53. Genesis Rabbah 36:1.
54. Louis Finkelstein, *The Pharisees*, 260.
55. Genesis Rabbah 22:9.
56. Exodus Rabbah 30:11.
57. Exodus Rabbah 31:10.
58. Pesikta Rabbati 8:3.
59. Pesikta de Rab Kahana 15:4.
60. Lamentations Rabbah 1:37
61. Numbers Rabbah 14:6.
62. Exodus Rabbah 5:22, 6:1, 6:2.
63. David Hartman, *A Living Covenant*, 187.
64. Berakoth 5b.
65. Baba Metzia 58b.
66. Berakoth 17a.
67. Avot 4:15.
68. Baba Bathra 16a.
69. Menahoth 29b.
70. Yomah 22b.
71. Urbach, *The Sages*, 519; Fishbane, *The Kiss of God*, 115.
72. Voltaire, *Philosophical Dictionary*, 74.

CHAPTER THREE
THEODICIES

1. Eliezer Schweid, *To Declare That God Is Upright*, 9; cf. 42.
2. Richard Rubenstein, *After Auschwitz*, 1st ed., x.
3. Emil Fackenheim, *To Mend the World*, 195.
4. Gershom Scholem, "Revelation and Tradition as Religious Categories in Judaism," 282.
5. Scholem, "Martin Buber's Conception of Judaism," 159.
6. Steven Kepnes, *The Text as Thou*, 135–36.

7. Ibid., 121.

8. Martin Buber, *The Prophetic Faith*, 1.

9. Ibid., 171–72.

10. Buber, "The Election of Israel: A Biblical Inquiry," 85–86.

11. Buber, *The Prophetic Faith*, 187.

12. Ibid., 192.

13. Ibid., 197.

14. Ibid., 201.

15. Hermann Cohen, *Religion of Reason*, 149. Cf. 229, 233–35, 253.

16. Ibid., 266–67. Compare also how the Suffering Servant figured in the thought of Kaufman Kohler whose *Jewish Theology* was (like Cohen's *Religion of Reason*) published in 1919.

17. Buber, *The Prophetic Faith*, 234.

18. Buber, *Eclipse of God*, 119.

19. Ibid., 36.

20. Buber, *Israel and the World*, 82.

21. Ibid., 77.

22. Emil Fackenheim, *To Mend the World*, 196–97. See Chapter 6 below.

23. Fackenheim, *God's Presence in History*, 61.

24. Rubenstein, *After Auschwitz*, 1st ed., 245. See Chapter 4 below.

25. Buber, *On Judaism*, 214.

26. Ibid., 215.

27. Ibid., 223.

28. Ibid., 224–25.

29. Buber, *I and Thou*, 168.

30. Edward Kaplan, "Heschel's Poetics of Religious Thinking," 115.

31. Abraham Joshua Heschel, *A Passion for Truth*, 269.

32. Ibid., 264.

33. Ibid., 280.

34. Ibid., 298.

35. Ibid., 302–3.

36. Heschel, *Man Is Not Alone*, 151.

37. Note, however, how Heschel closed this chapter. Once again, complaint surreptitiously shifted back to God. Without explanation or comment, Heschel cited Psalm 44 in full! The psalmist prods a sleeping God. He badgers and rebukes. Himself a master stylist, Heschel never challenged God in his own voice. He accused God, but only under a clumsy guise of rhetorical device and biblical citation. In fact, no bridge eased the shift from Heschel's condemnation of human iniquity to his citation of Psalm 44. It is an entirely abrupt transition, obliquely indicating how Heschel shied away from the very complaint slipping into his own discourse.

38. Charles Taylor, *Sources of the Self*, 12–13. Strangely, however, the Holocaust does not appear in Taylor's account.

39. Abraham Joshua Heschel, *Man Is Not Alone*, 185. Heschel repeats this claim in *God in Search of Man*, 369. See Charles Taylor, *Sources of the Self*, x.

40. Heschel, "The Meaning of This Hour," 148.

41. Heschel, *Man Is Not Alone*, 283.

42. Ibid., 286–87. Heschel took this phraseology directly from the mishnaic ethical treatise Pirkei Avot 4:16, where R. Jacob says: "This world is like a lobby before the world to come. Prepare yourself in the lobby so that you may enter the banquet hall." It remains unclear, however, whether Heschel's "temple of light" was otherworldly.
43. Heschel, *God in Search of Man*, 367.
44. Heschel, *A Passion for Truth*, 273.
45. Heschel, *Israel: An Echo in Eternity*, 98.
46. Heschel, *The Prophets*, 283.
47. Heschel, *Israel: An Echo of Eternity*, 113.
48. Ibid., 137.
49. Edward Kaplan, "Mysticism and Despair in Abraham J. Heschel's Religious Thought," 37.
50. Ibid., 47.
51. Joseph Soloveitchik, "Kol Dodi Dofek," 53.
52. Ibid., 52–53.
53. Ibid., 54.
54. Ibid., 54–56.
55. Ibid., 53–54.
56. Ibid., 56.
57. Ibid., 51.
58. Job 1:1.
59. Soloveitchik, "Kol Dodi Dofek," 58–62.
60. Ibid., 63.
61. Ibid., 66–68.
62. Ibid., 69.
63. Ibid., 76.
64. Mordecai Kaplan, *The Meaning of God in Modern Jewish Religion*, 72–73.
65. Ibid., 72.
66. Ibid., 71–76.
67. Ibid., 132–33.
68. Eliezer Berkovits, *Major Themes in Modern Philosophies of Judaism*, 158–59.
69. Ibid., 173–78.
70. Kaplan, *The Meaning of God*, 144. Cf. 136–44.
71. Ibid., 139–40.
72. Ibid., 140.
73. Mordecai Kaplan, *Questions Jews Ask*, 119–20.
74. Berkovits, *Major Themes in Modern Philosophies of Judaism*, 155–56.
75. Kaplan, *The Meaning of God*, 63.
76. Ibid., 63–64.
77. Friedrich Nietzsche, *The Gay Science*, #299.
78. Nietzsche, *Beyond Good and Evil*, #108.
79. *Sifre to Deuteronomy*, #43.
80. Nietzsche, *The Gay Science*, #326.
81. Steven Katz, *Post-Holocaust Dialogues*, 127–28.

CHAPTER FOUR
"HITLER'S ACCOMPLICE"?!

1. Richard L. Rubenstein, 1st ed. *After Auschwitz*, 68.
2. The "literature" on Rubenstein typically consists of potshots against him. Welcome exceptions can be found in Steven Katz, *Post-Holocaust Dialogues*, chapters 4 and 5; Michael Berenbaum, *The Vision of the Void*, chapter 7; William E. Kaufman, *Contemporary Jewish Philosophies*, chapter 5; and Daniel Cohn-Sherbok, *Holocaust Theology*, chapter 7.
3. Arthur E. Green, "A Response to Richard Rubenstein," 26.
4. Robert Gordis, "A Cruel God or None at All—Is There No Choice?" 278.
5. Katz, *Post-Holocaust Dialogues*, 198.
6. See Will Herberg's denigration of "Greco-Oriental spirituality" in *Judaism and Modern Man*, 47–66. Cf. Heschel's critique of Greek nature paganism in *God in Search of Man*, 88–98. See also the general importance accorded to "History" in the works of Heschel, Herberg, and the early Arthur Cohen.
7. Jacob Neusner, *Understanding Jewish Theology*, 184.
8. Katz, *Post-Holocaust Dialogues*, 184–85.
9. David Hume, *Dialogues Concerning Natural Religion*, 66.
10. Rubenstein, *After Auschwitz*, 1st ed., 86–87.
11. Ibid., 58.
12. Richard L. Rubenstein and John K. Roth, *Approaches to Auschwitz*, 301.
13. Peter Berger, *The Sacred Canopy*, 46.
14. Rubenstein, *After Auschwitz*, 2d. ed., 158.
15. Rubenstein, *After Auschwitz*, 1st ed., 46–58.
16. Rubenstein, *Approaches to Auschwitz*, 309–10. Rubenstein's use of the third person in this quote is explained by the fact that *Approaches to Auschwitz* was coauthored with John Roth. The chapter from which this passage was taken includes a discussion about Rubenstein in the third person. The material, however, was written by Rubenstein and much of it was republished in the second edition of *After Auschwitz*.
17. Rubenstein, *After Auschwitz*, 1st ed., 46.
18. Rubenstein, *The Religious Imagination*, 124.
19. Rubenstein, *After Auschwitz*, 1st ed., 46.
20. Rubenstein, *Morality and Eros*, 40.
21. Rubenstein, *The Religious Imagination*, 122.
22. Eliezer Schweid, *From Ruin to Salvation*, 10–14.
23. Deuteronomy 32:4–5.
24. Rubenstein, *After Auschwitz*, 1st ed., chapter 14. See also 151–52.
25. Ibid., 244–45.
26. Rubenstein, *After Auschwitz*, 2nd ed., xii.
27. Rubenstein, *After Auschwitz*, 1st ed., 130.
28. Ibid., 136.
29. Ibid., 139–40.
30. Judith Plaskow, *Standing Again at Sinai*, 149.
31. Rubenstein, *Morality and Eros*, 186. Cf. 185–89.
32. Rubenstein, *After Auschwitz*, 2nd ed., 297.

33. Ibid., xiii.

34. Ibid., 174.

35. Rubenstein, *After Auschwitz*, 1st ed., 44.

36. Steven Katz, *Post-Holocaust Dialogues*, 200.

37. Richard L. Rubenstein, *After Auschwitz*, 1st ed., 19.

38. Rubenstein, *Morality and Eros*, 40, 32–41.

39. Rubenstein, *After Auschwitz*, 1st ed., 124–26.

40. Paul Tillich, *Systematic Theology*, part I, 156. Cf. 156–59, 235–38.

41. Richard L. Rubenstein, *Morality and Eros*, 185.

42. Rubenstein, *After Auschwitz*, 1st ed., 80.

43. Ibid., 125.

44. Ibid., 124–25. Cf. 128.

45. Richard L. Rubenstein, *Morality and Eros*, 192–94. Cf. Rubenstein, *After Auschwitz*, 1st ed., 79–80, 141.

46. Rubenstein, *After Auschwitz*, 1st ed., 198.

47. Rubenstein, *Morality and Eros*, 190–91 (emphasis added).

48. Ibid., pp. 195–96 (emphasis added). Cf. Rubenstein, *After Auschwitz*, 1st ed., 182–83, 198, 209, 220, 260.

49. Rubenstein, *After Auschwitz*, 1st ed., 141 (emphasis added).

50. Walter Kaufmann, *Nietzsche*, 282–83.

51. Friedrich Nietzsche, *The Gay Science*, #341.

52. Rubenstein, *After Auschwitz*, 1st ed., 263–64.

53. Rubenstein, *After Auschwitz*, 2nd ed., 200.

54. Ibid., 174.

55. Katz, *Post-Holocaust Dialogue*, 199–200.

56. Rubenstein, *The Religious Imagination*, 21.

57. Ibid., 150. Cf 147–50.

58. Ibid., 171.

59. Ibid., 171–82.

60. Ibid., 183.

61. Van Austin Harvey, *The Historian and the Believer*, especially chapters 1 and 4.

62. Rubenstein, *The Religious Imagination*, 41–42.

63. Shabbat 55a.

64. David Kraemer, *Responses to Suffering in Classical Rabbinic Literature*, 187.

65. Rubenstein, *The Religious Imagination*, 47.

66. Ibid., 128.

67. Ibid., 130.

68. Ibid., 136–37.

69. Rubenstein, *After Auschwitz*, 1st ed., 87.

70. Ibid., 153.

71. Rubenstein, *The Religious Imagination*, xvi–xvii.

72. Rubenstein, "Job and Auschwitz," 422.

73. Ibid., 423.

74. Ibid., 426, 431–35. Rubenstein makes this bald claim on the basis of

Bruno Bettelheim and Eli Cohen's psychoanalytic studies of concentration camp life.

75. Ibid., 435–36.

76. Rubenstein, *The Age of Triage*, 132. See also Rubenstein, *The Cunning of History*, 88–90.

77. David Biale, *Gershom Scholem. Kabbalah and Counter-History*, 7.

78. Rubenstein, *After Auschwitz*, 1st ed., 230, cf. 219, 247–48. See also *Morality and Eros*, 185; *Approaches to Auschwitz*, 311, 314; *After Auschwitz*, 2nd ed., 303–4; "Jewish Theology and the Current World Situation," 25.

79. Daniel C. Matt, "Ayin: The Concept of Nothingness in Jewish Mysticism," 121–59.

80. Rubenstein, *After Auschwitz*, 1st ed., 110.

81. Ibid., 124.

82. Ibid., chap. 5.

83. Ibid., 222.

84. Ibid., 225.

85. In contrast to this reading of Leviticus, see Jacob Milgrom, *The Anchor Bible. Leviticus 1–16*, 44–45. Milgrom argues that the priestly cult represented a process by which the Israelites weaned themselves from pagan beliefs in malevolent demons. Human sin, not demons, carry impurity in the Book of Leviticus. A similar ethical impulse motivates Leviticus's prescribed sacrifices, its understanding of guilt, and its concern for the poor. But even Milgrom admits that "Israel's battle against demonic beliefs was not won in one stroke" and alludes to the story of divine fire consuming Aaron's sons Nadav and Abihu at the altar.

86. Milgrom, *The Anchor Bible. Leviticus 1–16*, 599.

87. Harold Bloom, *The Anxiety of Influence*, 30.

88. Bloom, *A Map of Misreading*, 200.

89. Bloom, *The Anxiety of Influence*, 141.

CHAPTER FIVE
DO I BELONG TO THE RACE OF WORDS?

1. For discussions of ultra-Orthodox response to suffering, see Eliezer Schweid, *From Ruin to Salvation*; Gershon Greenberg, "Orthodox Theological Responses to Kristallnacht: Chayyim Ozer Grodensky ('Achiezer') and Elchonon Wasserman," "Myth and Catastrophe in Simha Elberg's Religious Thought," and "Redemption after Holocaust according to Mahane Israel-Lubavitch 1940–1945."

2. Eliezer Berkovits, *Man and God*, 259. See also Pesach Schindler, *Hasidic Responses to the Holocaust in the Light of Hasidic Thought*.

3. Ibid., 268.

4. Berkovits, *With God in Hell*, 128.

5. Charles M. Raffel, "Eliezer Berkovits," 6–8, 12.

6. A short list of some of the best writings on Berkovits would include Steven Katz, *Post Holocaust Dialogues*; Dan Cohn-Sherbok, *Holocaust Theology*; Michael

Berenbaum, *The Vision of the Void*; and Eliezer Schweid, *Wrestling until Daybreak*, 172, 180–82, 190. Only Schweid has suggested that Berkovits's traditionalism may have been more imagined than real.

7. Berkovits, *Faith after the Holocaust*, 90.

8. Berkovits, *Crisis and Faith*, 158.

9. Steven Katz, *Post-Holocaust Dialogues*, 270.

10. Berkovits, *Faith after the Holocaust*, 1.

11. Ibid., 3.

12. Ibid.

13. Ibid., 3–4.

14. Ibid., 5–6.

15. Berkovits, *Not in Heaven*, 104–5.

16. For discussions of women and Halakha, see Berkovits, *Crisis and Faith*, chap. 7. Cf. his *Jewish Women in Time and Torah* and also *Not in Heaven*. For a discussion of non-Orthodox conversions, see *Crisis and Faith*, chap. 8.

17. Berkovits discusses Klal Yisrael and Ahavat Yisrael in *Crisis and Faith*, 124–26, 171–76 and in *Not in Heaven*, 106–12.

18. Berkovits, *Faith after the Holocaust*, 68.

19. Ibid., 85.

20. Ibid., 101.

21. Ibid., 105–6 (emphasis added).

22. Ibid., 109.

23. Katz, *Post-Holocaust Dialogues*, 277–78. Dan Cohn-Sherbok, *Holocaust Theology*, 65–66. Eliezer Schweid, *Wrestling until Daybreak* 181–82.

24. Berkovits, *Faith after the Holocaust*, 111.

25. David Biale, *Power and Powerlessness in Jewish History*, 6.

26. Berkovits, *Faith after the Holocaust*, 113 (emphasis is mine).

27. Ibid., 136 (emphasis mine).

28. Ibid., 152 (emphasis is mine).

29. Ibid., 156.

30. Alan Berger, "Holocaust and History: A Theological Reflection," 204. Amos Funkenstein, "Theological Interpretations of the Holocaust," 71.

31. Berkovits, *Crisis and Faith*, 161.

32. Berkovits, *With God in Hell*, vii–ix.

33. Ibid., 76–77.

34. Ibid., 105–12.

35. Rakover's testimony can be found in Berkovits, *With God in Hell*, 128–31.

36. Ibid., chap. 5.

37. Ibid., 63.

38. Baba Batra 16a.

39. Berkovits, *Faith after the Holocaust*, 4. Cf. 69–70.

40. Ibid., 69.

41. Ibid.

42. Berkovits, *Not in Heaven*, 104–6; Berkovits, *Crisis and Faith*, 118–19.

43. Berkovits, *Not in Heaven*, 30. Cf. 28–32.

44. Ibid., 67. Cf. 64–70.

45. Berkovits, *Man and God*, 251.

46. The only exception to this rule is the *onan*—a mourner who has not yet buried his or her dead.

47. Berkovits, *Faith after the Holocaust*, 100–101.

48. Ibid., 102–3.

49. Ibid., 103–5.

50. Berkovits, *With God in Hell*, 118.

51. Joseph Soloveitchik, *The Rav Speaks*, 193–99.

52. Harold Bloom, *A Map of Misreading*, 62.

53. A paper could be written about Berkovits's own post-Holocaust "paganism" that details his use of Heidegger, Albert Camus, Ivan Karamazov, and the ideas of hubris and nemesis.

54. Bloom, *The Anxiety of Influence*, 141.

55. See Zvi Kolitz, ed., *Yossel Rakover Speaks to God*.

CHAPTER SIX
WHY IS THE WORLD TODAY NOT WATER?

1. The symposium first appeared in *Judaism* (16:3, summer 1967). Fackenheim has since republished his response in *The Jewish Return into History*, 19–24.

2. Fackenheim, *The Jewish Return into History*, 22.

3. Michael Wyschogrod, "Faith and the Holocaust," 286–94.

4. Fackenheim, *Metaphysics and Historicity*, 2.

5. Ibid., 68. Cf 67–69.

6. Fackenheim, *The Religious Dimension in Hegel's Thought*, 241–42. For the terms *post-Christian* and *postmodern*, see 235–36. Later, Fackenheim was to replace them with the term *post-Holocaust*. This early use of the term *postmodern* shares the same sense of rupture and fragmentation with which it has since come to be associated among broader circles.

7. Fackenheim, *Quest for Past and Future*, 205.

8. Ibid., 71.

9. Ibid., 52–65.

10. Ibid., 27.

11. Ibid., 34.

12. Ibid., 231.

13. Ibid., 51.

14. Ibid., 9.

15. Ibid., 91.

16. Ibid., 105.

17. Fackenheim, *God's Presence in History*, v.

18. Michael Berenbaum, *The Vision of the Void*, 6.

19. Fackenheim, *God's Presence in History*, 4.

20. Susan Shapiro, *Recovery of the Sacred*, 260.

21. Fackenheim, *God's Presence in History*, 8–14.

22. Ibid., 16.

23. Ibid., 49.

24. Steven Katz, *Post-Holocaust Dialogues*, 225.

25. Fackenheim, *God's Presence in History*, 83.

26. Ibid., 97.

27. Fackenheim, *The Jewish Return into History*, 23.

28. Fackenheim, *Quest for Past and Future*, 18.

29. Fackenheim, *God's Presence in History*, 39.

30. Ibid., 40.

31. Ibid., 52 (emphasis is Fackenheim's).

32. Arthur Cohen, "On Emil Fackenheim's *To Mend the World*: A Review Essay," 234.

33. Fackenheim, *God's Presence in History*, 78–79.

34. Fackenheim, *To Mend the World*, 193. Cf 189–90, 200, 216.

35. Ibid., 8, 107.

36. Ibid., 119. Cf. Emil Fackenheim, *The Religious Dimension in Hegel's Thought*, 11–12, 224.

37. Ibid., 11–12.

38. Ibid., 235–36.

39. Fackenheim, *To Mend the World*, 4.

40. Ibid., 55–56.

41. Ibid., 200.

42. Ibid., 216.

43. Ibid., 190.

44. Ibid., 200.

45. Ibid., 224, 248. Cf 23–4, 201.

46. Ibid., 216–23.

47. Ibid., 25, 217 (emphasis in the original).

48. Robert Alter, *Necessary Angels*, 109.

49. Steven Katz, *Post-Holocaust Dialogues*, 218.

50. Franz Rosenzweig, *The Star of Redemption*, 177. Rosenzweig modified this opposition in his open letter to Buber entitled "the Builders." Here Rosenzweig argued that one could transform *Gesetz* into *Gebot*.

51. Susan Shapiro, *Recovery of the Sacred*, 240–82.

52. Emil Fackenheim, *To Mend the World*, 255.

53. Ibid., 256.

54. Auschwitz, we suggested in the introduction to this study, is also an "icon." But this usage inverts the traditional sense of iconography. Traditionally, an icon depicts a lustrous image of the good within the midst of evil. Auschwitz is an icon, it is because it intensifies the image of death within the midst of life.

55. Emil Fackenheim, *The Jewish Return into History*, xiii.

56. Ibid., 208.

57. Fackenheim, *Encounters between Judaism and Modern Philosophy*, 167–68.

58. Ibid., 227. Fackenheim, *The Jewish Return into History*, 275.

59. Rene Girard, *Violence and the Sacred*, 24.

60. Ibid., 31.

61. Fackenheim, *The Jewish Return into History*, 83.

62. Ibid., 96. Cf. 54.

63. Ibid., 101.

64. Fackenheim, *To Mend the World*, 256–62. Incidentally, this critique of

Gadamer resembled the one posed by Jacques Derrida who asked whether "the precondition for [understanding the other], far from being the continuity of rapport . . . , is not rather the interruption of rapport, a certain rapport of interruption, the suspending of all mediation?" See Jacques Derrida, "Three Questions to Hans-Georg Gadamer," in Diane Michelfelder and Richard Palmer, eds., *Dialogue and Deconstruction*, 53.

65. Fackenheim, *The Jewish Bible after the Holocaust*, 16.

66. Ibid., vii–viii.

67. Fackenheim, *God's Presence in History*, 88. Cf. 76.

68. Fackenheim, *The Jewish Bible after the Holocaust*, 32.

69. William E. Kaufmann, *Contemporary Jewish Philosophies*, 119.

70. Emil Fackenheim, *The Jewish Bible after the Holocaust*, 26. See my discussion of Buber's "The Dialogue between Heaven and Earth" above in Chapter 3.

71. Ibid., 99.

72. Emil Fackenheim, *To Mend the World*, 329.

73. It occurs in two separate essays in Fackenheim, *Quest for Past and Future*, 20, 305. See also Fackenheim, "The Commandment to Hope: A Response to Contemporary Jewish Existence," in Walter H. Capps, ed., *The Future of Hope*, 91. The image of crown and scepter is found in Yoma 69b, where R. Joshua b. Levi describes how the Great Synod "restored [to God] the crown of the divine attributes to its ancient completeness."

74. Jacques Derrida, *Of Grammatology*, 145. We will leave it to the Derrideans to determine how the supplement operates in Derrida's own thought.

75. Fackenheim, *The Jewish Bible after the Holocaust*, 104.

76. Derrida, *Of Grammatology*, 314.

77. Moshe Barasch, *Icon*, 1–2.

CONCLUSION
DISCOURSE, SIGN, DIPTYCH

1. Foucault, *The Archaeology of Knowledge*, 4.

2. Ibid., 107, 117.

3. Ibid., 38, 62–64; cf. Foucault, "Politics and the Study of Discourse," 59–60.

4. Ibid., 126.

5. Irena Klepfitz is an American Jewish poet, a survivor born in Warsaw during the war and a founding member of the left-wing New Jewish Agenda. The Israeli poet Abba Kovner was a leader in the Vilna Ghetto Uprising. Dan Pagis was an Israeli poet. Dov Shilansky was Speaker of the Israeli Knesset in the 1980s. A survivor, he was known for vocally bringing up the Holocaust at politically sensitive moments. Avi Weiss is a rabbi in Riverdale, New York. Known alternatively as an activist and a rabble rouser, he was a central figure in the protest against the establishment of a Carmelite monastery at the site of Auschwitz in the late 1980s. Leon Uris, best known as the author of *Exodus*, also wrote *Mila 18*, a historical novel about the Warsaw Ghetto Uprising.

6. Foucault, *The Archaeology of Knowledge*, 179.

7. Foucault, *The History of Sexuality*, vol. 1, 43.

8. Arthur Green, *Seek My Face, Speak My Name*, 156–57.

9. Jonathan Sacks, *Crisis and Covenant*, 151. At the time that Rubenstein wrote *After Auschwitz*, he served as Hillel rabbi at the University of Pittsburgh and Carnegie-Mellon University.

10. Ibid., 228.

11. Judith Plaskow, *Standing Again at Sinai*.

12. Foucault, *The Archaeology of Knowledge*, 173–74.

13. The term *mutation* is, in my view, a more precise way to describe the strained lines of cultural transmission than the misleading *continuity*. Continuity implies stasis. Mutation implies the survival of a cultural pattern in modified form.

14. David Robey's introduction to Umberto Eco, *The Open Work*, xii.

15. Eco, *The Open Work*, 1–2.

16. Ibid., 90–93.

17. Mark C. Taylor, *Disfiguring*, 318. Cf. 46–47, 318–19.

18. Ibid., 299.

19. One might usefully compare post-Holocaust thought to various schools of German expressionism. The biblical figures and scenes of Emil Nolde, Wilhelm Gross, Jakob Steinhardt, Ernst Barlach, and Ludwig Meidner come especially to mind. At the same time, these woodcuts appear both understated and over-wrought, even to the point of being cartoonish. Using them as a model with which to invoke the Holocaust would invite suspicion that the artist/theologian tries to represent with figures that which lies beyond the scope of representation.

20. In presenting Kiefer's hesitant utopianism, I have drawn from Mark Rosenthal, *Anselm Kiefer*, John Hutchinson, "Kiefer's Wager"; and Peter Schjeldahl, "Reading the Rhine."

21. Taylor, *Disfiguring*, 300. Cf. 300–303.

22. Ibid., 307.

23. I thank Margaret Karalis for describing the sense of Kiefer's painting in terms of "opening."

24. Arthur A. Cohen, *The Tremendum*, 97–98.

25. Cf. Rosenthal, *Anselm Kiefer*, 121. The transition from *Shulamite* to *Departure from Egypt* (however unintentionally) resembles the transition from Wiesel's *Night* to *Dawn*.

26. Michael Wyschogrod, *The Body of Faith*, 9. Cf. 9–10.

27. Ibid., 18–19.

28. Ibid., 23.

29. Ibid., 25, Cf. 24–25.

30. Ibid., 224–26.

31. Ibid., 33.

32. Ibid., 254–56.

33. Ibid., 226.

BIBLIOGRAPHY

CLASSICAL JEWISH TEXTS

Babylonian Talmud. Isidore Epstein, ed. London: Soncino.
The Fathers According to Rabbi Nathan. Jullian Obermann, ed. Judah Goldin, trans. New Haven: Yale University Press, 1955.
The Holy Scriptures. Philadelphia: The Jewish Publication Society of America, 1917.
Midrash Rabbah. H. Freedman and Maurice Simon, trans. London and New York: Soncino, 1983.
Pirkei Avot. New York: Metsudah, 1980.
Pesikta Rabbati. William G. Braude, trans. New Haven: Yale University Press, 1968.
Sifre. A Tannaitic Commentary on the Book of Deuteronomy. Reuven Hammer, trans. New Haven: Yale University Press, 1986.

POST-HOLOCAUST AND OTHER SOURCES

Alter, Robert. *Necessary Angels. Tradition and Modernity in Kafka, Benjamin, and Scholem.* Cambridge, MA: Harvard University Press, 1991.
Bal, Mieke. *Death and Dissymmetry: The Politics of Coherence in the Book of Judges.* Chicago and London: The University of Chicago Press, 1988.
Barasch, Moshe. *Icon. Studies in the History of an Idea.* New York and London: New York University Press, 1992.
Bauman, Zygmunt. *Modernity and the Holocaust.* Ithaca: Cornell University Press, 1991.
Benisch, Pearl. *To Vanquish the Dragon.* Jerusalem and New York: Feldheim, 1991.
Berenbaum, Michael. *The Vision of the Void: Theological Reflections on the Works of Elie Wiesel.* Middletown, CT: Wesleyan University Press, 1979.
Berger, Alan. "Holocaust and History: A Theological Reflection." *Journal of Ecumenical Studies* 25, no. 2 (spring 1988): 194–211.
Berger, Peter. *The Sacred Canopy. Elements of a Sociological Theory of Religion.* Garden City, NY: Anchor, 1969.
Berger, Peter, and Thomas Luckmann. *The Social Construction of Reality: A Treatise on the Sociology of Knowledge.* Garden City, NY: Doubleday, Inc., 1966.
Berkovits, Eliezer. *Man and God. Studies in Biblical Theology.* Detroit: Wayne State University Press, 1969.
———. *Faith after the Holocaust.* New York: Ktav, 1973.
———. *Major Themes in Modern Philosophies of Judaism.* New York: Ktav, 1974.
———. *Crisis and Faith.* New York: Sanhedrin, 1976.
———. *With God in Hell.* New York and London: Sanhedrin, 1979.
———. *Not in Heaven. The Nature and Function of Halakha.* New York: Ktav, 1983.

———. *Jewish Women in Time and Torah*. Hoboken, NJ: Ktav, 1990.

Biale, David. *Gershom Scholem. Kabbalah and Counter-History*. 1979; 2d ed. Cambridge, MA and London: Harvard University Press, 1982.

———. *Power and Powerlessness in Jewish History*. New York: Schocken, 1986.

Bloom, Harold. *The Anxiety of Influence. A Theory of Poetry*. New York: Oxford University Press, 1973.

———. *A Map of Misreading*. New York: Oxford University Press, 1975.

Bouchard, Larry. *Tragic Method and Tragic Theology*. University Park and London: Pennsylvania State University Press, 1989.

Boyarin, Daniel. *Intertextuality and the Reading of Midrash*. Bloomington: Indiana University Press, 1990.

Buber, Martin. *Israel and the World. Essays in a Time of Crisis*. New York: Schocken, 1948.

———. *The Prophetic Faith*. New York: Collier Books, 1949.

———. *Eclipse of God. Studies in the Relation between Religion and Philosophy*. New York and Evanston: Harper and Row, 1952.

———. *On Judaism*. Ed. Nahum N. Glatzer. New York: Schocken, 1967.

———. "The Election of Israel: A Biblical Inquiry." In *On the Bible: Eighteen Studies*, ed. Nahum Glatzer. New York: Schocken, 1968, pp. 80–92.

———. *I and Thou*. 1923; rpt., trans. Walter Kaufmann, New York: Charles Scribner's Sons, 1969.

———. *The Letters of Martin Buber: A Life of Dialogue*. Ed. Nahum Glatzer and Paul Mendes-Flohr. Trans. Richard Winston, Clara Winston, and Harry Zohn. New York: Schocken Books, 1991.

Buchler, Adolph. *Studies in Sin and Atonement in the Rabbinic Literature of the First Century*. London: Oxford University Press, 1928.

Cohen, Arthur A. *The Tremendum. A Theological Interpretation of the Holocaust*. New York: Crossroad, 1981.

———. "On Emil Fackenheim's *To Mend the World*: A Review Essay." *Modern Judaism* 3, no. 2 (May 1983).

Cohen, Hermann. *Religion of Reason: Out of the Sources of Judaism*. New York: Frederick Ungar, 1971.

Cohn-Sherbok, Daniel. *Holocaust Theology*. London: Lamp, 1989.

Culler, Jonathan. *The Pursuit of Signs. Semiotics, Literature, Deconstruction*. Ithaca: Cornell University Press, 1981.

Daly, Mary. "After the Death of God the Father." In *Womanspirit Rising*, ed. Carol P. Christ and Judith Plaskow. San Francisco: Harper and Row, 1979, pp. 53–62.

Derrida, Jacques. *Of Grammatology*. Trans. Gayatri Chakravorty Spivak. Baltimore and London: Johns Hopkins University Press, 1976.

———. "Three Questions to Hans-Georg Gadamer." In *Dialogue and Deconstruction. The Gadamer-Derrida Encounter*, ed. and trans. Diane Michelfelder and Richard Palmer. New York: State University of New York Press, 1989, pp. 52–54.

———. *The Gift of Death*. Trans. David Wills. Chicago and London: The University of Chicago Press, 1995.

Dostoyevsky, Fyodor. *The Brothers Karamazov*. Trans. Constance Garnett. New York: W. W. Norton, Inc., 1976.

Eco, Umberto. *The Open Work.* Trans. Anna Cancogni. Cambridge, MA: Harvard University Press, 1989.

Eisen, Arnold. *The Chosen People in America: A Study in Jewish Religious Ideology.* Bloomington: Indiana University Press, 1983.

———. "Covenant." In *Contemporary Jewish Religious Thought*, ed. Arthur Cohen and Paul Mendes-Flohr. New York: The Free Press, 1987, pp. 107–12.

———. "Constructing the Usable Past: The Idea of Tradition in Twentieth-Century American Judaism." In *The Uses of Tradition*, ed. Jack Werthheimer. New York and Jerusalem: Jewish Theological Seminary, 1992, pp. 429–61.

Fackenheim, Emil L. "The Commandment to Hope: A Response to Contemporary Jewish Existence." In *The Future of Hope*, ed. Walter H. Capps. Philadelphia: Fortress, 1970, pp. 68–91.

———. *God's Presence in History: Jewish Affirmations of Philosophical Reflections.* New York: Harper Torch, 1970.

———. *Encounters between Judaism and Modern Philosophy: A Preface to Future Jewish Thought.* New York: Schocken, 1973.

———. *The Jewish Return into History: Reflections in the Age of Auschwitz and a New Jerusalem.* New York: Schocken, 1978.

———. *To Mend the World: Foundations of Future Jewish Thought.* New York: Schocken, 1982.

———. *The Jewish Bible after the Holocaust: A Re-Reading.* Bloomington and Indianapolis: Indiana University Press, 1990.

———. *Metaphysics and Historicity.* Milwaukee: Marquette University Press, 1961.

———. *The Religious Dimension in Hegel's Thought.* Bloomington and London: Indiana University Press, 1967.

———. *Quest for Past and Future: Essays in Jewish Theology.* Bloomington and London: Indiana University Press, 1968.

Finkelstein, Louis. *The Pharisees.* Philadelphia: Jewish Publishing Society, 1938.

Fishbane, Michael. *The Garments of Torah: Essays in Biblical Hermeneutics.* Bloomington and Indianapolis: Indiana University Press, 1989.

———. *The Kiss of God: Spiritual and Mystical Death in Judaism.* Seattle and London: University of Washington Press, 1994.

Flew, Anthony. "Divine Omnipotence and Human Freedom." In *New Essays in Philosophical Theology*, ed. Anthony Flew and Alasdair MacIntyre. New York: Macmillan, 1955, pp. 144–69.

Foucault, Michel. *The Archaeology of Knowledge.* Trans. A. M. Sheridan Smith. New York: Pantheon, 1972.

———. *The History of Sexuality. Volume I: An Introduction.* Trans. Robert Hurley. 1978; rpt. New York: Vintage, 1980.

———. "Politics and the Study of Discourse." In *The Foucault Effect: Studies in Governmentality*, ed. Graham Burchell, Collin Gordon, and Peter Miller. Chicago: The University of Chicago Press, 1991, pp. 53–72.

Funkenstein, Amos. "Theological Interpretations of the Holocaust." *The Tel Aviv Review* 1, no. 1 (1988): 67–100.

Geertz, Clifford. *The Interpretation of Culture.* New York: Basic Books, 1973.

Giddens, Anthony. *The Consequences of Modernity*. Stanford: Stanford University Press, 1990.

Girard, René. *Violence and the Sacred*. Trans. Patrick Gregory. Baltimore and London: Johns Hopkins University Press, 1977.

Glazer, Nathan. *American Judaism*. 1957; 2d ed. Chicago and London: The University of Chicago Press, 1972.

Good, Edwin M. *In Turns of Tempest. A Reading of Job with a Translation*. Stanford: Stanford University Press, 1990.

Gordis, Robert. *The Book of God and Man. A Study of Job*. Chicago and London: University of Chicago Press, 1965.

———. "A Cruel God or None at All—Is There No Choice?" *Judaism* 21, no. 3 (summer 1972): 277–84.

Green, Arthur. "A Response to Richard Rubenstein." *Conservative Judaism* 18, no. 4 (summer 1974): 26–32.

———. "The Role of Jewish Mysticism in a Contemporary Theology of Judaism." *Conservative Judaism* 30, no. 4 (1976): 10–24.

———. *Seek My Face, Speak My Name: A Contemporary Jewish Theology*. Northvale, NJ, and London: Jason Aronson, 1992.

Greenberg, Blu. *On Women and Judaism. A View from Tradition*. Philadelphia: Jewish Publication Society, 1981.

Greenberg, Gershon. "Myth and Catastrophe in Simha Elberg's Religious Thought." *Tradition* 26, no. 1 (fall 1991): 39–59.

———. "Orthodox Theological Responses to Kristallnacht: Chayyim Ozer Grodensky ('Achiezer') and Elchonon Wasserman." *Holocaust and Genocide Studies* 3, no. 4 (1988): 431–41.

———. "Redemption after Holocaust according to Mahane Israel-Lubavitch 1940–1945." *Modern Judaism* 12 (1992): 61–84.

Greenberg, Irving. "Cloud of Smoke, Pillar of Fire: Judaism, Christianity, and Modernity after the Holocaust." In *Auschwitz: Beginning of a New Era*, ed. Eva Fleischner. New York: Ktav, 1977, pp. 7–55.

———. "Voluntary Covenant." In his *Perspectives. A Clal Thesis*. New York: Clal, The National Jewish Center for Learning and Leadership, 1982.

Griffin, David Ray. *God, Power, and Evil: A Process Theology*. Philadelphia: Westminster, 1976.

Habel, Norman. *The Book of Job. A Commentary*. Philadelphia: Westminster, 1985.

Hartman, David. *A Living Covenant. The Innovative Spirit in Traditional Judaism*. New York: Free Press, 1985.

———. "Suffering." In *Contemporary Jewish Religious Thought*, ed. Arthur Cohen and Paul Mendes-Flohr. New York: Free Press. 1987, pp. 939–46.

Harvey, Van Austin. *The Historian and the Believer. The Morality of Historical Knowledge and Christian Belief*. New York: Macmillan, 1966.

Hefner, Philip. "Is Theodicy a Question of Power?" *The Journal of Religion* 59, no. 1 (Jan. 1979): 87–93.

———. "God and Chaos: The Demiurge versus the Urgrund." *Zygon* 19, no. 4 (December 1984): 469–85.

Herberg, Will. *Judaism and Modern Man: An Interpretation of Jewish Religion*. New York: Atheneum, 1951.

Heschel, Abraham Joshua. *Man Is Not Alone. A Philosophy of Religion.* Philadelphia: Jewish Publication Society, 1951.

———. "The Meaning of This Hour." In *Quest for God. Studies in Prayer and Symbolism.* New York: Crossroad, 1954.

———. *God in Search of Man. A Philosophy of Judaism.* New York: Meridian Books and Jewish Publication Society, 1955.

———. *The Prophets.* Philadelphia: Jewish Publication Society, 1962.

———. *Israel: An Echo in Eternity.* New York: Farrar, Straus, and Giroux, 1967.

———. *A Passion for Truth.* New York: Farrar, Straus, and Giroux, 1973.

Hick, John. *Evil and the God of Love.* New York: Harper and Row, 1978.

Hume, David. *Dialogues Concerning Natural Religion.* New York: Hafner, 1948.

Hutchinson, John. "Kiefer's Wager." In Anselm Kiefer, *Jason.* Dublin: The Douglas Hyde Gallery, 1990.

Jabes, Edmond. *The Book of Questions.* Trans. Rosmarie Waldrop. Vol. 1. Hanover and London: Wesleyan University Press, 1972.

Kadushin, Max. *The Rabbinic Mind.* New York: Blaisdell, 1965.

Kaplan, Edward. "Mysticism and Despair in Abraham J. Heschel's Religious Thought." *The Journal of Religion* 57 (January 1977): 33–47.

———. "Heschel's Poetics of Religious Thinking." In *Abraham Joshua Heschel. Exploring His Life and Thought,* ed. John Merkle. New York: Macmillan, 1985, pp. 103–19.

Kaplan, Mordecai. *Questions Jews Ask: Reconstructionist Answers.* New York: Reconstructionist Press, 1956.

———. *The Meaning of God in Modern Jewish Religion.* New York: Reconstructionist Press, 1962.

Katz, Steven. *Post-Holocaust Dialogues: Critical Studies in Modern Jewish Thought.* New York and London: New York University Press, 1985.

Kaufmann, Walter. *Nietzsche. Philosopher, Psychologist, Antichrist.* Princeton, NJ: Princeton University Press, 1974.

Kaufman, William E. *Contemporary Jewish Philosophies.* Lanham, MD: University Press of America, 1985.

Kepnes, Steven. *The Text as Thou. Martin Buber's Dialogical Hermeneutics and Narrative Theology.* Bloomington and Indianapolis: Indiana University Press, 1992.

Kohler, Kaufman. *Jewish Theology. Systematically and Historically Considered.* New York: Macmillan, 1928.

Kolitz, Zvi, ed. *Yossel Rakover Speaks to God: Holocaust Challenges to Religious Faith.* Hoboken, NJ: Ktav, 1995.

Kraemer, David. *Responses to Suffering in Classical Rabbinic Literature.* New York and Oxford: Oxford University Press, 1995.

Kristeva, Julia. *Desire in Language. A Semiotic Approach to Literature and Art.* Trans. Thomas Gura, Alice Jarding, and Leon S. Roudiez. New York: Columbia University Press, 1980.

Laytner, Anson. *Arguing with God. A Jewish Tradition.* Northvale, NJ, and London: Jason Aronson, 1990.

Levi, Primo. *Survival in Auschwitz. The Nazi Assault on Humanity.* Trans. Stuart Woolf. 1960; rpt. New York: Collier, 1993.

Lyotard, Jean-François. *The Differend. Phrases in Dispute.* Trans. Van Den Abbeele. Minneapolis: University of Minnesota Press, 1988.

———. *Heidegger and "the jews."* Trans. Andreas Michel and Mark S. Roberts. Minneapolis: University of Minnesota Press, 1990.

Mackie, John. *The Miracle of Theism: Arguments for and against the Existence of God.* Oxford: Clarendon Press. 1982.

Matt, Daniel C. "Ayin: The Concept of Nothingness in Jewish Mysticism." In *The Problem of Pure Consciousness in Mysticism and Philosophy,* ed. Robert K.C. Forman. New York and Oxford: Oxford University Press, 1990, pp. 121–59.

McCloskey, H. J. *God and Evil.* The Hague: Martinus Nijhoff, 1974.

Milgrom, Jacob. *The Anchor Bible. Leviticus 1–16. A New Translation with Introduction and Commentary.* New York: Doubleday, 1991.

Mintz, Alan. *Hurban: Responses to Catastrophe in Hebrew Literature.* New York: Columbia University Press. 1984.

Neusner, Jacob. *Understanding Jewish Theology.* New York: Ktav, 1973.

———. *The Canonical History of Ideas. The Place of the So-Called Tannaite Midrashim: Mekhilta Attributed to R. Ishmael, Sifra, Sifre to Numbers, and Sifre to Deuteronomy.* Atlanta: Scholars Press, 1990.

Nietzsche, Friedrich. *The Antichrist.* In *The Portable Nietzsche,* ed. Walter Kaufmann. New York: Viking, 1954.

———. *Beyond Good and Evil.* Trans. Walter Kaufmann. New York: Vintage, 1966.

———. *The Gay Science.* Trans. Walter Kaufmann. New York: Vintage, 1974.

Plaskow, Judith. *Standing Again at Sinai. Judaism from a Feminist Perspective.* San Francisco: Harper Collins, 1990.

Rad, Gerhard von. *Deuteronomy. A Commentary.* Philadelphia: Westminster, 1966.

Raffel, Charles M. "Eliezer Berkovits." In *Interpreters of Judaism in the Late Twentieth Century,* ed. Steven T. Katz. Washington, DC: B'nai B'rith Books, 1993, pp. 1–15.

Rosenthal, Mark. *Anselm Kiefer.* Chicago and Philadelphia: Prestel-Verlag, 1987.

Rosenzweig, Franz. *The Star of Redemption.* Trans. William H. Hallo. New York: Holt, Rinehart and Winston, 1970.

Roskies, David G. *Against the Apocalypse: Response to Catastrophe in Modern Jewish Culture.* Cambridge, MA, and London: Harvard University Press, 1984.

Rubenstein, Richard L. *After Auschwitz: Radical Theology and Contemporary Judaism.* 1st ed. Indianapolis: Bobbs-Merrill, 1966.

———. *The Religious Imagination.* Boston: Beacon Press. 1968.

———. "Job and Auschwitz." *Union Seminary Quarterly* 25, no. 4 (summer 1970): 421–37.

———. *Morality and Eros.* New York: McGraw Hill, 1970.

———. "Jewish Theology and the Current World Situation." *Conservative Judaism.* 18, no. 4 (summer 1974): 3–25.

———. *The Cunning of History.* New York: Harper and Row, 1975.

———. *The Age of Triage: Fear and Hope in an Overcrowded World.* Boston: Beacon, 1983.

————. *Power Struggle. An Autobiographical Confession.* University Press of America, 1985.

————. *After Auschwitz. History, Theology, and Contemporary Judaism.* 2d ed. Baltimore and London: Johns Hopkins University Press, 1992.

Rubenstein, Richard L., and John K. Roth. *Approaches to Auschwitz. The Holocaust and Its Legacy.* Atlanta: John Knox, 1987.

Sacks, Jonathan. *Crisis and Covenant. Jewish Thought after the Holocaust.* Manchester and New York: Manchester University Press, 1992.

Schechter, Solomon. "The Doctrine of Divine Retribution." In *Origins of Judaism: History of the Jews in the Second Century of the Common Era*, vol. 1, part 3, ed. Jacob Neusner. New York and London: Garland, 1990, pp. 362–79.

Schjeldahl, Peter. "Reading the Rhine." In *The Books of Anselm Kiefer. 1969–1990*, ed. Gotz Adriani, trans. Bruni Mayor. New York: George Braziller, 1991, pp. 21–23.

Schindler, Pesach. *Hasidic Responses to the Holocaust in Light of Hasidic Thought.* Hoboken, NJ: Ktav, 1990.

Scholem, Gershom G. *Major Trends in Jewish Mysticism.* New York: Schocken, 1946.

————. "Revelation and Tradition as Religious Categories in Judaism and Other Essays on Jewish Spirituality." In *The Messianic Idea in Judaism.* New York: Schocken, 1971, pp. 282–303.

————. "Martin Buber's Conception of Judaism." In his *On Jews and Judaism in Crisis.* New York: Schocken, 1976, pp. 126–71.

Schweid, Eliezer. *Wrestling until Daybreak.* (Hebrew) Tel Aviv: Hakibbutz Hameuchad, 1990.

————. *To Declare That God Is Upright: Theodicy in Jewish Thought.* (Hebrew) Jerusalem: Tag Hoza'at L' 'or, 1994.

————. *From Ruin to Salvation. Contemporary Ultra-Orthodox Response to the Holocaust.* (Hebrew) Tel Aviv: Hakibbutz Hameuchad, 1994.

Shapiro, Susan. *Recovery of the Sacred. Hermeneutics and Theology after the Holocaust.* Ph.D dissertation, University of Chicago, 1983.

Soloveitchik, Joseph. "Kol Dodi Dofek." In *Theological and Halakhic Reflections on the Holocaust*, ed. Bernhard Rosenberg and Fred Heuman. Hoboken, NJ: Ktav, 1992.

————. *The Rav Speaks. Five Addresses.* Jerusalem: Tal Orot Institute, 1982–83.

Sontag, Frederick. *The God of Evil: An Argument from the Existence of the Devil.* New York, Evanston, and London: Harper and Row, 1970.

Stern, David. *Parables in Midrash. Narrative and Exegesis in Rabbinic Literature.* Cambridge, MA, and London: Harvard University Press, 1991.

Surin, Kenneth. *Theology and the Problem of Evil.* Oxford and New York: Basil Blackwell, 1986.

Sutzkever, Abraham. *Siberia.* London, New York, and Toronto: Abelard-Schuman, 1961.

Taylor, Charles. *Sources of the Self. The Making of the Modern Identity.* Cambridge, MA: Harvard University Press, 1989.

Taylor, Mark C. *Disfiguring: Art, Architecture, Religion.* Chicago and London: University of Chicago Press, 1992.

Tilley, Terrence W. *The Evils of Theodicy*. Washington, DC: Georgetown University Press, 1991.

Tillich, Paul. *Systematic Theology*. Chicago: University of Chicago Press, 1967.

Tracy, David. *Plurality and Ambiguity. Hermeneutics, Religion, Hope*. San Francisco: Harper and Row, 1987.

Trible, Phyllis. *God and the Rhetoric of Sexuality*. Philadelphia: Fortress, 1978.

Urbach, Ephraim E. *The Sages: Their Concepts and Beliefs*. Trans. Israel Abrahams. Cambridge, MA, and London: Harvard University Press, 1987.

Voltaire, François-Marie Arouet. *Philosophical Dictionary*. Ed. and trans. Theodoere Besterman. New York: Penguin Books, 1972.

Weber, Max. *The Sociology of Religion*. Boston: Beacon, 1963.

Weinfeld, Moshe. *Deuteronomy and the Deuteronomic School*. Oxford: Oxford University Press, 1972.

Wiesel, Elie. *The Accident*. 1962; rpt. New York: Hill and Wang, 1985.

———. *Messengers of God*. New York: Summit, 1976.

Wright, G. Ernest. *The Interpreter's Bible. Book of Deuteronomy*. New York and Nashville: Abingdon, 1953.

———. "The Lawsuit of God: A Form-Critical Study of Deuteronomy 32." In *Israel's Prophetic Heritage*, ed. Bernhard Anderson and Walter Harrelson. New York: Harper and Brothers, 1962, pp. 26–67.

Wyschogrod, Edith. *Spirit in Ashes: Hegel, Heidegger and Man-Made Mass Death*. New Haven and London: Yale University Press, 1985.

Wyschogrod, Michael. *The Body of Faith. Judaism as Corporeal Election*. Minneapolis: Seabury Press, 1983.

———. "Faith and the Holocaust." *Judaism* 20, no. 3 (summer 1971): 286–94.

Yehoshua, A. B. *Between Right and Right: Israel Problem or Solution*. Trans. Arnold Schwartz. Garden City, NY: Doubleday, 1981.

Zuckerman, Bruce. *Job the Silent*. New York and Oxford: Oxford University Press, 1991.

INDEX

Abraham, 32–33, 43, 50, 58, 70, 150, 155. See also *akeidah*
affect. *See* emotion
aggadah, 6, 36, 101–2, 132. *See also* midrash; tradition
ahavat Yisrael. *See* Israel; love
Aḥer, 132. *See also* Elisha b. Abuyeh
AIDS, 3
akeidah (Binding of Isaac), 176. *See also* Abraham
R. Akiba, 15, 20, 36, 43, 44–46, 56–57, 58, 82, 123, 129–30, 132
alchemy, 11, 82, 171
Alter, Robert, 148
Altizer, Thomas, 94
amcha, 147, 151. *See also* Israel
Amery, Jean, 7, 84, 162. *See also* "logic of destruction"
R. Ammi, 41, 102–3
amor fati, 99–100. *See also* Nietzsche
anger, 37, 58, 69, 110, 113, 115, 118, 125, 167, 168, 177
Anielewicz, Mordecai, 153
antitheodicy, 12, 31–34, 47–59; avowals of incomprehension and mystery as, 55–57, 57–58, 143; covenant and, 31–33, 50; definition of, 4 and n.3, 5, 20, 31, 37; and God, 5, 37, 47–57, 57–59, 115–25, 155–56; goodness and, 37, 116; instability of, 5, 37, 57–59; and messianism, 58, 124, 143; and modern Jewish thought, 10–11, 59; and post-Holocaust Jewish thought, 11, 14–15, 109–11, 113–15, 115–25, 128, 132–33, 151, 163–68; protest and complaint as, 11, 14, 20, 32, 47, 47–54, 69n.37, 84, 103, 110, 113, 115, 117, 118–19, 120, 125, 126, 127, 129, 155–56; solidarity as, 9, 32, 37, 47, 54–55, 74, 100, 117–18, 132, 155–56, 158, 165, 167. *See also* anger; Job
apologetics, 19–20, 28–31
Arendt, Hannah, 7, 15, 162
Armenian genocide, 3
art, artists, aesthetics, 3, 6, 81–83, 166, 168–78, 170n.19. *See also* icons

assimilation, 20, 30, 76, 142
astonishment, wonder, 141, 142, 147, 152
Athens, 88–89
Auschwitz, as icon, 84, 152n.54, 163
authenticity, 8. *See also* Judaism

Baal Shem Tov, 68, 70
Bal, Mieke, 37
Barasch, Moshe, 160
Bar Kochba, 153
Bauman, Zygmunt, 3, 15
belief, 113
Benisch, Perl, 24
Berenbaum, Michael, 8, 88n.2, 140
Berger, Alan, 122
Berger, Peter, 19, 25–27, 31
Berkovits, Eliezer, 8–9, 16, 23, 24, 32–33, 112–13, 161, 163–65, 166–68, 170, 174–75, 177–78; centrality to post-Holocaust discourse, 3–4, 113; critique of Kaplan, 78, 80; on "holy disbelief," 117; and modern Jewish thought, 60–62; and Rubenstein, 35–36, 58, 112–13, 116, 129, 131–33, 164–65; and Soloveitchik, 60, 126, 127; on theodicy and antitheodicy, 113–15, 115–26, 132, 164; "traditionalism" and "conservatism" of, 8–9, 12, 113, 114–15, 125–26; on the uniqueness of the Holocaust, 114; use of tradition, 35–36, 125–33
Bettelheim, Bruno, 7, 84, 104n.74, 162
Biale, David, 105, 120
Bialik, Hayim Nahman, 6, 13
Bible, 6, 8, 9, 20, 33, 166; Buber's use of, 62–63, 65, 66–67, 155; Fackenheim on, 136, 154–58; and post-Holocaust thought, 35–36, 88, 90, 97, 127, 135–36, 154–58. *See also* Job; theodicy; tradition
Blanchot, Maurice, 171
blasphemy, 4, 71, 118, 143, 164
Bloom, Harold, 88, 101, 110–11, 131–32, 132–33
Bosnia, 3
Boyarin, Daniel, 33

Brecht, Bertoldt, 110

Buber, Martin, 14, 62–67, 80–84, 105, 107, 139, 143, 148, 149; attitude toward modernity, 6, 64–65; on biblical theodicies, 63–64; critique of, 62, 65–66, 87; Fackenheim and, 60, 65–66, 139, 143, 148, 155, 156; on Holocaust, 62–63, 65–67, 87, 104, 162; on reading the Bible today, 155; realism regarding evil, 62; on suffering as catharsis, 64, 65, 67; and theodicy, 9, 10–11, 66–67, 121, 156, 163; and tradition, 59, 163. *See also* theology, modern Jewish

Cain and Abel, 31, 52, 62
Cambodia, 3, 69
catastrophe. *See* suffering
catharsis, 64, 65, 67, 71, 82, 84
Celan, Paul, 171
Chagall, Marc, 3, 6
children, 7, 16, 21, 50, 51, 53, 79–80, 83, 89, 118, 139, 143, 147, 150, 155, 156, 163
Chmelniki, 13, 15, 114
chosenness, 90, 92; belief in undermined by modernity, 6. *See also* covenant
Christianity, 8, 76, 90, 91–92, 118, 121; in post-Christian world, 136 and n.6, 145; *tikkun* of, 149–50. *See also* Gruber; Justin Martyr; Lewinska; Lichtenberg
Cohen, Arthur, 12–13, 23, 144, 162, 174; and postmodernism, 170
Cohen, Eli, 7, 104n.74
Cohen, Hermann, 10, 64, 107, 121
Cohn-Sherbok, Dan, 88n.2, 114, 119
compassion, 21, 51, 69, 82, 118
complaint. *See* antitheodicy
courage, 21, 46, 82
covenant: and antitheodicy, 31–33, 50; with God, 23–25, 31–33, 38–39, 113, 175; Israel and, 10, 27–28, 32, 38–39, 90; in post-Holocaust Jewish thought, 8, 87, 90, 113, 124, 127, 175; and problem of evil, 20, 23–25, 27–28; and theodicy, 10, 38
Cox, Harvey, 94
Crusader massacres, 13, 36, 114

Daly, Mary, 28–29
Dawidowicz, Lucy, 7, 162

death, 3, 5, 15–16, 38, 41, 44, 45, 46, 55, 83, 98, 102–3, 125, 145–46, 148, 149, 152n.54, 154, 159, 177
death of God, 8; Rubenstein on, 11, 87, 92–94. *See also* God
Derrida, Jacques, 9, 15, 32–33, 155n.64, 159–60
despair, 7, 71, 78, 139–40, 142, 143, 150, 153
Des Pres, Terrence, 7, 125, 162
Deuteronomy, 14, 20, 36, 38, 38–39, 45, 164; Berkovits on, 121, 132; Buber on, 63; Heschel and, 69; Rubenstein on, 94, 106, 108; Soloveitchik on, 75, 77
Diaspora, 120, 159. *See also* exile
disbelief. *See* Berkovits; blasphemy
discourse: formation of, 12, 161–65; of Holocaust, 7–8, 12, 83–84, 161–68
Dostoyevsky, Fyodor. *See* Karamazov, Ivan
Dionysus, 97, 99, 101

Eco, Umberto, 12, 165–68
Eichmann trial, 7, 84, 162
Ele Ezkera. See Yom Kippur
Elisha b. Abuyeh, 33, 35, 58, 89, 129–31, 163, 168. *See also* Aḥer
emotion, feelings, sentiment, sentimentalism, 24–25, 144, 146–47. *See also* anger; astonishment; despair; joy
Enlightenment, 6, 15, 27, 137. *See also* modernity
Epicurus, 23, 89
evil: covenant and, 20, 23–25, 27–28; meaning of, 33, 43, 61, 67, 68, 69, 70, 71, 74–75, 78, 80, 80–84, 90–91, 101, 103, 110, 121–22, 143; problem of, 13–15, 19–20, 21, 23, 25, 28, 35, 89–92, 100; realism regarding, 11, 61, 62, 72, 73, 77, 80; social dimension of, 25–28, 89–91; textual dimension of, 28–31. *See also* Holocaust: uniqueness of; suffering; theodicy
exile, 8, 64, 114. *See also* Diaspora

Fackenheim, Emil, 9, 23, 114, 120, 134–60, 161, 163–65, 166–68, 174–75, 177–78; and astonishment and wonder, 141, 142; and Bible, 136, 154–58; and Buber, 60, 65–66, 139, 143, 148, 155, 156; centrality to post-Holocaust discourse, 3–4, 134; on divine attributes,

CPSIA information can be obtained at www.ICGtesting.com
Printed in the USA
BVOW010515060613

322471BV00009B/171/P